BYTES

COLORADO'S FAMILY-FRIENDLY COOKBOOK

BYTES

Published By
Graland Country Day School
Denver, Colorado

COLORADO'S FAMILY-FRIENDLY COOKBOOK

Copyright © Graland Country Day School 1984
All Rights Reserved

No portion of this book may be reproduced—mechanically, electronically, or by any other means, including photocopying—without the express written consent of the publisher.

Library of Congress Cataloging in Publication Data
Main entry under title:

Bytes : Colorado's family-friendly cookbook.

  Includes index.
    1. Cookery—Colorado.   I. Graland Country Day School.
TX715.B9883   1984   641.5   84-24663
ISBN 0-9613742-0-9

Additional copies may be obtained by addressing:
BYTES
Graland Country Day School
30 Birch Street
Denver, Colorado 80220

Design by Christina Weber Graphic Design
Cover illustration by Lynn Dougherty

Printed by A.B. Hirschfeld Press, Denver, Colorado

Proceeds from the sale of this book go to
Graland Country Day School, Denver, Colorado

Manufactured in the United States of America
First Printing November 1984

ACKNOWLEDGMENTS

We wish to thank the following individuals and companies for their invaluable support and assistance on this project:

Regina Biederman
Century Bank
Sally Clayton
Copac Payroll
Dixon Paper Company
Eldridge & Company Realty
FBC Foods International
Flower Design
Marilyn Foster
Barbara and Richard Hamman
A.B. Hirschfeld Press
Patty Mack
Peg McKechnie
Rosemarie Murane
pdg Real Estate
Harry Pforzheimer III
Candi Rogers

A special thanks goes to Peter McLaughlin of McLaughlin and Company and the Wine Store at Larimer Square, and to Rich Martin of Ledo-Dionysus Inc. for the wine selections in this book and the engaging comments which accompany them.

Why Bytes?	9
ELEGANT BITS — Seasonal menus, recipes and wine selections for elegant entertaining	11
GLOBAL BITS — International menus and recipes adapted to American tastes	83
PORTABLE BITS — Menus and recipes for picnics and brown bag lunches	117
FAMILY BITS — Recipes for everyday, family fare including make-ahead mixes	145
KID BITS — Recipes for children's snacks and meals	177
COOKIE BITS — Recipes for cookies, bars and small tarts	193
MERRY BITS — Party themes, activities and food suggestions	211
PARITY BITS — Equivalents, substitutions and high altitude adjustments	229
Contributors	236
Index	238

Project Chairpersons

Charlotte Kagan Katz
Carolyn Miller
Barbara Volpe

Promotion

Charlie Eldridge

Editing

Andrea Watson

Index

Barbara Hamman
Richard Hamman

Chapter Coordinators

Elegant Bits:
Addie Valentine

Global Bits:
Sue Beasley

Portable Bits:
Linda Broughton

Family Bits:
Gayle Renick

Kid Bits:
Linda Averbach
Joan Mankwitz

Cookie Bits:
Barbara Stanton

Merry Bits:
Edie Buchanan
Nancy Parker

Parity Bits and
Make-Ahead Mixes:
Linda Matthews

Chapter Advisor

Marilyn McWilliams

Testers

Karen Allen
Lieba Alpert
Nancy Anschutz
Betsy Beatty
Marge Bender
Joan Betz
Phyllis Bollman
Betty Brownson
Joan Byrne
Jan Cantrill
Jill Crow
Maureen Douglass
Ginny Ennis
Rosemary Esty
Regina Falbo
Cathy Falk
Karen Frankel
Nancy Franks
Patricia Goodman
Karen Gralow
Barbara Hamman
Norma Heinschel
Carol Heller
Jeannie Herrick-Stare
Arlene Hirschfeld
Diane Hoagland
Rebecca Holman
Robert Holman
Donna Hultin
Julie Johnson
Kate Johnson
Charlotte Kagan Katz
Fred Katz
Debbie Keller
Urling Kingery
Evelyne Lafond
Eleanor Lauer
Paulette Louie
Lois MacPhee
Jan Mallory
Diane Mariash
Joyce Martin
Marilyn McWilliams
Carolyn Miller
Frederick Miller
Gegertha Mozia
Janie Narcisi
Nancy Neusteter
Judy Parcel
Ann Petkun
Susie Precourt
Barbara Radosevich

Michele Right
Mary Robbins
Dee Schranz
Nancy Scott
Kathleen Sheldon
Nathalie Simsak
Carole Stolper
Judith Sullivan
Ellen Susman
Jane Thalman
Kristin Tracy
Karen Van De Water
Beth Vinton
Barbara Volpe
Les Volpe
Pamela Warner
Connie Watts
Joy Wilhelm
Karen Zimmerman
Sara Zimmerman
Ali Zinn

The Children of
Graland Country Day School
who happily tested Kid Bits

Why Bytes?

A clever, relevant and timely title is the dream of every cookbook editor. The connection between bites and food is obvious to all. Moreover, the homonym, "bytes", in computer language, is a unit of information and a "bit" is a smaller unit of information. Eight bits equal a byte; the first seven bits carry the information and the eighth, the parity bit, checks the information on the other seven. As computers make their way into the kitchen, which they are doing with increasing frequency, computer terms will no longer be foreign to the world of cooking and cookbooks.

Some of us already have a computer in our kitchens; others are only contemplating the computer's arrival in the kitchen. However, the computer is rapidly developing into a kitchen tool that many will want to use. For example, it can file and retrieve our recipes, analyze the nutritional and caloric content of menus to promote better health, and make swift calculations when we wish to alter recipes. Furthermore, the computer can inventory the contents of our pantry and generate shopping lists each week or month. With the advancement of computer technology and the reduction in the cost of hardware and software, more and more households will turn to the computer for invaluable assistance in food preparation and kitchen management.

So .... GOTO *Bytes!* Since a relatively small INPUT will yield a healthy, tasty OUTPUT worth sharing with family and friends, you often will RETURN to *Bytes*.

ELEGANT BITS

ELEGANT BITS

HORS D'OEUVRES:

Beef Rolls
Makes 40

16 large scallions
2 tablespoons sesame oil
8 ⅛-inch thick slices boneless rib roast, with fat removed
1½ cups flour
oil for deep frying

Marinade:
4 teaspoons thinly sliced fresh ginger
1 teaspoon dried crushed red pepper, no seeds
¼ cup rice vinegar
7 tablespoons sugar
7 tablespoons soy sauce
5 tablespoons sweet sake

Cut off the whites of the scallions and cut equal lengths of the green tops.

In a heavy skillet, heat the sesame oil. Add the scallions and sauté until lightly browned. Remove from the heat.

Cut the beef slices in half and wrap each piece around one scallion white portion and several green pieces. Secure with a toothpick.

Dredge the beef rolls in the flour.

Heat one inch of oil in a skillet and deep-fry the beef until golden brown. Place the beef in one layer in a dish.

Combine the ginger, red pepper, vinegar, sugar, soy sauce and sweet sake in a saucepan. Heat just to the boiling point.

Pour the marinade over the beef rolls while they are still hot. Marinate for 30 minutes, turning occasionally.

Cut the beef rolls into bite-sized pieces. Serve warm or at room temperature.

Tomato-Shrimp Mold
8 Cups

1 10½-ounce can tomato soup
10½ ounces water
6 ounces cream cheese, softened
2 packages unflavored gelatin
½ cup cold water
1 cup mayonnaise
¾ cup minced celery
½ cup minced onion
1 pound tiny shrimps, cooked and chopped

This recipe can be prepared a day in advance and kept refrigerated until serving time.

In a medium saucepan, combine the soup and the water and bring to a boil.

Add the cream cheese and whisk to blend well.

Dissolve the gelatin in the cold water and add to the hot soup, stirring until liquefied.

Remove the saucepan from the heat and fold in the mayonnaise, celery, onion and shrimps.

Cool the mixture slightly and pour into a 2-quart mold.

Chill for at least 4 hours before unmolding to serve.

Mushroom and Endive Cheese Bites
Makes 30

1 head Belgian endive
½ pound small mushrooms, cleaned with stems removed
1 bunch watercress, washed with tough stems removed
2 4-ounce packages Boursin or Alouette cheese, softened

Remove the leaves from the endive head and place the leaves and mushrooms on a serving platter.

Garnish the leaves and mushroom caps with sprigs of watercress.

Place the cheese in a pastry bag fitted with a star tip. Pipe the cheese on the bottom ends of the endive leaves, using the cheese to hold the watercress in place. Repeat the process with the mushroom caps, filling the cavities.

Snail and Walnut Stuffed Mushrooms
Makes 48

48 small mushroom caps, cleaned with stems removed
6 tablespoons butter
2 cloves garlic, minced
12 walnut halves
2 tablespoons minced parsley
2 7-ounce cans snails, drained and rinsed
salt and freshly ground pepper to taste
French bread

Melt 2 tablespoons of the butter in a large skillet. Sauté the mushrooms, turning them in the butter, until just browned. Transfer to a warmed platter and keep warm.

Drain the skillet and melt the remaining butter.

Add the garlic, walnuts and parsley and sauté until the garlic is transparent.

Add the snails and heat through, turning carefully.

Season with the salt and the pepper.

Place a snail or a walnut in each mushroom cap.

Pour the sauce over the tops. Serve hot with the French bread.

Stuffed Figs
24 Figs

24 dried figs
sherry or port
pecan or walnut halves
8 ounces cream cheese or to taste
24 partially cooked bacon strips

Soak the figs in sherry for 36 hours.

Split each fig and fill it with a nut and some cream cheese.

Wrap the figs with the bacon and secure with toothpicks.

Broil the figs until the bacon is crisp and the figs are well heated.

Caviar in Kumquat Shells
Makes 24

12 kumquats
1 2-ounce jar red caviar or salmon roe

Wash the kumquats and cut in half lengthwise.

Scoop out the pulp from each half, using a melon baller.

Fill with a dab of caviar.

Caviar Supreme
30 Servings

This hors d'oeuvre makes a dazzling presentation when displayed on a pedestal dish and is well garnished.

2 packages unflavored gelatin
½ cup cold water

In a small bowl, dissolve the gelatin in the cold water. Set the small bowl in a larger bowl of hot water to liquefy the gelatin.

Egg Layer:
8 hard-boiled eggs, finely chopped
1 cup mayonnaise
½ cup minced parsley
2 large scallions, minced
1 teaspoon salt
dash of hot pepper sauce
freshly ground white pepper to taste

Combine the eggs, mayonnaise, parsley, scallions, salt, pepper sauce and pepper with one tablespoon of the liquefied gelatin. Blend well.

Spread the mixture in the bottom of a greased 9-inch spring form pan and refrigerate until the next layer is prepared.

Avocado Layer:
2 ripe avocados, puréed
2 ripe avocados, diced
2 large shallots, minced
4 tablespoons fresh lemon juice
4 tablespoons mayonnaise
1 teaspoon salt
dash of hot pepper sauce
freshly ground pepper to taste

Combine the avocados, shallots, lemon juice, mayonnaise, salt, pepper sauce and pepper with one tablespoon of the liquefied gelatin and blend.

Spread the mixture evenly over the egg layer and refrigerate until the next layer is prepared.

Sour Cream-Onion Layer:
2 cups sour cream
½ cup finely minced onion

Combine the sour cream, onion and one tablespoon of the liquefied gelatin. Spread the mixture over the avocado layer. Refrigerate for 2-3 hours.

2 3½- to 4-ounce jars black or red caviar
2 tablespoons freshly squeezed lemon juice

Just before serving, rinse the caviar in a sieve under cold water. Sprinkle the lemon juice over the caviar and drain well.

Remove the layers from the spring form pan and place on a serving dish.

Spread the caviar evenly over the sour cream layer.

lemon curl
lemon slices
parsley

Garnish the top with a curl of lemon peel. Garnish the bottom edge with scalloped lemon slice halves and parsley sprigs.

1 loaf very thinly sliced white bread, crust removed and lightly toasted

Serve chilled with toast triangles.

Cream Fondue
Serves 6

2 cups heavy cream
4 tablespoons butter or margarine
8 flat anchovy fillets, rinsed and finely chopped
1 teaspoon garlic, finely chopped
bread sticks
sweet red pepper strips
scallions
fresh mushrooms
fennel sticks
cauliflower florets
turnip wedges
red radishes
celery sticks
carrot sticks

In a heavy, one-quart enameled saucepan, bring the cream to a boil. Cook it, stirring frequently, for 30-45 minutes, or until it is thick and has reduced to about one cup.

In another one-quart saucepan, sauté the anchovies and the garlic in the butter for 1-2 minutes. Add the reduced cream and bring the sauce to a simmer, stirring constantly.

Pour the fondue into a flameproof dish with a candle warmer or other heat source.

Serve the cream fondue accompanied by the bread sticks and cold vegetables for dipping.

If the butter and cream separate while the sauce stands, beat the mixture with a whisk.

Eggplant Relish
3 Cups

½ cup extra virgin olive oil
4 Japanese eggplants, thinly sliced
2 onions, very thinly sliced
1-3 tablespoons water
2-4 tablespoons soy sauce or to taste
½ cup yogurt or sour cream

table water crackers

Heat the oil in a skillet and sauté the eggplant and the onion until tender. As the oil is absorbed, add a small amount of water to the skillet.

Add the soy sauce and place the lid on the skillet. Continue to cook over low heat until the eggplant and onions are soft.

Chill the eggplant mixture and then add the yogurt or sour cream.

Serve with the table water crackers.

Kennedy Crackers
15 Crackers

1 8-ounce package cream cheese, softened
1 egg yolk
pinch of pepper
garlic powder to taste
Ritz Crackers

Blend the cream cheese, egg yolk, pepper and garlic powder together until smooth.

Mound the mixture on the crackers, to produce a mini-mountain effect.

Place the crackers on a cookie sheet and broil until golden brown. The broiling time will be approximately 1-2 minutes. Watch closely when broiling.

Serve hot.

Moroccan Bastillo
Serves 12

½ cup butter
1 teaspoon salt
1 3-pound chicken with giblets
    and liver
5 cloves garlic, minced
1 medium onion, finely chopped
3 tablespoons fresh coriander <u>or</u>
    1 teaspoon dried coriander
¼ cup minced parsley
1 teaspoon ground ginger
½ teaspoon ground cumin
3 cinnamon sticks
1 large pinch saffron
¾ teaspoon cayenne pepper
½ teaspoon turmeric
3 cups water

Melt the butter in a large pot over medium heat.

Salt the chicken and place it in the pot with the garlic. Brown the chicken and remove from the pot.

Add to the pot the onion, chicken giblets and liver. Cook until the onions are transparent.

Add the coriander, parsley, ginger, cumin, cinnamon sticks, saffron, cayenne and turmeric. Stir to blend.

Add the water gradually, stirring to mix the spices.

Return the chicken to the pot and simmer for one hour.

¼ cup oil <u>or</u> butter
¾ pound whole blanched almonds
⅓ cup powdered sugar
1½ teaspoons cinnamon

In a skillet, heat the oil and lightly brown the almonds. Drain the almonds on paper towels and allow to cool. Reserve 10-15 almonds for garnish.

Grind the almonds coarsely and mix with the powdered sugar and cinnamon. Set aside

Remove the chicken, giblets, liver and cinnamon sticks from the pot. Skin and debone the chicken. Mince the meat with the giblets and liver. Set aside.

½ cup lemon juice
10 eggs, beaten well

Reduce the chicken broth over high heat to 1¾ cups. Lower the heat and add the lemon juice. Slowly add the eggs to the liquid, stirring continuously. The eggs will become curdy, stiff and dry. Set the mixture aside, off the heat.

1 package frozen filo dough
1 cup butter, melted

Preheat the oven to 350° F.

To assemble the bastillo, butter a pizza pan and lay 6 sheets of filo dough across the pan, one at a time, brushing each sheet with melted butter and crisscrossing the rectangular sheets. The ends will be hanging over the edge of the pan.

Brush 6 more sheets with butter, fold them in half and place in the center of the first 6 sheets.

Sprinkle half of the nut mixture over a 12"-13" diameter of the dough-lined pizza pan. Continue with layers of half the egg mixture, the entire chicken mixture, the second half of the egg mixture and the second half of the nut mixture.

Fold the overhanging filo dough to the center and brush with butter.

Crisscross 8 buttered sheets of filo dough across the top of the filling.

Place another pizza pan on top and invert the pans. Remove the top pan and again fold the overlapping dough to the center and brush with butter. Pat the bastillo to form a round loaf.

Place one pizza pan on top and invert again.

Crisscross two more sheets of filo dough over the loaf, brush with butter and tuck under the overhanging edges.

Bake for 25 minutes and drain the excess butter from the pan. Bake another 20 minutes.

3 tablespoons powdered sugar
1 tablespoon cinnamon

Combine the powdered sugar and cinnamon and sift a heavy coating over the top of the bastillo.

Garnish the bastillo with the reserved toasted almonds.

Marinated Crab Claws   *Serves 6*

18 fresh crab claws, shells removed or 3 6½-ounce cans crab legs, drained
1 cup minced green onion
½ cup minced parsley
2 stalks celery, minced
1 clove garlic, crushed
1 cup extra virgin olive oil
½ cup tarragon vinegar
2 tablespoons fresh lemon juice
1 tablespoon Worcestershire sauce

Rinse, drain and pat dry the fresh crab claws and set aside. If the canned crab legs are to be used, drain them and remove any tendons from the meat.

In a medium bowl, mix together the onion, parsley, celery, garlic, olive oil, vinegar, lemon juice and Worcestershire sauce. Whisk the mixture to blend well.

Pour the marinade over the crab claws and refrigerate for several hours.

Serve at room temperature. The crab legs will require a cracker or bread when served.

ELEGANT BITS

Bolder Boulder Breakfast

Milk-with-a-Punch

Flagstaff Casserole
Mangoes with Lime
Strawberry Bread
Chocolate Tea Cake

Chandon Blanc de Noirs

Chandon Blanc de Noirs is a sparkling white wine with a blush. It is excellent with a casserole. This wine has good body and elegant nose, and is produced by one of California's most talented women winemakers.

Milk-with-a-Punch
Serves One

1½ ounces dark rum
1½ ounces brandy
1½ teaspoons powdered sugar
ice cubes
whole milk
nutmeg or cinnamon

In a tall glass, combine the rum, brandy and sugar. Stir well.

Add the desired amount of ice cubes and then fill the glass with the milk. Stir the drink.

Sprinkle the top of the drink with the nutmeg or the cinnamon.

Flagstaff Casserole
Serves 6

2 9-ounce packages frozen artichoke hearts
2 cups diced ham
8 hard-boiled eggs, quartered
1 bay leaf
2 10½-ounce cans cream of mushroom soup
1 tablespoon chopped onion
¼ cup sherry
½ teaspoon salt
¼ teaspoon garlic powder
4 slices American cheese

Preheat the oven to 400° F.

Cook the artichoke hearts according to the package directions and drain.

In an ovenproof casserole, arrange the ham, eggs and artichokes to cover the bottom of the dish.

Combine the bay leaf, soup, onion, sherry, salt and garlic powder. Blend well. Pour the mixture over the ham, eggs and artichokes.

Top with the cheese.

Bake for 25-30 minutes.

Mangoes with Lime
Serves 6

4 ripe mangoes, peeled
2 teaspoons lime juice

Cut the mango fruit from the stones in strips. Place in a serving dish.

Pour the lime juice over the mangoes and toss gently.

Serve at room temperature or chilled.

Strawberry Bread
2 Loaves

1 cup butter or margarine
1½ cups sugar
1 teaspoon vanilla
½ teaspoon grated lemon zest
4 eggs
½ cup sour cream
1 cup strawberry jam
3 cups flour
1 teaspoon salt
1 teaspoon cream of tartar
½ teaspoon baking soda
½ cup chopped nuts

Preheat the oven to 350° F.

Grease two regular loaf pans or 5 4"x2"x2" loaf pans.

Cream the butter, sugar, vanilla and lemon zest. Add the eggs, one at a time, beating well after each addition.

Add all of the dry ingredients alternately with the sour cream and the jam. Blend in the chopped nuts.

Pour the batter into the loaf pans and bake 50-55 minutes for the large loaves. Test at 30-35 minutes for the smaller loaves.

Cool on a rack.

Chocolate Tea Cake
1 Loaf

butter
4 tablespoons fine bread crumbs
1¾ cups flour
1 teaspoon baking soda
½ teaspoon salt
4 tablespoons butter
⅔ cup sugar
1 egg
1 cup buttermilk
½ teaspoon vanilla
1 teaspoon powdered instant coffee or espresso
⅓ cup unsweetened cocoa powder
3 - 6 ounces miniature chocolate chips
1 cup chopped walnuts

This cake may be stored in the refrigerator for one week or frozen for later use. It is best when it is refrigerated overnight after baking.

Preheat the oven to 350° F.

Adjust the oven rack to ⅓ of the way up from the bottom.

Butter a 9"x5"x3" pan, dust with the fine bread crumbs and set aside.

Sift together the flour, baking soda and salt and set aside.

In a large mixing bowl, cream the butter and the sugar. Continue to beat and add the egg, milk and vanilla, blending well.

Add the coffee and the cocoa.

Add the sifted flour mixture, alternating with the buttermilk. Scrape the bowl and beat only until mixed after each addition.

Stir in the chocolate chips and the nuts. Turn the batter into the prepared pan and smooth the top.

Bake for 45 minutes, or until a cake tester inserted in the center comes out clean.

Cool the cake in the pan for 10 minutes. Then, turn it onto a wire rack.

ELEGANT BITS

Blake Street Brunch

Kir Double Royale

Egg Curry
Carrot and Lemon Salad
Cinnamon Pitas

Poppy Seed Cake

Kir Double Royale *Serves 1*

1 sugar cube, dipped in Angostura bitters
champagne, very dry
1 teaspoon Crème de Cassis or to taste
dash of Curacao
twist of lemon

Place the dipped sugar cube in a champagne flute.

Fill the glass with the champagne. Add the Crème de Cassis and the Curacao.

Garnish the drink with the lemon twist.

Egg Curry *Serves 6*

4 tablespoons butter
2 tablespoons minced onion
3 tablespoons flour
1 teaspoon salt
½ teaspoon white pepper
1½ teaspoons curry powder
1 medium apple, pared and coarsely chopped
2 cups scalded milk
3 bananas, peeled and sliced diagonally
lemon juice
1 tablespoon butter
1 cup slivered almonds, toasted
8 hard-boiled eggs, quartered
3 cups cooked rice
shredded coconut
mango chutney

In a saucepan, melt the butter. Sauté the onions for 3 minutes.

Mix the flour, salt, pepper and curry powder together and stir into the butter and the onions. Stir in the apple and cook for about 3 minutes.

Add the milk and stir until the sauce boils and thickens. Keep the sauce hot.

Sprinkle the bananas with the lemon juice. Sauté them in the butter.

Pour the hot sauce over the warm rice. Mound the eggs, bananas and almonds on top. Sprinkle with the coconut.

Serve with the mango chutney.

Carrot and Lemon Salad
Serves 6

10 large carrots
2 tablespoons chopped parsley
2 tablespoons coarsely grated lemon peel
5 green onions, chopped
½ cup olive oil
3 tablespoons fresh lemon juice
¼ teaspoon dry mustard
¼ teaspoon salt
¼ teaspoon pepper

Peel the carrots and cut them into julienne strips.

Steam the carrots for about 4 minutes, or until barely tender. Remove the carrots from the steamer and plunge them into cold water. Drain well.

In a large bowl, combine the carrots, parsley, lemon peel and green onions. Mix thoroughly.

In a small bowl, whisk together the olive oil, lemon juice, mustard, salt and pepper.

Pour the mixture over the carrots and toss until the carrots are well covered with the dressing.

Cover the salad and chill until serving time.

Cinnamon Pitas
Serves 6

6 pita pockets
6 tablespoons butter, melted
cinnamon-sugar

Preheat the oven to 350° F.

Split the pitas in half and cut the halves into two pieces.

Brush each pita piece with the melted butter and sprinkle with the cinnamon-sugar. Place the pitas on a cookie sheet.

Bake for 5-8 minutes, or until the desired crispness is reached.

Poppy Seed Cake
One Cake

2¾ cups sugar
1½ cups vegetable oil
4 eggs
1 cup milk
1 teaspoon vanilla
3 cups flour
1 teaspoon baking soda
1 teaspoon salt
1 2¼-ounce package poppy seeds
powdered sugar

Preheat the oven to 350° F.

Cream the sugar and the oil.

Add the eggs, one at a time, while continuing to beat.

Stir in the milk and the vanilla.

Combine the flour, baking soda, salt and poppy seeds. Blend into the liquid mixture.

Pour the batter into a greased and floured 10-inch tube or Bundt pan.

Bake for 50-60 minutes.

Allow the cake to cool for 15 minutes before removing it from the pan.

Sprinkle with the powdered sugar.

ELEGANT BITS

Cherry Creek Luncheon

Chilled Plum Soup

Southwestern Sole with Crab Sauce
Strawberry and Spinach Salad

Monmousseau Muscadet   or
Bollini Pinot Grigio

Saronno Torte

Monmousseau Muscadet is flinty and crisp. This wine with its earthy flavors is from France's famed Loire Valley.

Bollini Pinot Grigio is an Italian white wine with enough fortitude and character to stand up to the Crab Sauce. It is dry and crisp with a short finish.

Chilled Plum Soup   Serves 6-8

2 1-pound 3-ounce cans plums, pitted
1 cup water
½ cup honey
1 cinnamon stick
¼ teaspoon pepper
pinch of salt
½ cup red wine
1 tablespoon cornstarch
½ cup cream
2 tablespoons fresh lemon juice
1 teaspoon grated lemon peel,
1 cup sour cream
3 tablespoons brandy
sour cream
ground cinnamon

Drain the plums, reserving the syrup. Chop the plums.

In a large saucepan, combine the plums, plum syrup, water, honey, cinnamon stick, pepper and salt. Bring to a boil. Reduce the heat and cook for 5 minutes.

Mix the wine with the cornstarch and stir into the mixture. Add the cream and cook, stirring until thickened.

Add the lemon juice and the lemon peel. Remove the pan from the heat and discard the cinnamon stick.

Whisk one cup of the soup with the sour cream and brandy in a separate bowl until smooth. Add to the hot mixture.

Chill at least 4 hours before serving.

Garnish each bowl of the soup with a teaspoon of sour cream sprinkled with the cinnamon.

Southwestern Sole with Crab Sauce *Serves 8*

2-2½ pounds fillet of sole <u>or</u> fillet of flounder
8 thick flour tortillas
oil for frying tortillas
¾ cup scallions, including green tops
1 tablespoon garlic, minced
1 tablespoon oil
1 tablespoon butter
3 6½-ounce cans crab legs, drained
¾ cup plain yogurt
⅓ cup mayonnaise
3 tablespoons lemon juice
1 teaspoon tarragon
⅛ teaspoon hot red pepper flakes, no seeds
1 cup flour
salt and pepper to taste
¼ cup minced parsley
sliced tomatoes

Wash the fillets well and set them in the milk for 20 minutes. Make sure the fish is coated by the milk.

Preheat the oven to 200° F.

Dampen each tortilla with water and keep wrapped for 5 minutes before frying. Fry the tortillas in one inch of hot vegetable oil until they are puffed and golden on both sides. Drain on paper towels.

Place the tortillas on oven racks to keep warm until ready to be assembled.

Sauté the scallions and the garlic in the oil and the butter until they are transparent. Remove the pan from the heat.

Add the crabmeat, yogurt, mayonnaise, lemon juice, tarragon and red pepper flakes to the pan. This mixture will be reheated just before assembling the dish.

Sprinkle the flour over a surface covered with wax paper. Add the salt and pepper, blending well.

Remove the fillets from the milk but do not drain them. Coat the fish on all sides with the seasoned flour, shaking to rid the fillets of excess flour.

Heat the butter in a large skillet and cook the fillets until golden. Turn once to cook both sides. The total cooking time for each fillet should be 4-5 minutes. Transfer the fillets to a warm platter as they are cooked.

To assemble the dish, warm the crab sauce and place the warm tortillas on the dinner plates. Place 2 fillets over each tortilla. Top with reheated crab sauce. Garnish with the parsley.

Serve hot with sliced tomatoes.

ELEGANT BITS

Strawberry and Spinach Salad
Serves 6

10 ounces fresh spinach, stems removed, washed and torn into pieces
1 pound fresh strawberries, halved
¼ cup sugar
3 tablespoons fresh lemon juice
1 egg yolk
6 tablespoons vegetable oil

Place the spinach and the strawberries in a salad bowl. Chill well.

In a bowl or a covered jar, combine the sugar and the lemon juice. Whisk to dissolve the sugar.

Add the egg yolk. Whisk to blend well.

Add the oil, a little at a time, whisking constantly until the dressing is thick and creamy.

Cover and refrigerate the dressing until ready to serve. Whisk or shake the covered jar before dressing the salad.

Toss the salad, making sure some of the strawberries are visible.

Serve chilled.

Saronno Torte
8 Servings

1 cup unsalted butter, softened
1 cup sugar
5 egg yolks
½ teaspoon almond extract
½ teaspoon vanilla extract
½ cup amaretti crumbs
½ cup flour, sifted
4 ounces semi-sweet chocolate chips
6 egg whites
powdered sugar

This delicious torte can be made a day ahead of serving. It also freezes well.

Preheat the oven to 350° F.

Butter and flour a 10" springform pan.

Cream the butter and the sugar until very fluffy. Beat in the egg yolks, one at a time, mixing well after each addition. Add the almond and vanilla extracts and stir thoroughly.

Gradually add the amaretti crumbs and the flour, beating well. Fold in the chocolate pieces.

In a separate bowl, beat the egg whites until stiff peaks form. Stir a small portion of the whites into the batter to loosen it. Then, fold in the remaining whites carefully.

Spread the batter into the prepared pan and bake for 35-45 minutes or until the torte tests done.

Cool in the pan for 30 minutes. Loosen the edges with a knife and remove the sides of the pan. Cool the torte completely.

Dust the torte generously with powdered sugar before serving.

Loveland Luncheon

Lemon Consommé

Papaya Baked with Cheese
Fennel Salad on Tomato Slices
Herbed Pita Toast

Clos Du Bois Johannisberg Riesling, Early Harvest   or Beringer Chenin Blanc

---

Chocolate Kahlua Tarts

Clos Du Bois Johannisberg Riesling, Early Harvest is made from grapes picked when the acids are high, resulting in a crisp, slightly-sweet, sipping wine.

Beringer Chenin Blanc has been a gold medal winner for 4 years in a row. Sweet aromas rise from a glass of this light-bodied wine that rivals the smallest estates in Loire.

Lemon Consommé   *Serves 6*

6 cups chicken broth
juice of 1½ large lemons
3 egg yolks, lightly beaten
6 very thin lemon slices
chopped parsley

In a large saucepan, bring the broth to a boil.

Combine the lemon juice and the egg yolks, mixing thoroughly.

Remove the broth from the heat and gradually pour in the egg and lemon mixture, stirring very rapidly.

Serve the soup hot or cold. Garnish each bowl with a lemon slice and a sprinkling of the chopped parsley.

Papaya Baked with Cheese   *Serves 6*

2 cups cottage cheese
3 3-ounce packages cream cheese, softened
¾ teaspoon curry powder
2 tablespoons chopped chutney
3 tablespoons golden raisins
1 cup thinly sliced water chestnuts
3 papayas, halved and seeded
3 tablespoons cinnamon-sugar
3 tablespoons butter, melted
watercress <u>or</u> parsley

Preheat the oven to 450° F.

Blend the cottage cheese, cream cheese and curry powder until smooth.

Stir in the chutney, raisins and water chestnuts.

Fill the papaya halves with the cheese mixture and sprinkle the tops with the cinnamon-sugar and the melted butter.

Bake for 15-20 minutes.

Serve hot. Garnish with the watercress or the parsley.

ELEGANT BITS

Fennel Salad on Tomato Slices
Serves 6

2 fennel bulbs
½ cup extra virgin olive oil
1 tablespoon fresh lemon juice
salt and pepper to taste
2-3 ripe tomatoes, peeled and thinly sliced

Wash the fennel bulbs. Remove the green tops, any tough outer leaves and a thin slice from the bottom.

Slice the bulbs wafer-thin and place in a bowl.

Add the olive oil, lemon juice, salt and pepper and toss. Refrigerate for 1-2 hours.

Before serving, again toss the fennel slices in the dressing. Serve on thin slices of ripe tomatoes.

Herbed Pita Toast
Serves 6

6 pita pockets
6 tablespoons butter, melted
crushed basil
salt and pepper to taste

Preheat the oven to 350° F.

Split the pitas in half and cut the halves into two pieces.

Brush each pita piece with the melted butter and sprinkle with the basil, salt and pepper.

Bake for 5-8 minutes, or until the desired crispness is reached.

Serve hot or at room temperature.

Chocolate Kahlua Tarts

See page 210.

Mountain Weekend Dinner

Leek Salad

Scallops in Mushroom-Tomato Cream
Baked Rice
Grated Zucchini

Concannon Chardonnay   or
Stevenot Sauvignon Blanc

Pueblo Cream

Concannon Chardonnay is a "find". The mellow fruitiness is a great blend with the mushroom-scallop combination.

Stevenot Sauvignon Blanc is not as dry as most Sauvignon Blancs. It is more mellow in body with a bit of lemon grass in the after taste.

Leek Salad *6-8 Servings*

10 leeks, green tops removed
¼ cup vegetable oil
¼ cup olive oil
3 tablespoons wine vinegar
1 clove garlic, finely minced
¼ cup chopped parsley
¼ cup thinly sliced green onions
2 tablespoons green peppercorns
2 tablespoons chopped pimiento
salt and pepper to taste
fresh spinach leaves

Wash the leeks well. Slice the leeks thinly.

Steam the leeks for about 4 minutes, or until the desired tenderness is reached.

Cool the leeks.

Mix the remaining ingredients, except the spinach leaves, and toss with the leeks. Refrigerate until serving time.

Serve on a bed of fresh spinach leaves.

Scallops in Mushroom-Tomato Cream *Serves 6*

3 pints scallops, about 3 pounds
⅓ cup butter
¼ cup finely chopped shallots
3 cups quartered mushrooms
1 pint cherry tomatoes, peeled
⅓ cup dry white wine
1½ cups heavy cream
salt and freshly ground pepper to taste
1½ tablespoons finely chopped parsley

Rinse any sand from the scallops and let them drain.

Heat all but one tablespoon of the butter in a large skillet over medium heat. When the butter is hot but before it is browned, add the scallops.

Cook the scallops, shaking the skillet and stirring until lightly golden, about 1-2 minutes. Do not overcook.

Remove the scallops from the pan with a slotted spoon and set aside in a covered dish.

Add the remaining butter to the skillet with the shallots, mushrooms and tomatoes. Cook and stir for 2 minutes.

Add the wine to the skillet and reduce the liquid by half.

Add the cream, salt and pepper and cook over high heat for 3-4 minutes.

Add the scallops and stir to reheat them.

Pour the mixture into a serving dish and sprinkle with the parsley.

Serve immediately.

Baked Rice *Serves 6*

3 tablespoons butter
3 tablespoons minced onion
2 cups uncooked rice
3 cups chicken broth
1 tablespoon minced parsley
¼ teaspoon dried thyme
⅛ teaspoon cayenne pepper

Preheat the oven to 400° F.

Melt the butter in a large saucepan and cook the onion until it is transparent.

Add the rice and stir to coat the grains.

Stir in the chicken broth, parsley, thyme and pepper.

Place the rice in a covered baking dish.

Bake for 20 minutes.

Keep the rice covered in a warm place until serving time.

Grated Zucchini

Serves 6

4 tablespoons butter or margarine
6 small zucchini, grated
salt and pepper to taste
½ cup cream, optional

In a large skillet, melt the butter over medium heat. Sauté the zucchini stirring constantly, for about 4 minutes. The squash should be tender and the liquids reduced to no more than a tablespoon.

Season with the salt and pepper and add the cream. Heat through.

Serve hot.

Pueblo Cream

Serves 6

This unusual dessert is very rich. Thus, small servings are appropriate. Do not prepare it more than two to three hours in advance because it darkens after a few hours.

To reduce the chilling time, refrigerate the ingredients and the serving dishes before preparation begins.

2 avocados, halved and peeled
¼ cup fresh lime juice
½ cup plus 1 tablespoon powdered sugar
2 tablespoons white crème de cacao
¾ cup chopped unsalted pistachio nuts
1½ cups heavy cream, whipped
lime slices

Using a blender or a food processor fitted with a steel blade, blend the avocado, lime juice, sugar and crème de cacao until smooth.

Stir in the pistachio nuts, reserving one tablespoon for garnish.

Fold in the whipped cream.

Divide the dessert among 6 clear glass serving dishes or wine glasses.

Garnish with the chopped nuts and the lime slices.

Chill the dessert before serving.

ELEGANT BITS

Springtime Supper

Cauliflower Soup

Baked Snapper on Lettuce
Steamed Asparagus with Olive Oil
Tarragon Sautéed New Potatoes

Olarra Blanco Seco or
Julian Robaire Graves

Strawberry-Orange Sorbet
Marie Antoinette Lace Cookies

Olarra Blanco Seco is one of the best values on the market. Produced in the Rioja, south of France, this wine is similar to a California Fumé Blanc. Today, Spain is producing fine wines at great prices.

Julian Robaire Graves is produced in a California style and blended with a large amount of Semillion. It is made in a "restaurant style" — ready to drink when released.

Cauliflower Soup
Serves 6-8

2 tablespoons vegetable oil
½ cup chopped onion
1 small carrot, grated
1 head cauliflower, cut into small florets
1 cup chopped celery
8 cups chicken broth
½ teaspoon peppercorns
1 teaspoon tarragon
½ bay leaf
¼ cup butter or margarine
¾ cup flour
2 cups milk
1 cup half and half
salt to taste
1 cup sour cream
2 tablespoons minced parsley

Heat the oil in a large saucepan over medium heat. Sauté the onions and the carrot until the onions are transparent.

Add the cauliflower and the celery. Lower the heat and cover. Cook for 15 minutes, stirring occasionally.

Add the broth.

Tie the peppercorns, tarragon and bay leaf in cheese cloth and add the bouquet garni to the broth. Simmer for 15 minutes.

In a medium saucepan, melt the butter. Add the flour, stirring to blend the roux.

Slowly whisk in the milk and bring to a boil. Cook until the sauce is thick and smooth, stirring constantly. Remove from the heat and stir in the half and half.

Stir the sauce into the simmering soup. Season to taste and continue simmering for 15 minutes.

Just before serving, remove the bouquet garni and whisk in the sour cream.

Add the chopped parsley. Reheat the soup but do not boil. Serve hot.

Baked Snapper on Lettuce

Serves 6

4 cups shredded iceberg lettuce
2 pounds fresh red snapper fillets
1 cup mayonnaise
1 cup grated Parmesan cheese
2 green onions, chopped
chopped parsley

Preheat the oven to 350° F.

Cover the bottom of a greased, ovenproof serving dish with the shredded lettuce. Place the fish on top of the lettuce bed.

In a medium bowl, mix together the mayonnaise, cheese and green onions. Spread the mixture on the top of the fillets.

Bake for 30 minutes. Sprinkle the fish with chopped parsley and serve at once.

Steamed Asparagus with Olive Oil

Serves 6

3 pounds fresh asparagus
salt and pepper to taste
2 tablespoons extra virgin olive oil

Snap off the tough bottoms of the asparagus.

Place the asparagus in the top of a steamer over boiling water. Steam slender stalks for 2-3 minutes and thick stalks for 5-6 minutes.

Remove the asparagus from the steamer and arrange on a warm serving platter.

Season with the salt, pepper and olive oil.

Tarragon Sautéed New Potatoes

Serves 6

2 pounds small new potatoes
4 tablespoons butter
2 teaspoons tarragon
salt and freshly ground pepper
    to taste

Wash and dry the potatoes.

Melt the butter in a large skillet. Slice the potatoes very thinly into the butter.

Add the tarragon and cover the potatoes. Cook turning with a spatula, until they are tender and lightly browned.

Season with the salt and pepper. Serve hot.

Soak fish in milk for 15-20 minutes to freshen the taste.

Measure the thickest part of a piece of fish. Cook 10 minutes per inch at the thickest part.

ELEGANT BITS

Strawberry-Orange Sorbert

Serves 6

1½ cups orange juice
½ cup freshly squeezed lemon juice
3 10-ounce packages frozen
    strawberries
1 cup sugar
3 cups champagne
fresh strawberries or orange slices

Combine the orange juice, lemon juice, strawberries, and sugar. Place the mixture in a blender in batches and blend until smooth.

Add the champagne and pour into a 9"x12"x2" pan. Freeze for 4 hours.

Whip the sorbet and refreeze.

Garnish the sorbet with fresh strawberries or orange slices when served.

Marie Antoinette's Lace Cookies

See page 205.

Aspen Alfresco

Cucumber-Watercress Soup

Vitello Tonnato
Tomatoes Provençal
French Bread

Freemark Abbey Chardonnay

White Chocolate Strawberries
Currant Cookies

Freemark Abbey Chardonnay is mouth-filling and beautifully balanced. The fruit is not so forward and the softness matches the veal and tuna sauce combination.

Cucumber-Watercress Soup   *Serves 6*

3 cucumbers, peeled, seeded and sliced
1 bunch watercress, stems removed and leaves chopped
3 tablespoons butter
1½ cups diced cooked potatoes
1 quart chicken broth
1 cup heavy cream
salt and pepper to taste
cucumber slices
watercress sprigs

In a large saucepan, sauté the cucumbers and the watercress in the butter until the cucumbers are soft and the watercress is wilted.

Add the potatoes and the chicken broth. Cover and simmer for 10-15 minutes.

Remove the saucepan from the heat and cool.

Purée the soup in a food processor or a blender.

Add the heavy cream, salt and pepper, stirring well.

Refrigerate the soup for several hours to chill thoroughly before serving.

Pour the soup into chilled bowls. Garnish with a cucumber slice and a watercress sprig.

ELEGANT BITS

Vitello Tonnato
Serves 6

Plan to prepare this marvelous hot-weather fare a day in advance.

1 3-pound round <u>or</u> loin of veal, boned, rolled and tied
water
2 stalks celery, leaves included
2 carrots, peeled
1 small onion
2 cups dry white wine

In a large pot, cover the veal with the water. Add the celery, carrots, onion and wine.

Bring the liquid to a boil and lower the heat. Cover the pot and simmer for 1½ hours.

Remove the pot from the heat and let the meat cool in the broth.

2 7-ounce cans white tuna, packed in oil
1 2-ounce can anchovies, packed in oil
2 tablespoons wine vinegar
juice of one lemon
1 cup extra virgin olive oil

In a food processor or a blender, prepare the tuna sauce. Add the tuna with its oil, anchovies with their oil, vinegar, lemon juice and olive oil to the work bowl. Process until the sauce is creamy in texture.

When the meat is cool, remove it to a carving board and cut it into ¼-inch slices. Arrange the slices on a serving dish in an overlapping pattern.

Pour the tuna sauce over the veal, lifting the sliced veal to coat all sides of it.

Refrigerate covered for one day before serving.

3 tablespoons capers, drained
1 8-ounce jar gherkins, drained
1 2¼-ounce can ripe olives, sliced
1 2-ounce can rolled anchovies, drained
¼ cup pickled red pepper strips <u>or</u> pimiento strips

At serving time, garnish the veal with the capers, gherkins, olives, anchovy curls and pickled red peppers or pimientos.

Tomatoes Provencal
Serves 6

This recipe is best prepared in the summer with vine ripened tomatoes.

Preheat the oven to 350°F.

6 ripe tomatoes
1 cup chopped parsley
½ cup pine nuts
½ teaspoon seasoned salt
1 tablespoon minced garlic
juice of ½ lemon
3 tablespoons olive oil
2 tablespoons dry white wine

Halve the tomatoes and remove the seeds with a small spoon. Place the tomatoes in an oiled baking dish.

Combine the remaining ingredients and use the mixture to fill the hollow seed cavities in the tomato halves.

Bake for 15-20 minutes, or until heated through.

White Chocolate Strawberries

Serves 6

2 pints fresh strawberries
1 pound bulk white chocolate
1 cup chopped unsalted pistachio nuts or 1 cup chopped pine nuts or 1 cup toasted, chopped cashews or 1 cup almond brickle chips

Clean and dry the strawberries, leaving the green stems on the berries. Set aside.

In the top of a double boiler, melt the chocolate over boiling water.

Remove the pan from the heat and dip each berry in the chocolate. Then dip the tip of the berry in one type of the chopped nuts or the almond brickle chips.

Place the berries on serving dishes. Allow the chocolate to harden before serving.

Currant Cookies

See page 204.

ELEGANT BITS

Central City Supper

Carpaccio

Vosne Romanée Red Burgundy

Lobster and Chicken Marengo
Italian Steamed Rice
Braised Scallions

Concannon Sauvignon Blanc   or
Rutherford Hill Sauvignon Blanc

Lettuce and Orange Salad

Opera House Pie

Vosne Romanée Red Burgundy is perfection! It is smooth and mellow with elegant fire for the capers and truffles. Burgundy, in fact, is the center of the truffle area in France.

Concannon Sauvignon Blanc has slightly grassy flavors which is very typical of French Graves. It is dry and crisp with a straw-golden color.

Rutherford Hill Sauvignon Blanc is a very fruity wine balanced by oak ageing. It is not as grassy as many California Sauvignon Blancs.

Carpaccio *Serves 6*

12 very thin slices sirloin steak, about ½ pound
juice of one lemon
12 thin slices Parmesan cheese
2 tablespoons capers, drained
1 truffle, thinly sliced

Cover the steak slices with the lemon juice and let marinate for 2 hours in the refrigerator.

Return the meat to room temperature and place several slices on each serving plate.

Garnish with the Parmesan cheese slices, capers and truffles.

Lobster and Chicken Marengo

Serves 6-8

This is a great make-ahead dish. Everything can be done a day in advance except for the addition of the lobster and the tomatoes. This dish can also be used for a buffet and served in a chafing dish with the chicken cut into bite-sized pieces.

4 chicken breasts, skinned, boned and split
¼ cup butter
2 tablespoons dry sherry
½ pound fresh mushrooms, sliced
2 tablespoons flour
1½ cups chicken stock
1 bay leaf, crushed
1 tablespoon tomato paste
2 tablespoons chopped fresh chives
½ teaspoon salt
¼ teaspoon pepper
1½ pounds lobster meat, cooked and cut into bite-size pieces
1 pint cherry tomatoes

Preheat the oven to 300° F.

In a skillet, heat the butter until it foams. Add the chicken and brown until golden. Spoon the sherry over the chicken.

Remove the chicken to a shallow baking dish, reserving the skillet and drippings. Cover the chicken with foil and bake for 25-30 minutes, or until tender.

Add the mushrooms to the reserved skillet and sauté for 4-5 minutes.

Blend in the flour. Add the chicken stock and simmer, stirring constantly until thickened.

Season with the bay leaf, tomato paste, chives, salt and pepper. Simmer the mixture slowly for 15 minutes.

Add the lobster meat and the tomatoes to the sauce and simmer slowly for 5-8 minutes more, or until the lobster and tomatoes are well heated.

Serve the chicken breasts on a large platter topped with the sauce. Arrange rice or curly endive around the edge of the platter.

Italian Steamed Rice

Serves 6

3 tablespoons butter
2 shallots, sliced
2 cups uncooked Italian rice
3 cups chicken broth or water
3 tablespoons freshly grated Parmesan cheese

In a large saucepan, melt the butter over medium heat.

Sauté the shallots until they are transparent.

Add the rice and stir briefly.

Add the chicken broth or water and increase the heat. When the broth boils, stir once with a fork and reduce the heat to the lowest setting. Place the lid on the pan and cook for 20 minutes.

Add the cheese and fluff the rice once.

Serve hot.

ELEGANT BITS

Braised Scallions
Serves 6

3 bunches scallions, roots trimmed
½ cup water
3 tablespoons butter or margarine
1 tablespoon dry white wine
salt and pepper to taste

Place the scallions, water and butter in a large skillet.

Cook over high heat for about 4 minutes. The water should evaporate. Continue to cook in the butter to just brown the scallions.

Add the wine, shaking the pan to blend the flavor.

Season with the salt and pepper. Remove the scallions from the heat and serve immediately.

Lettuce and Orange Salad
Serves 6-8

1 medium head leaf lettuce, torn into small pieces
1 small cucumber, thinly sliced
1 large orange, peeled and thinly sliced or
　1 16-ounce can Mandarin orange sections, drained
3 green onions, thinly sliced
1 avocado, seeded, peeled and sliced

In a large salad bowl, combine the lettuce, cucumber, orange sections, onions and avocado.

Just before serving, pour the desired amount of Orange Salad Dressing over the salad and toss lightly.

Orange Salad Dressing
One Cup

½ teaspoon grated fresh orange peel
¼ cup fresh orange juice
½ cup vegetable oil
1 tablespoon sugar
2 tablespoons red wine vinegar
1 tablespoon lemon juice
½ teaspoon salt

Combine all of the ingredients in a blender. Cover and blend until well mixed.

Opera House Pie
Serves 8

1 cup butter
½ cup sugar
½ cup brown sugar
2 eggs
½ cup flour
1 cup chopped walnuts
1 6-ounce package semi-sweet chocolate morsels
1 9-inch pie shell, unbaked
whipped cream or ice cream

Preheat the oven to 325° F.

In a large bowl, cream the butter and the sugars. Add the eggs and mix well.

Add the flour and blend well.

Add the walnuts and the chocolate morsels and stir to blend.

Pour the mixture into the pie shell and bake for one hour.

Before serving, garnish the pie with the whipped cream or ice cream.

Grand Lake Regatta Supper

Pistachio Soup

Brochettes of Shrimp and Zucchini
Apricot Rice
Sautéed Cherry Tomatoes

Kenwood Chenin Blanc   or
Pecota French Colombard

A Cake for All Seasons

Ridge Zinfandel, Late Harvest

Kenwood Chenin Blanc is a light-bodied and fruity wine. It is produced in a dry style from the grape that produces the famous Vouvray wines of the Loire Valley in France.

Pecota French Colombard is an oak-aged wine similar to a Sauvignon Blanc at half of the price. It is dry and simple and easy to drink. Save the label — it is a true piece of art!

Ridge Zinfandel, Late Harvest, is a red wine to try with chocolate if you have the entrepreneurial spirit. This is California's version of a fine ruby port.

Pistachio Soup   *Serves 6*

1½ **cups shelled pistachio nuts, unsalted**
1½ **cups chicken broth**
1 **cup heavy cream**
1 **cup plain yogurt**
¼ **cup white wine**
salt and pepper to taste
flowers or rose petals

Blend the pistachio nuts and the chicken broth for one minute in a blender.

Add the cream and the yogurt, blending until well mixed.

Stir in the wine and season with the salt and pepper.

Chill the soup for 2-3 hours before serving.

Pour into chilled bowls and garnish the soup with small flowers or rose petals.

ELEGANT BITS

⅓ cup oil
3 tablespoons lemon juice
¼ teaspoon salt
½ teaspoon lemon pepper
½ teaspoon garlic powder
1 teaspoon oregano
2 pounds large shrimp, shelled and deveined
1-3 zucchini, sliced into one-inch pieces
1 6-ounce can pitted ripe olives

Brochettes of Shrimp and Zucchini *Serves 6*

Mix the first 6 ingredients together in a large bowl. Add the shrimp. Cover and chill overnight.

Thread the zucchini onto skewers, alternating with the shrimp and the olives. Reserve any remaining marinade.

Cook the kabobs over hot coals for 10-15 minutes, turning and basting with the reserved marinade. Do not overcook.

¼ cup butter
2 cups long-grained rice, rinsed and drained
3½ cups water
¼ teaspoon salt
½ cup white raisins
⅔ cup diced dried apricots

Apricot Rice *Serves 6*

Melt the butter in a large, heavy saucepan over medium heat.

Add the rice and stir until golden, about 2-3 minutes.

Add the water and the salt and bring to a boil. Reduce the heat to low, cover the pan and simmer for 5 minutes.

Stir in the raisins and the apricots. Cover and continue to cook until the rice is dry and soft, about 12 minutes.

3 tablespoons butter
3 cups cherry tomatoes, washed, stemmed and dried
salt to taste
chopped fresh basil or dried basil

Sautéed Cherry Tomatoes *6 Servings*

Melt the butter in a large skillet.

Add the tomatoes and sauté until the tomatoes begin to split. Stir often so that the tomatoes do not burn.

Season with the salt.

Sprinkle heavily with the basil and serve at once.

A Cake for All Seasons
Serves 8

A Cake for All Seasons is best if prepared a day in advance. This delicious cake can serve as a birthday cake for children and adults.

Pound Cake

1 cup butter or ½ cup butter and
    ½ cup margarine
2 cups sugar
6 eggs
2 teaspoons vanilla
2 cups flour
¼ teaspoon salt

Preheat the oven to 350° F.

In a large mixing bowl, cream the butter and the sugar.

Add the eggs, one at a time, while continuing to beat.

Add the vanilla and blend well.

Add the flour with the salt, one cup at a time, and blend well.

Pour the batter into a greased and floured 8"x4" loaf pan.

Bake for one hour, or until a cake tester inserted in the center comes out clean.

Cool and chill the cake. Split it into 3 layers.

Ricotta Cheese Filling

1 16-ounce container ricotta cheese
2 tablespoons heavy cream
¼ cup sugar
3 tablespoons orange liqueur
4 tablespoons chopped candied fruit
    or white raisins
2 ounces semi-sweet chocolate,
    coarsely chopped

Mix the cheese, cream, sugar and liqueur, beating until smooth.

Add the fruit and the chopped chocolate. Blend well.

Spread the filling between the pound cake layers. Cover and chill.

Chocolate Frosting

6 ounces semi-sweet chocolate
⅓ cup black coffee
½ pound unsalted butter, cut into
    one-inch pieces
orange or almond liqueur to taste

In a double boiler, melt the chocolate in the coffee. Remove from the heat.

Beat in the butter, one piece at a time, until smooth.

Stir in the orange or almond liqueur.

Frost the cake on the top and sides or spread a very thick layer on the top only. Chill at least 24 hours before serving.

ELEGANT BITS

Summer Reunion Dinner

Chilled Tomato-Dill Soup

Blueberry Chicken
Corn Custard
Whole Wheat French Bread

Geyser Peak Chardonnay   or
Beringer Riesling

Palm Hearts, Avocado and Lettuce Salad

Strawberry Tart

Geyser Peak Chardonnay is a lighter Chardonnay with the taste of some butter and oak. It is not too complex so it does not overmatch the chicken.

Beringer Riesling is dry and fruity. It perfectly complements the chicken. Serve it well chilled.

Chilled Tomato-Dill Soup   *Serves 6*

2 medium onions, chopped
1 clove garlic, chopped
2 tablespoons margarine
4 large ripe tomatoes, cored, seeded and quartered
½ cup water
1 chicken bouillon cube
1 teaspoon dried dill weed
⅛ teaspoon salt
⅛ teaspoon pepper
½ cup mayonnaise
chopped fresh dill or chopped parsley

In a 2-quart saucepan, sauté the onion and the garlic in the margarine until wilted.

Add the tomatoes, water, bouillon cube, dill weed, salt and pepper and simmer covered for 10 minutes.

Remove the soup from the heat and allow it to cool.

Place the mixture in a blender one half at a time, and blend until smooth.

Whisk in the mayonnaise.

Cover and chill overnight.

Serve in chilled bowls with a sprinkling of dill or chopped parsley.

Blueberry Chicken
Serves 6

3 - 3½ pound chicken, cut into 8 pieces or an equal amount of chicken breast
1 tablespoon vegetable oil
1 tablespoon unsalted butter
⅔ cup dry white wine
¼ cup blueberry vinegar or wine vinegar
1 tablespoon minced garlic
1 10¾-ounce can chicken broth
1 tablespoon tomato paste
1 cup fresh or frozen blueberries, unthawed

In a large stainless steel or enameled skillet, brown the chicken in the oil and butter over medium heat. Transfer the chicken to a platter after browning.

Add the wine, vinegar, and garlic to the skillet. Deglaze the skillet, scraping up the brown bits clinging to the bottom and the sides.

Stir in the chicken broth and the tomato paste.

Bring the liquid to a boil and add the browned chicken.

Cover the mixture and simmer for 35-40 minutes, or until the chicken is tender.

Transfer the chicken to a warm plate. Cover it and keep it warm.

Skim the fat from the pan juices and reduce the juices over high heat to about one cup.

The blueberries should be added just before serving. Spoon the blueberries into the boiling juices and remove the pan from the heat immediately. Stir just to warm the berries.

Top the chicken with the sauce and serve at once.

Corn Custard
Serves 6

3 eggs, well beaten
¼ cup flour
½ teaspoon salt
½ teaspoon freshly ground white pepper
1 10-ounce package frozen corn, thawed
1 tablespoons butter or margarine, melted
2 cups light cream

Preheat the oven to 325° F.

In a large mixing bowl, beat together the eggs, flour, salt and pepper.

Stir in the corn, butter and light cream.

Pour the mixture into a greased 3-quart baking dish and place the dish in a pan of hot water.

Bake for 1½ hours, or until a knife inserted in the center comes out clean.

ELEGANT BITS

Palm Hearts, Avocado and Lettuce Salad *Serves 6*

2 heads Bibb lettuce, torn into bite-sized pieces
2 avocados, seeded, peeled and cut into cubes
1 16-ounce can hearts of palm, drained and sliced
6 tablespoons olive oil
2 tablespoons vinegar
½ teaspoon salt
freshly ground black pepper

In a large salad bowl, combine the lettuce, avocados and palm hearts.

In a small bowl, whisk together the olive oil, vinegar and salt.

Just before serving, pour the dressing over the salad and toss gently.

Sprinkle the top of the salad with the freshly ground pepper or pass a peppermill at the table.

Strawberry Tart *Serves 6*

This tart can also be made with fresh blueberries and blackberry jelly.

After the tart shell has been baked and cooled, it can be left in the pan, covered with foil and frozen for later use.

1 cup flour
2 tablespoons powdered sugar
½ cup butter

Preheat the oven to 425° F.

Combine the flour, powdered sugar and butter in the work bowl of a food processor. Process with a steel blade until the mixture forms a dough ball. Stop immediately.

Press the dough into a greased 9-inch tart pan.

Bake for 10-12 minutes or until golden in color.

Cool and remove from the pan. Place the shell on a plate covered with a doily.

3 cups fresh strawberries, washed and dried, with stems removed
1 10-ounce jar red raspberry jelly or strawberry jelly
chopped pistachio nuts or slivered almonds
ice cream or whipped cream

Arrange the strawberries, pointed ends up, in the tart shell.

Melt the jelly over low heat. Allow it to cool slightly while stirring.

Brush each strawberry liberally with the jelly, making sure to completely cover and seal each berry. Pour any remaining jelly between the strawberries.

Chill for at least 2 hours before serving.

Serve as is or garnish with chopped pistachio nuts, slivered almonds, ice cream or whipped cream.

Symphony Supper

Salad Gruyère
French Bread

Veal with Prosciutto
Buttered Egg Noodles
Eggplant with Sun-Dried Tomatoes

Simi Chardonnay   or
Pine Ridge (Oak Knoll) Chardonnay

Summer Berries

Simi Chardonnay is an "insider's" wine and one of California's very best. The fruit of the grape is very forward, yet the oak ageing adds delicious vanilla flavors. If Burgundy is Beethoven, then Chardonnay is Dvořák.

Pine Ridge (Oak Knoll) Chardonnay is produced by former Colorado resident, Gary Andrus. It is a very rich and full-bodied wine with a lingering finish. The Oak Knoll Vineyard produces Andrus' best Chardonnay grapes. In texture, this wine is like Brahm's Fourth Symphony.

Salad Gruyère *Serves 6-8*

3 cups diagonally sliced celery
1 cup julienne strips of Gruyère cheese
2 cups sliced fresh mushrooms
6 tablespoons olive oil
1½ tablespoons wine vinegar
1½ teaspoons Dijon mustard
salt and freshly ground pepper to taste
Bibb lettuce
chopped parsley

Combine the celery, cheese and mushrooms in a large bowl.

Mix the olive oil, vinegar, mustard, salt and pepper. Pour the dressing over the cheese and the vegetables.

Marinate the salad for 10-15 minutes before serving.

Serve the salad on beds of the Bibb lettuce and sprinkle with the chopped parsley.

ELEGANT BITS

8 3-ounce veal loin scallops, pounded
salt and freshly ground pepper to taste
2 tablespoons flour
⅓ cup butter or margarine
2 cups sliced fresh mushrooms
6 ounces prosciutto, diced
2 teaspoons chopped shallots
1 cup port wine
1 cup heavy cream
1 tablespoon chopped parsley
1 teaspoon fresh lime juice
lime slices, Italian parsley or tomato roses

Veal with Prosciutto
Serves 6

Season the veal with the salt and pepper and dust lightly with the flour.

Sauté the veal in the butter until tender and cooked through. Transfer it to a warm platter.

Sauté the mushrooms in the butter remaining in the pan until tender.

Add the prosciutto, shallots and wine. Cook to reduce the liquid.

Add the cream and continue to reduce the sauce until fairly thick.

Add the parsley and the lime juice, stirring to blend.

Return the veal to the sauce and heat through.

Serve hot and garnish with lime slices, Italian parsley or tomato roses.

1 8.8-ounce package egg noodles
2 tablespoons butter, softened or olive oil

Buttered Egg Noodles
Serves 6

Cook the noodles according to the package directions. Drain and add the butter or olive oil. Serve hot with the Veal with Prosciutto.

Eggplant with Sun-Dried Tomatoes
Serves 6

7 Japanese eggplants
1 tablespoon salt
⅓ cup vegetable oil
6 scallions, cut into ½-inch pieces
5 sun-dried tomatoes, rinsed and chopped (If oil packed sun-dried tomatoes are used, drain the oil and chop.)
salt and pepper to taste

Slice the eggplants lengthwise into thin 2-inch strips and place in a colander. Sprinkle with the salt and let them stand for 15 minutes.

Rinse the eggplant and pat it dry.

In a large skillet, sauté the eggplant in the oil, stirring until it is tender and lightly browned. The cooking time will be about 4-5 minutes.

Add the scallions and the tomatoes. Cover and continue cooking for 1 minute.

Season with the salt and pepper and serve hot.

Summer Berries
Serves 6

1 pint fresh blueberries, cleaned and dried
2 pints fresh strawberries, washed, dried and halved
grated zest of one orange
½ cup honey
⅓ cup blueberry vinegar or cider vinegar
1 pint fresh raspberries

Combine the blueberries, strawberries and the grated orange zest in a bowl.

In a small bowl, whisk together the honey and vinegar. Pour it over the blueberries and strawberries. Cover and refrigerate for two hours.

Just before serving, add the raspberries and toss gently.

ELEGANT BITS

Telluride Barbecue

Marinated Leeks
___

Barbecued Leg of Lamb
Barley and Mushrooms
Spinach with Red Onions

Simi Pinot Noir   or
Rutherford Hill Merlot
___

Raspberries Sabayon

Simi Pinot Noir is soft and velvety, dry and medium-bodied. Winemaker Zelma Long produces in a style similar to a French Burgundy.

Rutherford Hill Merlot is a softer wine than the Cabernet Sauvignon. It has a good balance of fruit and oak flavors. In Bordeaux, Merlot is blended with Cabernet to produce the famed wines of Lafite and Mouton.

Marinated Leeks   *Serves 6*

⅓ cup extra virgin olive oil
2 tablespoons balsamic **or** wine vinegar
1 clove garlic, chopped
1 cup white wine
1 teaspoon salt
½ teaspoon freshly ground black pepper
1 sprig parsley
¼ teaspoon thyme

12 small leeks
water **or** white wine
1 tablespoon chopped parsley
dash of Tabasco

Mix together the oil, vinegar, garlic, wine, salt, pepper, parsley and thyme to make the sauce.

Trim away 2 or 3 inches of the toughest tips of the green leaves of the leeks. Split the leeks down to halfway through the white part, separate the layers and wash the leeks under running water to remove the sand.

Arrange the leeks in a flat pan and pour the sauce over them. Add enough water or a white wine-water mixture, to cover. Simmer until just tender. Cool in the broth.

Remove the leeks to a serving dish and cook the broth down by one-third. Add the chopped parsley and the Tabasco, and pour over the leeks.

Chill before serving.

Barbecued Leg of Lamb
Serves 6-8

6-8 pound leg of lamb, trimmed, boned and butterflied
3 tablespoons Dijon mustard
3 tablespoons red wine vinegar
3 tablespoons olive oil
½ teaspoon pepper

Arrange the lamb, boned side up, in a glass baking dish.

In a small bowl, whisk together the mustard, vinegar, olive oil and pepper.

Spread the mixture over the lamb and marinate at room temperature for 2 hours or refrigerate overnight.

3 cups canned tomato sauce
2 tablespoons Worcestershire sauce
¼ teaspoon celery salt
2 garlic cloves, minced
1 cup minced onion
2 tablespoons dry sherry
2 tablespoons red wine vinegar
2 tablespoons olive oil
salt and pepper to taste

In a large saucepan, combine the tomato sauce, Worcestershire sauce, celery salt, garlic, onion, sherry, vinegar, oil, salt and pepper.

Grill the lamb over hot coals, basting with the sauce and turning every 10 minutes for 45 minutes, for medium rare. A meat thermometer should register 140° F. when inserted.

Let the meat stand for 10 minutes before slicing it across the grain.

Warm the remaining sauce and serve it with the meat.

Barley and Mushrooms
Serves 6

1 tablespoon vegetable oil
1 medium sized onion, chopped
¼ pound fresh mushrooms, finely chopped
1 4-ounce jar pimientos, chopped
2 10¾-ounce cans chicken broth
⅓ cup water
1 cup medium barley
⅛ teaspoon thyme, optional
pepper to taste

Preheat the oven to 350° F.

In a stove top, ovenproof casserole, heat the oil over a medium high heat. Add the onions and mushrooms. When the onions become transparent, add the pimientos, chicken broth, water, spices and barley.

Increase the heat to high and bring the mixture to a boil. Cover with a tight fitting lid, remove from the heat and transfer the casserole to the oven.

Bake for 40 minutes.

ELEGANT BITS

Spinach with Red Onions *Serves 6*

5 tablespoons olive oil
2 medium red onions, thinly sliced
2 pounds fresh spinach, washed, with stems removed
2 teaspoons fresh lemon juice
freshly ground pepper to taste

Heat the oil in a large skillet over medium heat until hot.

Add the onions and sauté, stirring constantly, until the onions begin to brown.

Add the spinach and cook, stirring until just wilted.

Remove the pan from the heat and add the lemon juice and the pepper. Toss and serve immediately.

Raspberries Sabayon *Serves 6*

2 pints fresh red raspberries
5 egg yolks
2 tablespoons sugar
⅓ cup Grand Marnier liqueur
½ cup heavy cream

Divide the raspberries between six serving dishes and refrigerate.

In the top of a double boiler, with an electric mixer at medium speed, beat the egg yolks until thick. Gradually beat in the sugar and continue to beat until the mixture is light and soft peaks form when the beater is slowly raised.

Place the double boiler top over simmering water and slowly beat in the Grand Marnier. Continue beating until the mixture is fluffy, about 3-5 minutes.

Remove the double boiler top from the hot water and set it in ice water. Beat the custard over the ice water until completely cooled.

In a chilled mixing bowl, whip the cream until stiff. Gently fold the whipped cream into the custard.

Top each dish of raspberries with the sabayon sauce and serve cold.

Aspen-Turning Supper

Ham and Belgian Endive Roulade

Simi Rosé of Cabernet

Plum Good Duck
Puréed Parsnips and Potatoes
Sautéed Escarole and Red Peppers

Beringer Gamay Beaujolais

Chocolate Cream Torte

Simi Rosé of Cabernet, produced from the most expensive red wine grape, has all of the flavors and aromas of the famous Bordeaux grape variety. It is not as sweet as most California Rosé wines but is medium dry with slight bitterness in the finish.

Beringer Gamay Beaujolais is fresh and fruity. It is a dry, but very light-bodied wine for drinking — not sipping. It is at its best in its youth.

Ham and Belgian Endive Roulade — Serves 6

6 whole Belgian endives, washed

Steam the endives until just tender, about 3-4 minutes. Remove them from the heat to avoid overcooking and keep warm.

4 tablespoons butter or margarine
4 tablespoons flour
2 cups milk
salt and freshly ground pepper to taste

Melt the butter in a small saucepan over moderate heat. Do not let the butter brown.

Whisk in the flour to blend well.

Add the milk in a thin stream, whisking constantly to blend. Continue cooking and stirring until the mixture boils and thickens.

Season with the salt and pepper. Keep the sauce warm.

6 thin slices boiled ham

To assemble the roulade, wrap each whole endive in a slice of ham. Place on warmed plates. Divide the sauce among the rolls, pouring it over the tops. Serve immediately.

ELEGANT BITS

Plum Good Duck
Serves 6-8

2 ducklings, washed and quartered
4 oranges, halved
1 medium onion, chopped
1 garlic clove,
    minced

1 6-ounce can frozen lemonade
⅓ cup catsup
¼ cup soy sauce
1 teaspoon Worcestershire sauce
1 teaspoon powdered ginger
1 teaspoon chili powder
1 teaspoon dried tarragon
2 teaspoons dry mustard
4 drops Tabasco sauce
1 16-ounce can purple plums,
    drained, pitted and mashed

Preheat the oven to 350° F.

Place the duckling quarters over the orange halves on a roasting rack. Sprinkle the onion and the garlic over the top of the pieces. Place the rack in a roasting pan.

Bake for one hour before beginning to baste the duckling.

In a blender or a food processor, blend the lemonade, catsup, soy sauce Worcestershire sauce, ginger, chili powder, tarragon, mustard and Tabasco sauce on high speed.

Pour the mixture into a saucepan and add the plums.

Simmer the sauce for 15 minutes.

After the duckling has cooked for the first hour, begin to baste it with the sauce every 10 minutes for 30 minutes.

The total cooking time for the duckling will be one hour and 30 minutes.

Puréed Parsnips and Potatoes
Serves 6

5 small parsnips, peeled
4 medium potatoes, peeled
4 tablespoons butter, softened
⅓ cup half and half
1 egg, lightly beaten
salt and white pepper to taste

Preheat the oven to 350° F.

Cube the parsnips and the potatoes. Boil them in water to cover for 20-25 minutes, or until they are soft.

Drain the vegetables and return the pan with the vegetables to the heat. Shake the pan over the heat to dry the vegetables slightly.

Place the vegetables and the butter in a food processor or a food mill and process until smooth.

Beat in the half and half, egg, salt and pepper.

Transfer the mixture to a buttered baking dish.

Bake for 30 minutes, or until it is puffed and brown.

Sautéed Escarole and Red Peppers

Serves 6

3 cloves garlic, crushed
¼ cup extra virgin olive oil
1½ pounds fresh broad-leaf escarole, washed, dried and cut into 3-inch pieces
1 large red pepper, sliced into 3-inch strips
salt and pepper to taste

In a large skillet over medium heat, sauté the garlic in the olive oil for 4 minutes. Remove the garlic if it begins to brown.

Add the escarole and the pepper to the skillet and cook over high heat, stirring until the escarole is wilted.

Remove the vegetables from the heat and season with the salt and pepper.

Chocolate Cream Torte

12 Servings

The torte may be prepared ahead and frozen. Freeze uncovered until firm. Then, wrap and return the torte to the freezer. To serve, thaw the torte in the refrigerator for 2-3 hours.

2 4-ounce packages sweet cooking chocolate
½ cup sugar
½ cup water
½ teaspoon cinnamon
2 teaspoons vanilla
1 11-ounce package dry pie crust mix
2 cups heavy cream, whipped

From one end of one bar of chocolate, shave 3 of the squares into curls. Set the curls aside for garnishing the torte.

Break the remaining chocolate into pieces and combine with the sugar, water and cinnamon in a small pan. Cook and stir over low heat until the mixture is smooth.

Remove the pan from the heat and add the vanilla.

Cool to room temperature.

Preheat the oven to 425° F.

Mix ¾ cup of the chocolate sauce into the dry pie crust mix.

Divide the dough into 4 parts and press each part on the bottom of inverted 9-inch layer pans.

Bake for 6-8 minutes, or until the pastry is almost firm. If the pastry has spread over the edge of the pan, trim the excess with a sharp knife.

Cool the layers on the pan just until firm. Then, carefully remove the layers to wire racks to cool completely.

Fold the remaining chocolate sauce into the whipped cream. Spread the cream between the layers and on top of the torte.

Garnish with the reserved chocolate curls. Chill at least 8 hours or overnight.

ELEGANT BITS

Autumn Buffet

Assorted Hors d'Oeuvres

Seafood Lasagne
Sweet and Sour Carrots
Endive and Pomegranate Salad

Hanns Kornell Extra Dry Champagne

Inventive Tarts

Hanns Kornell Extra Dry Champagne displays a touch of sweetness. It is produced in the classic French "Methode Champenoise" by California's best. The bubbles are minute and never-ending. This can be served all evening long — from the first hors d'oeuvre to the last bite of tart.

Seafood Lasagne *Serves 10-12*

1 tablespoon butter
1 tablespoon minced shallots
1¼ pounds shrimp, shelled and deveined
1¼ pounds bay scallops
½ cup dry white wine

Béchamel Sauce:
4 tablespoons butter
4 tablespoons flour
2 cups milk
salt and pepper to taste

2 cups mushrooms, sliced
1 cup plum tomatoes, drained and chopped
½ cup heavy cream
¼ teaspoon hot red pepper flakes
3 tablespoons minced parsley
salt to taste
9 strips lasagne noodles
1½ cups grated Swiss cheese

In a large skillet, heat the butter over medium heat. Sauté the shallots for 30 seconds.

Add the shrimp and the scallops and cook until the shrimp starts to turn pink.

Add the wine and continue cooking and stirring just until the liquid begins to boil. Immediately remove the skillet from the heat and transfer the shellfish to a bowl with a slotted spoon. Reserve the liquid in the skillet.

Prepare the Béchamel sauce in a medium saucepan. Melt the butter and whisk in the flour. Continue to beat the mixture as the milk is gradually added. Stir continuously until the sauce thickens. Remove it from the heat and set aside.

Bring the fish cooking liquid to a simmer. Add the mushrooms and simmer for 5 minutes.

Add the Béchamel sauce and the tomatoes to the mushrooms and simmer for 5 minutes, stirring frequently.

Add the cream, red pepper flakes, parsley and any liquid that has accumulated around the shellfish. Stir to blend, season with the salt and set the mixture aside.

Cook the lasagne noodles according to the package directions.

Preheat the oven to 375° F.

Butter a 13"x9"x2" pan or a large ovenproof serving platter.

Spoon a thin layer of the sauce over the bottom of the dish. Add ⅓ of the shellfish mixture, cover with three of the lasagne noodles and top with the sauce.

Repeat the process two more times, ending with the remaining sauce. Top the dish with the cheese.

Bake for 30 minutes. The Seafood Lasagne should be bubbling hot with a golden top.

Sweet and Sour Carrots *Serves 12*

3 pounds whole baby carrots or thinly sliced carrots
1½ cups honey
1 cup wine vinegar
¼ teaspoon cinnamon
¼ teaspoon ginger
¼ teaspoon cloves
¼ teaspoon cardamom
¼ teaspoon salt
1 cup slivered green pepper
3 tablespoons Marsala wine

Steam the carrots over boiling water for 5-6 minutes. Remove the carrots from the steamer and set aside.

In a large saucepan, combine the honey, vinegar, cinnamon, ginger, cloves, cardamom and salt and bring to a boil.

Add the carrots, peppers and Marsala wine.

Reheat the mixture to boiling, stirring the vegetables to coat them with the sauce.

Remove from the heat and serve at once.

Endive and Pomegranate Salad *Serves 12*

4 bunches watercress, washed, with stems removed
12 whole Belgian endives trimmed
4 large scallions, tops removed
4 tablespoons red wine vinegar
8 tablespoons extra virgin olive oil
salt and freshly ground pepper to taste
⅔ cup pomegranate seeds

Rinse the watercress. Drain and pat it dry gently with paper towels.

Cut the endives into quarters lengthwise and separate the leaves. Place the endive in a salad bowl.

Add the watercress to the endive and refrigerate covered until ready to serve.

Slice the scallions into very thin rounds and keep them separate until ready for use.

Whisk the vinegar, oil, salt and pepper in a small bowl until thoroughly blended.

To serve, add the onions to the endive and watercress. Add the dressing and toss thoroughly.

Garnish the salad with the pomegranate seeds.

Inventive Tarts

Serves 12

Allowing dinner guests to invent their own dessert tart is an enticing way to satisfy individual sweet tastes.

On a dessert table, arrange a tray of the empty pastry shells and bowls of the various fillings and toppings. Each guest may then create his or her own magnificent tart.

12 prepared individual pastry shells
Citrus Filling
Chocolate Filling
Vanilla Filling
Toppings:
whipped cream
chopped nuts
strawberries, raspberries or blueberries, sliced and sugared
kiwi, peeled and sliced
semi-sweet chocolate, shaved
maraschino cherries
candied violets
peppermint candy, crushed
candied orange peel, chopped
toffee candy bars, crushed

Citrus Filling

3 Cups

6 eggs
2 tablespoons grated lemon zest
2 tablespoons grated orange zest
½ cup fresh lemon juice
4 tablespoons fresh orange juice
pinch of salt
1¼ cups sugar
1¼ cups butter, softened

In the top of a double boiler over simmering water, beat the eggs until lemon colored.

Stir in the lemon zest, orange zest, lemon juice, orange juice, salt, sugar and butter. Continue cooking and stirring until the filling thickens. Chill.

For a quicker filling, follow package directions for lemon pudding and pie filling mix, adding 2 tablespoons grated orange zest during the cooking.

Chocolate Filling
2 Cups

1½ cups milk
4 ounces semi-sweet chocolate, chopped
2 eggs plus 1 egg yolk
½ cup sugar
¼ cup flour
1 teaspoon vanilla
¼ teaspoon cinnamon

In a saucepan over medium heat, scald the milk with the chocolate, stirring to blend.

In the top of a double boiler over simmering water, beat the eggs and egg yolk until lemon colored.

Combine the sugar and the flour. Whisk into the eggs until creamy.

Pour the chocolate mixture gradually into the egg mixture, stirring constantly until the filling reaches the boiling point and thickens, about 5-6 minutes.

Remove the mixture from the heat and add the vanilla and the cinnamon. Stir to blend and keep stirring until almost cool.

Chill until serving time.

For a quicker filling, follow package directions for chocolate pudding and pie filling mix, adding ¼ teaspoon cinnamon before cooling.

Vanilla Filling
2 Cups

1½ cups milk
1 vanilla bean
½ cup sugar
¼ cup flour
4 egg yolks, beaten
1 tablespoon brandy

In a saucepan over medium heat, scald the milk with the vanilla bean.

In the top of a double boiler over simmering water, blend the sugar, flour and egg yolks. Cream this mixture until light.

After removing the vanilla bean, add the scalded milk gradually to the egg mixture. Blend well.

Cook the mixture, stirring constantly, until it reaches the boiling point and thickens. Remove it from the heat and stir in the brandy. Keep stirring to release the steam while cooling.

For a quicker filling, follow package instructions for vanilla pudding and pie filling mix, adding 1 tablespoon of brandy after cooking.

ELEGANT BITS

Tech Center Company Dinner

Marinated Herring
French Bread

Lamb Chops in Paper
Carrot Pudding
Sautéed English Cucumbers

Clos du Val Cabernet or
Château Lafon-Rochet Bordeaux

Black Bottom Pie

Clos du Val Cabernet is big and lush, like Brahms. It is a fine match for lamb and mushrooms. Remember, the wine should fit the sauce more than the meat. In this case, the wine is perfect for both.

Château Lafon-Rochet Bordeaux is a bit more austere than the Clos du Val Cabernet. It has good tannin to match the lamb. The wine is a blend of Cabernet and Merlot and is a classified fifth growth.

Marinated Herring 2 Quarts

This herring can be eaten immediately after it is prepared. However, it ages well in the refrigerator for several months.

1½ pounds herring tidbits in wine sauce, drained
1 cup coarsely chopped apple
1 cup coarsely chopped onion
1 cup coarsely chopped dill pickle
1 10¾-ounce can tomato purée
1 cup wine vinegar
1 cup sugar
1 teaspoon prepared mustard
¼ cup white wine
2 tablespoons oil

Combine the herring, apple, onion and pickle.

Combine the tomato purée, wine vinegar, sugar, mustard, wine and oil.

Combine the two mixtures and refrigerate.

6 2-rib lamb chops, fat trimmed and bones scraped
1 tablespoon olive oil
1 pound fresh mushrooms, finely chopped
1 tablespoon butter
salt and freshly ground pepper to taste
6 medium slices Canadian bacon
6 10"x15" pieces parchment paper
olive oil

Lamb Chops in Paper

Serves 6

Preheat the oven to 450° F.

In a large skillet, over high heat, quickly brown the lamb chops on all sides in the olive oil. Remove the chops from the pan and allow them to cool.

Add the butter and the mushrooms to the skillet and cook over medium heat, stirring until the mushroom liquid has evaporated.

Remove the mushrooms and place them in a towel. Twist the towel to remove any remaining liquid. Set the mushrooms aside.

Use 6 10"x15" sheets of parchment paper folded in half to cut a large heart shape for each lamb chop.

To assemble the recipe, oil one parchment heart. Place one slice of the Canadian bacon on one side of the heart. Then place a lamb chop on the bacon and top with one heaping tablespoon of mushrooms.

To close the parchment heart, fold the paper over the top. Beginning at the top of the heart, fold several times in the direction of the lamb to seal the paper. Continue folding around the heart, crimping the paper to seal tightly. Repeat the procedure for each lamb chop.

The lamb can be refrigerated at this point. It should then be returned to room temperature and cooked just before serving.

Place the lamb on a cookie sheet and bake for 10 minutes.

To serve, split the top of the parchment paper.

ELEGANT BITS

Carrot Pudding
Serves 6

1½ pounds carrots, peeled and sliced
4 tablespoons butter or margarine, melted
¼ cup sugar
1 egg, beaten
¼ cup milk
⅓ cup flour
1½ teaspoons baking powder
1½ teaspoons cinnamon

Preheat the oven to 350° F.

Boil or steam the carrots until just tender.

Drain the carrots and place them in a food processor in batches. Process until smooth.

Add the butter, sugar, egg and milk to the carrots. Blend well.

Mix together the flour, baking powder and cinnamon and add to the carrot mixture. Stir well to blend.

Pour the mixture into a greased, 1½-quart souffle dish.

Bake for 45 minutes and serve hot.

Sautéed English Cucumbers
Serves 6

1 seedless English cucumber, peeled
2 tablespoons butter
pinch of garlic powder
salt to taste

Cut the English cucumber into 2-inch matchstick pieces or thin diagonal slices.

In a medium skillet, sauté the cucumber in the butter, stirring until it is slightly transparent but still firm. The cooking time will be 2-3 minutes.

Remove the cucumber from the heat and season with the garlic powder and salt.

Black Bottom Pie *Serves 12*

The flavor and texture of this dessert is improved if prepared at least 8 hours before serving.

10 graham crackers 3 tablespoons sugar 5 tablespoons butter, melted	Preheat the oven to 300° F. Break the graham crackers into a blender and blend at high speed until they are fine crumbs. Pour the crumbs and the sugar into a 9"x12"x1¾" pan. Stir to mix. Add the butter to the crumbs and stir to blend. Press the crumbs into the bottom of the pan to form the crust. Bake for 10 minutes. Set aside to cool.
6 egg yolks 3 cups half and half ¾ cup sugar 2 tablespoons cornstarch	In the top of a double boiler over simmering water, beat the egg yolks. Gradually add the half and half. Combine the sugar and the cornstarch and whisk into the liquid mixture. Cook the custard, stirring constantly, until slightly thickened.
2¼ ounces bitter chocolate, melted 1½ teaspoons vanilla	Remove one cup of custard from the double boiler and stir it into the melted chocolate. Add the vanilla and blend well. Spread a layer of the chocolate custard over the crumb crust and allow to cool.
1 package unflavored gelatin 4 tablespoons cold water	Dissolve the gelatin in the water and set aside.
6 egg whites ⅜ teaspoon cream of tartar ¾ cup sugar 1½ teaspoons vanilla	Beat the egg whites with the cream of tartar until soft peaks are formed. Add the sugar, a little at a time, and beat until stiff peaks are formed. Add the gelatin and the vanilla to the remaining warm custard. Cool. Fold the cooled custard into the egg white mixture. Spread it over the chocolate custard layer and refrigerate.
1 cup whipping cream 1 teaspoon vanilla 3 tablespoons sugar	Whip the cream in a chilled bowl until stiff peaks are formed. Add the vanilla and the sugar, beating just to blend well. Before serving, pipe whipped cream rosettes over the top of the custard.

Upland Hunters' Dinner

Beet and Watercress Salad

Braised Quail
Wild Rice
Steamed Green Beans and Turnips

David Bruce Pinot Noir   or
Pine Ridge Cabernet

Almond Shells with Lemon Curd
Stilton Cheese and Apples

Calem '75 Port

David Bruce Pinot Noir is a big wine to match the fowl. It has a taste of the earth which would match a Ralph Lauren tent ad — wild and romantic!

Pine Ridge Cabernet has soft tannin and lots of fruit. It is big but mellow. Former Copper Mountain developer, Gary Andrus, is the winemaker.

Calem '75 Port, along with the Stilton cheese, is a combination that the British could not do without and neither should you. Match it with Beethoven and a crackling fire.

Beet and Watercress Salad   Serves 6

¼ cup wine vinegar
2 teaspoons Dijon mustard
¾ cup walnut oil
salt and pepper to taste
2 16-ounce cans small whole beets, drained
3 bunches watercress, washed with coarse stems removed

In a small bowl, whip together the vinegar, mustard, walnut oil, salt and pepper.

Pour the dressing over the beets and marinate in the refrigerator for one hour or more.

Remove the beets from the salad dressing and whip the dressing. Pour it over the watercress and toss.

Divide the watercress among 6 chilled serving plates.

Garnish with the marinated beets.

Braised Quail

Serves 6

12 domestic quail
6 tablespoons butter
¾ cup Madeira
1½ cups chicken broth

Preheat the oven to 325° F.

Split the quail down the backbone, leaving the halves attached by the breastbone. Wash the birds well and pat dry.

In a large ovenproof and stove top pan, over medium high heat, sauté the quail in the butter for 5 minutes, turning them until they are golden.

Transfer the quail to a dish with a slotted spoon. Drain the fat from the pan and add the Madeira and the chicken broth. Stir the liquid to deglaze the pan.

Return the quail to the pan and cover the pot.

Bake for 15-20 minutes, or until the quail are tender. Remove the lid and bake another 10 minutes.

Serve hot with wild rice.

Wild Rice

Serves 6

2 tablespoons butter
½ cup minced celery
½ cup minced onion
1½ cups wild rice, washed and drained
1 4-ounce jar pimientos, drained
3 cups chicken broth
salt and freshly ground pepper to taste

Preheat the oven to 325° F.

In a heavy, lidded casserole, melt the butter and sauté the celery and the onion until wilted but not browned.

Add the rice and stir to coat with the butter.

Slowly add the broth, stirring continually.

Add the pimientos, salt and pepper.

Cover tightly and bake for 35-40 minutes, or until the liquid is absorbed.

Steamed Green Beans and Turnips

Serves 6

1 pound fresh green beans, stemmed and cut into 2½-inch pieces.
1 pound white turnips, peeled and cut into matchstick pieces
2 tablespoons butter
salt and pepper to taste

Steam the green beans 8-10 minutes over boiling water. Test for doneness after 8 minutes. Drain when done.

Steam the turnips 10-12 minutes over boiling water. Test for doneness. The turnips should be firm.

In a large saucepan, melt the butter. Add the cooked beans and the turnips. Stir over high heat just to coat the vegetables with the butter.

Season with the salt and pepper.

Almond Shells with Lemon Curd

See page 209.

ELEGANT BITS

Vail Après Ski Supper

Swordfish Soup
Vegetable Salad with Sherried Dressing
French Bread

Burgess Cellars Chardonnay or
Grgich-Hill Chardonnay

Sweet Cheese Fondue

Tokaji Aszú, 3 Puttonos

Burgess Cellars Chardonnay is both fermented and aged in oak. The wine is very rich and buttery and will not be overpowered by the spices of the soup.

Grgich-Hill Chardonnay is from Napa Valley's Rich Valley Vineyards. It is the product and loving child of Mike Grgich. This is a big wine which is not for the beginning wine drinker.

Tokaji Aszú, 3 Puttonos, is a Hungarian dessert wine with a hint of fruit and honey.

Swordfish Soup *Serves 4-6*

1 tablespoon vegetable oil
1 small onion, chopped
2 medium potatoes, cut into small cubes
1 garlic clove, peeled
2 cups water
2 8-ounce bottles clam juice
¼ cup dry white wine
1 16-ounce can tomatoes, seeded and crushed
1½ teaspoons tarragon
⅛ teaspoon basil
salt and pepper to taste
1 - 1¼ pounds swordfish steaks, skin and darkest meat removed, cut into bite-sized pieces

In a large pot, sauté the onion and the potatoes in the oil until the onion is transparent.

Add the garlic, water, clam juice, wine, tomatoes, tarragon, basil, salt and pepper. Simmer the liquid until the potatoes are tender but firm.

Add the swordfish and continue to simmer for 10-12 minutes. Test a piece of the fish to determine if it is cooked through.

Serve immediately or remove from the heat and reheat just before serving.

Vegetable Salad with Sherried Dressing
Serves 6

½ cup cauliflower florets
8 stalks fresh asparagus, cut on the diagonal
½ cup slivered celery
1 small zucchini, thinly sliced
½ cup fresh Brussels sprouts, cut in half
1 quart boiling water
½ cup sliced raw mushrooms
2 Belgian endives, sliced
1 small cucumber, thinly sliced
¼ cup sliced green onion
4 radishes, thinly sliced

6 green onion brushes
2 tablespoons chopped parsley

Place the cauliflower, asparagus, celery, zucchini and Brussels sprouts in a colander.

Pour the boiling water over the vegetables. Allow them to drain and cool.

In a large bowl, mix all of the vegetables together, tossing well.

Pour a desired amount of the Sherried Dressing over the vegetables and refrigerate for at least one hour before serving.

To serve the salad, remove it from the bowl with a slotted spoon and place on chilled plates. Garnish with the onion brushes and the parsley.

Sherried Dressing
5 cups

1 egg
1 teaspoon sugar
1 teaspoon salt
2 cups extra virgin olive oil
2 cups vegetable oil
½ cup wine vinegar
½ cup dry sherry
2 cloves garlic, crushed

Add all of the ingredients, except the sherry and garlic, to a blender. Blend at high speed for one minute.

Stir in the sherry and the garlic.

Sweet Cheese Fondue
Serves 6

¼ cup butter or margarine
¼ cup flour
2 cups light cream
8 ounces French triple cream cheese such as St. Andre
¼ - ½ cup sugar
⅓ cup Grand Marnier
peel of one orange, grated
strawberries, hulled
apples, cut into chunks
dried apricots
pound cake, cut into chunks

In a medium saucepan, melt the butter and stir in the flour.

Gradually add the light cream, stirring constantly until the sauce thickens.

Add the cheese and stir until the sauce is smooth and creamy.

Blend in the sugar, Grand Marnier and orange peel.

Pour the sauce into a fondue pot or chafing dish and keep warm while serving.

Arrange the fruit and the pound cake around the fondue for dipping. Provide each guest with a fondue fork and a dessert plate.

ELEGANT BITS

Celebration Dinner

Artichoke and Oyster Soup
French Bread

Concannon Sauvignon Blanc

Make-Ahead Beef Wellingtons
Bearnaise Cream Sauce
Basiled Vegetables

Jaboulet-Vercherre Gevrey Chambertin   or
Pommard

Belgian Endive and Hot Walnut Salad

Poached Pears with Raspberry Sauce

Jaboulet-Vercherre Gevrey Chambertin is a soft, subtle wine which slides down the throat just like the Beef Wellington. It is fatter than a Bordeaux.

Pommard is like the Jaboulet-Vercherre Gevrey Chambertin but even more elegant.

Artichoke and Oyster Soup   Serves 6

8 shallots, minced
4 garlic cloves, minced
¼ cup butter **or** margarine
2 tablespoons flour
2 14½-ounce cans chicken broth
1 15-ounce can artichoke hearts, drained and coarsely chopped
2 bay leaves
¼ teaspoon thyme
freshly ground pepper to taste
1 pint fresh oysters, about 24
2 tablespoons minced parsley

In a large saucepan, sauté the shallots and the garlic in the butter until they are softened.

Stir in the flour and cook the roux for 3 minutes, or until it is golden.

Remove the pan from the heat and slowly pour in the broth, whisking vigorously. Continue to whisk the mixture until it is smooth.

Add the artichoke hearts, bay leaves, thyme and pepper.

Cover the mixture and simmer for 30 minutes. Remove and discard the bay leaves after simmering.

Drain the oysters and add them to the simmering broth.

Poach the oysters in the broth for 5 minutes, or until they are plump and their edges are curled.

Ladle the soup into heated bowls, dividing the oysters among the bowls.

Sprinkle each serving with the parsley.

Make-Ahead Beef Wellingtons

Serves 6

This recipe is especially easy for entertaining because it must be made the day before it is to be served.

1 tablespoon butter
6 small beef fillets, 3-4 ounces, cut one-inch thick
10 tablespoons Madeira or sherry
1½ pounds mushrooms, finely chopped
1 package frozen patty shells, thawed
salt to taste

Melt the butter in a skillet over high heat. Sear the steaks on each side. Pour in 2 tablespoons of the Madeira and transfer the steaks to another container. Chill the steaks.

Add the remaining Madeira and the mushrooms to the skillet. Simmer this mixture, stirring until the liquid is almost absorbed. Chill the mixture.

On a floured board, roll out the thawed pastry, one piece at a time. Roll into a circle about 8 inches in diameter.

Place several tablespoons of the mushroom mixture in the center of the pastry. Add the steak and salt lightly. Place several tablespoons of the mushrooms on the top of the steak.

Fold the pastry over the steak to enclose and pinch it together to seal. Place the folded side down on an ungreased rimmed baking sheet. Repeat the process for each steak.

Cover the steaks and refrigerate overnight. Do not remove the steaks from the refrigerator until they go into the oven.

Preheat the oven to 475° F.

Bake for a total of 13 minutes. The first 10 minutes, bake on the lowest rack in the oven. The last 3 minutes, bake on the highest rack.

Serve at once, passing the Bernaise Cream Sauce to spoon over each steak.

ELEGANT BITS

Bearnaise Cream Sauce

4 tablespoons minced onion
2 tablespoons wine vinegar
1 teaspoon dried tarragon
½ cup butter
½ pound mushrooms, sliced or quartered
1 cup whipping cream
4 egg yolks, lightly beaten

In a medium saucepan, combine the onion, vinegar and tarragon. Boil the mixture, stirring constantly, until the liquid has evaporated.

Add the butter and the mushrooms, cooking until the mushrooms are lightly browned. Pour in the cream and bring the mixture to a boil.

Stir some of the mixture into the egg yolks and then add the egg yolks to the sauce in the pan. Cook the sauce briefly, stirring until slightly thickened.

The sauce can be reheated if warmed gently, stirring, over hot, not simmering, water. The sauce can be made ahead and frozen, if desired.

Basiled Vegetables *Serves 6*

2 ripe medium tomatoes
2 zucchini
½ head cauliflower
⅓ cup extra virgin olive oil
8 leaves fresh basil or
    1 tablespoon fresh tarragon
salt and pepper to taste

Preheat the oven to 400° F.

Thinly slice the vegetables and arrange them in a lightly oiled, shallow ovenproof serving dish, alternating the slices of vegetables.

Coat the vegetables with the oil and sprinkle with the herbs, salt and pepper.

Bake for 30 minutes and test for tenderness. Serve hot.

Belgian Endive and Hot Walnut Salad *Serves 6*

6 whole Belgian endives
½ cup walnut oil
1 cup walnut pieces
¼ cup balsamic vinegar
salt and freshly ground pepper
    to taste

This unusual salad gets its flavors from the walnut oil and balsamic vinegar. Olive oil and wine vinegar can be used if necessary but will produce a milder flavor.

Slice the endives lengthwise into narrow strips and place in a warm serving dish.

In a small skillet, heat the oil. Toast the walnuts until lightly browned.

Stir in the vinegar and pour the dressing over the endive. Season with the salt and pepper. Toss the salad and serve immediately.

Poached Pears with Raspberry Sauce

Serves 6

3 cups water
3 tablespoons lemon juice
1 cup sugar
6 Bosc pears or other firm, ripe pears

Combine the water, lemon juice and sugar in a saucepan. Bring to a boil. Reduce the heat and simmer.

Peel the pears and leave the stems intact. Use a melon baller to remove the seeds from the bottom of the pear.

Slice the rounded bottoms of the pears to provide a flat bottom so that the pears will stand upright.

Lower the pears into the liquid as soon as they are peeled.

Cover the pan and simmer about 8 minutes or until the pears are tender, yet firm.

Remove the pan from the heat and allow the pears to cool in the liquid.

Chill the pears in the liquid.

1 10-ounce package frozen raspberries

Add the raspberries and their juice to a blender and blend at high speed for 30 seconds.

Strain the raspberry liquid and divide it among six serving dishes.

Place the drained pears in the raspberry sauce.

ELEGANT BITS

Fireside Dinner

Parsnip Soup
French Bread

Hartley and Gibson Manzanilla Sherry

Braised Tongue
Rice with Vermicelli
Brussels Sprouts with Herb Butter

Bollini Cabernet   or
Clos du Roi Châteauneuf-du-Pape

Sherry-Macaroon Freeze

Hartley and Gibson Manzanilla Sherry can be served in a small glass at each place. Each guest can then pour half of the sherry in his or her soup and the other half goes "down the hatch" — after a lovely toast, of course.

Bollini Cabernet is a light red Cabernet from Italy. It is dry and medium-bodied with a bit of sandpaper on the tongue.

Clos du Roi Châteauneuf-du-Pape is bigger, more elegant and fuller-bodied than the Bollini Cabernet and it has a sense of history to match.

Parsnip Soup   *Serves 4-6*

4 tablespoons butter <u>or</u> margarine
1 pound parsnips, peeled and sliced
1 cup chopped celery
4 cups chicken broth
3 tablespoons flour
white pepper to taste
1/3 cup chopped parsley
1 cup water
3/4-1 cup freshly grated Parmesan cheese

Melt the butter in a heavy saucepan. Sauté the parsnips and the celery, stirring until the vegetables are coated with the butter. Cover and cook over medium low heat for 10 minutes, stirring occasionally.

Add half of the parsnips and celery to a blender. Add two cups of the chicken broth, the flour, pepper and parsley. Blend at high speed. Repeat the process with the remaining parsnip mixture and the broth.

Return all of the blended soup to the saucepan. Add the water and simmer over low heat for 10 minutes. The soup can be reheated briefly before serving.

Just before serving, sprinkle the soup with the freshly grated Parmesan cheese.

Braised Tongue
6 Servings

3 pounds veal or beef tongue
4 teaspoons powdered beef bouillon
2 quarts water or to cover

2 tablespoons margarine
1 teaspoon salt
¼ teaspoon powdered ginger
1 teaspoon paprika
1 large onion, chopped
2 large cloves garlic, minced
1 medium tomato, chopped
1 cup tongue broth
1 tablespoon cornstarch

Boil the tongue with the bouillon in 2 quarts of water in a large pot. Cook for 2-2½ hours, or until the tongue is tender.

Remove the tongue from the broth and peel it, reserving 1 cup of the broth. Slice the tongue into ½-inch pieces.

Melt the margarine over medium heat in a large skillet. Brown the tongue slices in the margarine.

Season with the salt, ginger and paprika. Remove the tongue and set it aside.

Sauté the onion and the garlic and then the tomato in the margarine remaining in the skillet.

Return the tongue to the skillet.

Combine the tongue broth with the cornstarch and stir until smooth. Add it gradually to the tongue and vegetables. Continue to cook over a medium heat until everything is well heated.

Adjust the seasonings and serve.

Rice with Vermicelli
Serves 6

3 tablespoons butter
1 cup finely chopped onion
1 clove garlic, finely chopped
3 cups chicken broth
¾ cup vermicelli pieces
1½ cups uncooked rice
salt to taste

Heat the butter in a heavy saucepan. Sauté the onion and the garlic briefly, stirring well.

Add the chicken broth and bring it to a boil.

Add the vermicelli, rice and salt to the broth. Allow the broth to return to a boil.

Reduce the heat and cover the pot with a tight-fitting lid. Simmer for 30 minutes, or until all the broth is absorbed.

Turn the heat off, but do not remove the cover. Allow the rice to stand for 15 minutes before serving.

ELEGANT BITS

Brussels Sprouts with Herb Butter
Serves 6

1 ½ pounds fresh Brussels sprouts

Trim the bottoms of the Brussels sprouts, remove any old leaves and cut a cross into the bottom of each Brussels sprout.

Place the sprouts in a steamer rack over boiling water. Cook for 12-14 minutes.

Transfer the Brussels sprouts to a warmed serving dish and toss with the herb butter until they are well coated.

Herb Butter
¼ Cup

¼ cup butter
2 teaspoons lemon juice
¼ teaspoon salt
⅛ teaspoon pepper
1 tablespoon chopped parsley
1 teaspoon chopped chives
¼ teaspoon tarragon leaves

Melt the butter in a small saucepan over low heat. Add the remaining ingredients and mix thoroughly.

Sherry-Macaroon Freeze
Serves 10

18-24 almond macaroons, crumbled
½ cup sherry <u>or</u> bourbon
½ cup chopped pecans
1 16½-ounce can pitted Bing cherries, drained
½ gallon vanilla ice cream, softened

In a large mixing bowl, combine the macaroons and the sherry. Stir and allow time for the macaroons to absorb the sherry.

Add the pecans, cherries and ice cream. Stir to blend.

Return the ice cream mixture to the freezer for at least 2 hours before serving.

Serve in stemmed glasses.

Stock Show Dinner

Rodeo Soup

Denver Beef
Steamed Rice
Julienne of Carrots and Celery

Tinto Olarra   or
Stag's Leap Gamay Beaujolais

Bibb Lettuce Salad with Roquefort Cheese Dressing

Frozen Chocolate Mousse Torte

Fontpinot Brandy

Tinto Olarra is a smooth, velvety red Spanish wine with herbal overtones. It is an inexpensive complement to a hearty meal.

Stag's Leap Gamay Beaujolais is a light, gulping wine from California.

Fontpinot Brandy from France is less acidic than most brandies and is France's only estate-bottled brandy.

Rodeo Soup *Serves 6*

1 tablespoon minced onion
1 10-ounce package frozen spinach, thawed and drained
3 tablespoons butter
1 cup chicken broth
1 10½-ounce can cream of chicken soup
1 10½-ounce can condensed potato soup
1½ cups milk
1½ cups heavy cream
2 tablespoons dry sherry
pepper to taste
chopped parsley

In a large saucepan, sauté the onion and spinach until the onion is transparent.

Add the chicken broth and the 2 soups to the spinach mixture and heat to the boiling point.

Remove the soup from the heat. Stir in the milk, heavy cream and pepper.

Garnish the soup with the parsley and serve hot.

ELEGANT BITS

Denver Beef
Serves 4 to 6

1½ pounds beef tenderloin, cut into 1-inch pieces
1 tablespoon paprika
pepper to taste
5 tablespoons butter
2 tablespoons chopped shallots
1 clove garlic, minced
1 red pepper, cut into 1-inch squares
1 green pepper, cut into 1-inch squares
½ pound mushrooms, quartered
1 tablespoon minced parsley
1 10¾-ounce can beef consommé
⅓ cup red wine
2 teaspoons cornstarch
¼ cup water
2 cups cherry tomatoes, peeled

Assemble all of the ingredients before beginning to prepare this recipe. The cooking time is very short and careful attention should be given to avoid overcooking.

Coat the meat with the paprika and the pepper.

Heat 3 tablespoons of the butter in a large skillet over high heat and add the beef all at once.

Cook the beef for approximately one minute, turning often to brown all sides. Remove the beef to a warm platter.

Return the skillet to the stove and add the remaining 2 tablespoons of butter, shallots, garlic, peppers and mushrooms. Sauté the vegetables for 2 minutes, stirring often. Do not overcook.

Add the beef, parsley, consommé, wine and cornstarch dissolved in the water. Heat the mixture to thicken slightly.

When the sauce has thickened, add the tomatoes and stir briefly to warm them. Serve immediately.

Steamed Rice
Serves 6

4 tablespoons butter
1½ cups uncooked rice
3 cups water or chicken broth
salt and pepper to taste

In a large saucepan, melt the butter. Add the rice, stirring to coat the grains. Continue to cook until the rice begins to look milky white.

Add the water or chicken broth, salt and pepper and increase the heat.

Boil the liquid for 2 minutes. Lower the heat to keep the liquid simmering slowly.

Cover the pan and cook for 18 minutes without removing the lid or until all the liquid is absorbed.

If the rice is not to be used immediately, wrap the lid in a clean towel and replace over the rice. This keeps the accumulated liquid from dripping back into the rice and creating a mushy area.

Julienne of Carrots and Celery *Serves 6*

2 cups julienne strips of carrot
2 cups julienne strips of celery
¼ cup butter, melted
2 tablespoons chopped parsley

Combine the strips of carrot and celery and place them in a steamer rack over boiling water.

Cook for 5 minutes, or until desired tenderness is reached.

Transfer the vegetables to a warmed serving dish. Toss them with the butter and the parsley.

Bibb Lettuce Salad *Serves 6*

1 large head Bibb lettuce, washed and dried
2 shallots, thinly sliced

Tear the lettuce leaves into bite-sized pieces and place in a chilled salad bowl with the shallots. Refrigerate the salad until ready to serve.

Just before serving on individual chilled salad plates, dress the salad with the Roquefort Cheese Dressing and toss well.

Roquefort Cheese Dressing *1 Cup*

¼ cup wine vinegar
¼ teaspoon salt
¼ teaspoon freshly ground pepper
½ cup extra virgin olive oil
2 tablespoons heavy cream
¼ cup crumbled Roquefort cheese
lemon juice to taste

In a small bowl, combine the vinegar, salt and pepper.

Add the oil and the cream in a steady stream, beating continuously until the dressing is emulsified.

Stir in the Roquefort cheese and the lemon juice.

Frozen Chocolate Mousse Torte

Serves 8

7 ounces almond paste
2 eggs
1 tablespoon cocoa powder

Preheat the oven to 350° F.

Crumble the almond paste in a food processor. Add the eggs and the cocoa powder. Process until the mixture is smooth.

Grease and flour a 9-inch springform pan.

Spread the mixture in the pan.

Bake for 15 minutes and cool.

6 ounces semi-sweet chocolate
3 eggs, separated
2 teaspoons dry instant coffee
1 tablespoon brandy
2 tablespoons sugar
½ cup heavy cream, whipped
1 ounce unsweetened chocolate, shaved

Melt the semi-sweet chocolate over a double boiler.

Beat the egg yolks well. Blend the yolks, coffee and brandy into the chocolate mixture. Remove from the boiling water to cool slightly.

In a large bowl, beat the egg whites until soft peaks form. Add the sugar. Continue to beat until stiff peaks form.

Fold in the cooled chocolate mixture.

Fold the whipped cream into the chocolate-egg white mixture. Spread evenly over the cooled cake layer.

Freeze the torte for 4 hours before serving.

To serve, remove the sides of the springform pan. Garnish with the shaved unsweetened chocolate.

Winter Carnival Dinner

Melon and Prosciutto

Cream Fondue

Shrimp and Sausage Arrezo
Rice
Zucchini Strips with Parmesan

Louis Max Beaujolais

Pistachio-Almond Sundaes

Calem Ruby Port

Louis Max Beaujolais is "the coward's wine." It is a French Beaujolais which is capable of both the shrimp, especially in a red sauce, and the sausage. This wine is fresh, light and very fruity.

Calem Ruby Port should follow the coffee which is served with the Sundaes.

Melon and Prosciutto
6 Servings

1 large cantaloupe, honeydew, <u>or</u> Crenshaw melon
6 very thin slices prosciutto
6 thin, round slices of lime
6 whole cloves

Cut the melon into 6 equal wedges. Cut the melon free from the rind, but leave the fruit resting on its rind.

Arrange a slice of prosciutto diagonally across each piece of melon.

Garnish each arrangement with a slice of lime which has a clove placed in the middle.

Cream Fondue

See page 15.

For this menu, serve the cream fondue as a salad course. Place the fondue in the center of the table. Provide each guest with an attractively arrayed assortment of vegetables and bread sticks for dipping.

ELEGANT BITS

Shrimp and Sausage Arrezo *6-8 Servings*

This can be made one day in advance. Add the shrimp at the last minute and heat thoroughly before serving.

4 stalks celery, chopped
4 medium onions, chopped
3 medium green peppers, chopped
1 clove garlic, finely chopped
2 tablespoons olive oil
1 28-ounce can peeled tomatoes
½ teaspoon oregano, ground
1½ pounds Italian sausage
salt and pepper to taste
1½ pounds shrimp, cooked and peeled

Sauté the celery, onions, peppers and garlic in the olive oil for 4-5 minutes but do not let them brown. Add the tomatoes and the oregano and stir well.

Sauté the sausage until it is thoroughly cooked and lightly browned. Cut the sausage into bite-sized pieces.

Add the sausage to the vegetable mixture and cook slowly for about 30 minutes. Season the mixture with the salt and pepper.

Just before serving, add the shrimp and cook only until heated.

Serve on a bed of white rice.

Zucchini Strips with Parmesan *6 Servings*

2 large zucchini
⅓ cup bread crumbs
salt and pepper to taste
½ teaspoon dried oregano
⅓ cup grated Parmesan cheese
⅓ cup olive oil
1 clove garlic, minced

Preheat the oven to 350° F.

Wash the zucchini and cut into long, thin strips. Place the zucchini in a shallow baking dish.

Combine the bread crumbs, salt, pepper and oregano. Sprinkle the zucchini with the crumb mixture, grated cheese, oil and garlic.

Bake for 20-25 minutes, or until the zucchini reaches the desired tenderness.

Serve hot or cold.

Pistachio-Almond Sundaes *6 Servings*

Chocolate dessert shells can be purchased at most gourmet food shops. They are nice to have on hand for quick but lovely desserts. They are delicious when filled with fresh fruit, sorbets or mousse.

6 scoops pistachio ice cream
6 chocolate dessert shells
Amaretto di Saronno liqueur
pink rose petals

Place one scoop of the ice cream into each dessert shell. Pour the desired amount of Amaretto over the ice cream.

Sprinkle each sundae with a few rose petals and serve at once.

Winter Holiday Dinner

Columbine Consommé
French Bread

Amontillado

Capillini with Caviar

Domaine Chandon Champagne

Pork Tenderloin with Hazelnuts
Brandied Hearts of Palm
French Peas

Clos du Bois Gewürztraminer, Early Harvest

Persimmon Pudding with Hard Sauce

Amontillado is straight out of Edgar Allan Poe's "The Cask of Amontillado". This sherry is dry and elegant, with a smooth, nutty aftertaste.

Domaine Chandon Champagne is a big, mouth-filling, yeasty wine which is perfect with caviar.

Clos du Bois Gewürztraminer, Early Harvest has a hint of nuts and raisins. It is a perfect match for pork — spicy with a slight spritz.

Columbine Consommé
Serves 6

2 14½-ounce cans clear chicken broth
2 8-ounce bottles clam juice
2 tablespoons finely grated carrot
watercress **or** parsley

Heat the chicken broth and clam juice in a saucepan until steaming hot, not boiling.

Divide the soup among the serving bowls. Add one teaspoon grated carrot to each bowl.

Garnish the soup with watercress or parsley. Serve the soup immediately.

Capillini with Caviar
Serves 6

1 pound cappillini pasta
2 tablespoons butter
2 ounces caviar, red **or** black
2 hard-boiled eggs, finely chopped
½ cup sour cream

Cook the pasta according to the package directions.

Drain the pasta well and add the butter and caviar to the pan. Toss to coat the pasta with the butter and caviar.

Divide the pasta between six warmed serving dishes and top with the chopped egg and sour cream.

Serve immediately.

ELEGANT BITS

Pork Tenderloin with Hazelnuts
Serves 6

2½-3 pounds pork tenderloin
¾ cup white vinegar
¾ cup sugar
8 tablespoons vegetable oil
½ cup dry sherry
1 cup shelled hazelnuts
½ cup currants or raisins

Cut the tenderloin into one-inch thick pieces across the grain.

In a shallow dish, combine the vinegar and the sugar, stirring until the sugar is dissolved. Place the tenderloin in the marinade for 20-30 minutes.

Heat 4 tablespoons of the oil in a small skillet and sauté the hazelnuts until golden brown. Set aside.

Heat the remaining 4 tablespoons of oil in a large skillet over medium heat. When it is hot, add the tenderloin and sauté for 4 minutes on each side, and until the pieces are caramelized. Set the pieces aside on a warm platter.

Deglaze the large skillet with the sherry and reduce the liquid slightly.

Add the hazelnuts, currants and pork tenderloin and simmer for 2 minutes, or until the meat is heated thoroughly.

Spoon the sauce over the pork tenderloin and serve.

Brandied Hearts of Palm
Serves 6

2 14-ounce cans hearts of palm
3 tablespoons butter or margarine
1 tablespoon brandy

Rinse and drain the hearts of palm. Slice them into ½-inch pieces.

Sauté the palms in the butter until glazed, stirring constantly.

Add the brandy and stir gently. Serve at once.

French Peas
Serves 6

4 tablespoons finely chopped scallions, including green tops
½ head Boston lettuce, finely shredded
1 tablespoon butter
2 10-ounce packages frozen petite green peas
salt and freshly ground pepper to taste

Sauté the scallions and the lettuce in the butter over low heat until the lettuce wilts, stirring occasionally.

Cook the peas according to the package directions.

Drain them and add to the lettuce. Season with the salt and pepper. Serve hot.

Persimmon Pudding with Hard Sauce
Serves 6

3-4 soft ripe persimmons
½ cup milk
1 cup flour
1 cup sugar, minus 2 tablespoons
1 teaspoon soda
½ teaspoon salt
dash of ground ginger
dash of ground cloves
½ cup raisins
½ cup chopped nuts

Preheat the oven to 350° F.

Peel openings in the persimmons and scoop out enough pulp to measure one cup.

In a large mixing bowl, combine the pulp and the milk, beating to mix well.

Sift together the dry ingredients. Add them to the persimmon mixture, blending well.

Stir in the raisins and the nuts.

Pour the pudding into a greased 9"x9" pan.

Bake for one hour. The pudding will look gooey at the end of the baking time. Do not overcook.

Serve warm with the warm Hard Sauce.

Hard Sauce
1 ½ Cups

1 cup powdered sugar
1 egg
2 tablespoons hot water
½ cup butter
1 teaspoon vanilla

In the top of a double boiler over boiling water, combine the sugar, egg, water, butter and vanilla.

Cook the sauce for 5 minutes, beating continuously.

GLOBAL BITS

Although the Japanese Dinner in this chapter may not be eaten with chopsticks, the flavors of the menu will conjure up images of kimonos and tea gardens. The Indian Dinner may not be served as the Indians would—with all courses brought to the table at the same time—but the flavor of curry and chutney will bring thoughts of sitar music and the Ganges River.

Global Bits has not been fashioned to duplicate foreign cuisines with total authenticity. Rather, these menus and recipes from around the globe have been adapted to fit American tastes and lifestyles. With foreign ingredients so readily available in markets throughout this country, many exotic meals can be created in the American kitchen.

GLOBAL BITS

Armenian Buffet

Stuffed Grape Leaves
Hummus with Pita Bread

Lamb and Eggplant
Bulgur Pilaf or
Tabouleh Salad
Sissar Salad

Yogurt Soup

Khourabia
Baklava
Candy Coated Almonds and Chick-Peas

Baklava and candy coated almonds and chick peas are available at specialty food stores.

Stuffed Grape Leaves   *72 Grape Leaves*

1 pound ground beef
1 onion, chopped
¼ cup long grain rice, uncooked
2 teaspoons dill weed
2 tablespoons chopped mint leaves
¼ cup currants
¼ cup pine nuts
2 cups chicken broth
salt and pepper to taste
2 8-ounce jars grape leaves
¼ cup lemon juice

Preheat the oven to 325° F.

Brown the beef and the onion. Add the rice, dill weed, mint leaves, currants, pine nuts and one cup of the chicken broth. Cover and cook the mixture until the rice absorbs the liquid. Season with the salt and pepper.

Soak the grape leaves in hot water for a few minutes. Drain the leaves.

Lay a grape leaf out flat, shiny side down. Place a heaping teaspoonful of the filling at the wide end of the leaf. Fold the wide end up and over the filling. Then, fold each side over. Roll the leaf toward the top. Place the rolled leaf in the bottom of a large, ungreased baking dish.

Continue this process until all of the leaves are completed. Pack them into the baking dish snugly so that they won't unroll.

Mix the remaining one cup of chicken broth with the lemon juice. Pour the mixture over the grape leaves. Place a plate on top of the grape leaves to hold them down. Seal the baking dish with foil.

Bake for 2 hours.

Stuffed Grape Leaves freeze well. When ready to use them, defrost the leaves first. To serve them warm, place them in a pan with enough water to cover the bottom. Steam the leaves gently until they are heated through.

Hummus

2½ cups

1 1-pound 4-ounce can garbanzos, drained
⅔ cup olive oil
⅓ cup lemon juice
½ cup sesame seed paste
2 large cloves garlic
½ teaspoon salt
minced parsley
toasted pita triangles or pitas, halved

Hummus makes a delicious spread for pita sandwiches.

In a food processor, fitted with a steel blade, add the garbanzos, oil, lemon juice, sesame seed paste, garlic and salt.

Process until the mixture is smooth.

Serve garnished with the parsley and the toasted pitas.

Lamb and Eggplant

Serves 8-10

2 medium eggplants
¼ cup vegetable oil
1 pound ground lamb or ground beef
1 egg
¼ cup bread crumbs
1 onion, finely chopped
¼ cup minced parsley
¼ teaspoon red chili pepper
1 teaspoon chopped fresh mint, or ½ teaspoon dried mint
1 teaspoon salt
½ teaspoon black pepper
3 green peppers, cut into 2-inch squares
3 tomatoes, thickly sliced
1 8-ounce can tomato sauce
1 teaspoon salt
½ teaspoon black pepper

Cut the eggplants in half lengthwise and slice them into ½-inch pieces. Brush the slices of eggplant with the oil. Place them on a cookie sheet and broil them on each side until golden brown.

Preheat the oven to 350° F.

Mix together the meat, egg, bread crumbs, onion, parsley, chili pepper, mint, salt and pepper.

Shape the mixture into flat, oval patties, approximately 2"x3".

In a large casserole dish with straight sides, arrange in rows the eggplant, green peppers, meat patties and tomatoes. Alternate the ingredients in a repeated pattern.

Dilute the tomato sauce with two parts water. Add the salt and the pepper. Pour the sauce over the arranged meat and vegetables. Cover the pan with foil.

Bake for two hours, checking occasionally to see that the ingredients remain moist. If necessary, add more tomato liquid. Uncover the pan during the last 30 minutes.

Lamb and Eggplant freezes well.

GLOBAL BITS

Bulgur Pilaf
6 Servings

Bulgur Pilaf can be made ahead and reheated before serving.

4 tablespoons butter
1 cup bulgur cracked wheat
1½ teaspoons salt
¼ teaspoon pepper
2½ cups chicken broth
2 tablespoons tomato paste
plain yogurt

Melt the butter in a large saucepan over medium heat. Add the bulgur wheat, salt and pepper. Saute for a few minutes or until the mixture is very lightly browned.

Stir in the chicken broth and tomato paste and bring to a boil. Cover and lower the heat.

Simmer for 30 minutes, or until the wheat is tender and the broth is absorbed.

Let stand, covered, for 15 minutes before serving. Top each serving with a dollop of yogurt or pass a small bowl of yogurt at the table.

Tabouleh Salad
Serves 4-6

1 cup bulgur cracked wheat
1 cucumber, seeded and diced
2 tomatoes, finely chopped
2 medium green onions, minced
15-20 sprigs parsley, minced
10 radishes, thinly sliced
⅓ cup fresh lemon juice
⅔ cup olive oil
salt to taste
½ teaspoon pepper
2 tablespoons minced fresh mint leaves

Rinse the bulgur and cover it with water. Soak it for one hour or overnight in the refrigerator. Drain well.

Mix together the cucumber, tomatoes, green onions, parsley and radishes. Add them to the bulgur.

Combine the lemon juice and the olive oil. Add the salt and the pepper.

Combine the dressing with the bulgur and vegetable mixture. Garnish with the mint leaves.

Chill the salad for one hour before serving.

Sissar Salad
Serves 4-6

1 15-ounce can garbanzos
2 tablespoons olive oil
2 tablespoons vinegar
1 teaspoon salt
½ teaspoon black pepper
5 scallions, chopped
2 medium tomatoes, diced
¼ cup chopped parsley
2 teaspoons fresh chopped mint leaves <u>or</u> 1 teaspoon dried mint leaves

Drain the liquid from the can of garbanzos.

Add the olive oil, vinegar, salt and pepper.

Refrigerate the mixture for 30 minutes.

Add the scallions, tomatoes, parsley and mint to the beans. Toss to mix.

Serve cold.

Yogurt Soup
Serves 6

Armenians frequently serve this soup at the end of a meal. It is very refreshing in hot weather.

2 cups plain yogurt
¾ cup cold water
1½ cups minced cucumber
1 clove garlic, quartered
1 tablespoon minced dill
½ teaspoon salt
¼ teaspoon white pepper

Beat the yogurt until smooth.

Blend in the cold water.

Add the remaining ingredients, blending well.

Chill the soup thoroughly or add an ice cube to each bowl.

Serve cold.

Khourabia
36 Cookies

½ pound unsalted butter, clarified
1 cup superfine sugar
2 cups flour

Filling:
4 ounces walnuts, ground
3 tablespoons sugar
1¼ teaspoons cinnamon

Preheat the oven to 350° F.

To clarify the butter, melt it over low heat. When it is completely melted, let it stand until the milk solids settle to the bottom. Skim the clarified butter fat from the top.

Cream the butter and the sugar until they are light and fluffy. Gradually add the flour until a stiff dough is formed.

The dough may be shaped into small crescents and baked without filling.

If a filling is desired, combine the walnuts, sugar and cinnamon.

Shape a walnut-size piece of dough into a cone. Make a hollow at one end and fill it with the nut mixture. Seal and shape the dough into a crescent.

Bake for 25 minutes, or until lightly browned.

GLOBAL BITS

Chinese Banquet

Spiced Chicken Wings
Green Onion Cakes

Hot and Sour Soup

Bean Sprout Salad

Spicy Orange Chicken
Gingered Pork and Cauliflower
Pepper Beef with Sweet and Sour Sauce
Szechwan Beef
Steamed Rice

Chinese Chews
Chinese Fried Cookies

Spiced Chicken Wings *Serves 12*

12 chicken wings, tips removed
1 small onion, sliced
½ cup soy sauce
¼ cup sugar
1 slice fresh ginger, finely chopped
several points star anise
½ teaspoon cinnamon

Place the chicken wings and the tips in a large saucepan. Cover them with 2 quarts of water. Add the onion.

Simmer the ingredients until the wings are tender, about 15-20 minutes.

Remove the wings from the pan and discard the tips.

Combine the remaining ingredients in a heavy skillet. Add the wings and simmer, turning until they are well coated, about 15 minutes.

Remove the wings from the sauce and serve hot or cold.

Green Onion Cakes
Serves 12

The tortilla offers a quick way to prepare these cakes. In fact, tortilla dough is nearly identical to the dough used by Chinese chefs for their onion cakes and is, therefore, a perfect substitute for the busy American cook.

1 cup vegetable or peanut oil
12 flour tortillas, 7-8 inches in diameter
9 tablespoons sesame oil
4 eggs, lightly beaten
salt to taste
1½ cups finely chopped green onions
½ pound bacon, cooked and crumbled, optional

Pour the oil in a heavy frying pan which is slightly larger than one of the tortillas. Heat the oil over medium heat to about 360°F., or hot enough to brown a tortilla in about one minute.

Place a tortilla flat on a work area. Brush it with the sesame oil and then with the egg. Sprinkle it lightly with the salt and 2-3 tablespoons of the green onions and the bacon. Align a second tortilla over the first one and press them firmly together.

Slide this onion cake into the hot oil. When it has browned on one side, use a pair of tongs to turn it over to brown the other side. When the cake has browned on both sides, hold it vertically over the oil to drain it.

Repeat the process until all of the cakes are cooked.

Cut each cake into 6 parts and serve warm.

Hot and Sour Soup
Serves 4-6

4 dried Chinese mushrooms
4 ounces lean pork
½ cup bamboo shoots
9 ounces tofu (bean curd)
4 cups chicken stock
1 teaspoon salt
1 tablespoon soy sauce
2 tablespoons vinegar
½ teaspoon freshly ground pepper, or more to taste
2 tablespoons cornstarch
¼ cup cold water
1 egg, beaten
1 green onion, chopped
1 tablespoon sesame oil

Soak the mushrooms in warm water to cover for 20 minutes. Drain them and reserve the liquid.

Cut the mushrooms, pork, bamboo shoots and bean curd into thin strips. Set them aside, keeping each ingredient separate.

Combine the chicken stock and the mushroom water in a saucepan and bring to a boil.

Add the salt, soy sauce, pork, bamboo shoots and mushrooms. Cover and simmer the mixture for 5 minutes.

Add the vinegar, pepper and bean curd and bring the mixture back to a boil.

Mix the cornstarch and the cold water. Add some hot liquid from the soup to the cornstarch-water mixture and then pour it into the hot soup. Boil for 1-2 minutes more.

Slowly add the egg to the hot soup. Stir once, gently.

Before serving the soup, sprinkle the top with the green onion and the sesame oil.

GLOBAL BITS

Bean Sprout Salad *Serves 4*

1 15-ounce can white asparagus
French or Italian dressing
½ pound fresh bean sprouts
1 8-ounce can sliced water chestnuts, drained
1 8-ounce can bamboo shoots, drained and sliced
½ cup sunflower seeds
¼ cup sesame seeds, toasted
¾ cup whole cashews

Marinate the asparagus in the dressing overnight.

Drain the asparagus. Set aside.

Toss the bean sprouts, water chestnuts, bamboo shoots, sunflower seeds and sesame seeds with the dressing.

Mound the sprout mixture on individual serving plates. Garnish with the asparagus and sprinkle with the cashews.

Spicy Orange Chicken *Serves 4*

2 whole chicken breasts, boned, skinned and cubed
1 teaspoon cornstarch
¾ teaspoon Szechwan chili paste with garlic
2 tablespoons dark soy sauce
1 tablespoon Hoisin sauce
2 tablespoons orange juice concentrate
¾ teaspoon sugar
2 tablespoons cooking oil
2 teaspoons minced fresh ginger
1 cup cubed onion
4 green onions, cut into 2-inch lengths
¼ cup orange zest, cut into thin 2-inch strips
1 teaspoon white vinegar
1 teaspoon sesame oil

Combine the chicken and the cornstarch, mixing well. Refrigerate for 30 minutes.

Combine the chili paste, soy sauce, Hoisin sauce, orange juice concentrate and sugar. Set the mixture aside.

Heat the oil in a wok or frying pan.

Add the ginger and stir-fry for 10 seconds. Add the chicken and stir-fry until it loses its pink appearance.

Pour in the chili paste mixture. Add the onions and the green onions and stir-fry for one minute.

Add the orange zest and stir-fry for 30 seconds. Add the vinegar and stir-fry for 30 seconds more.

Season with the sesame oil and mix well.

Gingered Pork and Cauliflower

Serves 4

1 tablespoon cornstarch
½ cup water
2 tablespoon soy sauce
2 tablespoons oil
2 cups sliced cauliflower
1 pound boneless pork, thinly sliced
¼ cup very thinly sliced fresh ginger
1 teaspoon chopped chives

In a small bowl, combine the cornstarch, water and soy sauce. Set aside.

Add the oil to a preheated wok or skillet.

Stir-fry the cauliflower for 1-2 minutes. Remove it to a plate.

Stir-fry the pork and the ginger slices until the pork loses its pink color.

Return the cauliflower to the wok with the pork.

Add the cornstarch mixture to the pork and cauliflower. Stir constantly until the mixture has thickened.

Serve on a warm platter and garnish with the chives.

Pepper Beef with Sweet and Sour Sauce

Serves 4

1 teaspoon soy sauce
½ teaspoon salt
1 teaspoon sugar
1 tablespoon cornstarch
1 egg, beaten
2 tablespoons water
1 pound flank steak or other lean beef, thinly sliced

2 tablespoons cooking oil
2 cloves garlic, minced
4 thin slices ginger, minced
2 green peppers, cut into triangles
3 green onions, cut into 2-inch pieces and sliced lengthwise

Combine the first 6 ingredients for the marinade.

Add the sliced beef to the marinade and marinate for 20 minutes.

Heat the oil in a wok. Add the garlic, ginger and green peppers. Stir-fry for 1-2 minutes. Remove the ingredients from the wok.

Add the beef to the heated wok and stir-fry for 5 minutes.

Return the peppers to the wok. Add the sauce and cook just to reheat the peppers and coat all of the ingredients with the sauce.

Add the green onions and serve immediately.

Sweet and Sour Sauce

1 Cup

2 tablespoons white wine
¼ cup white vinegar
⅓ cup sugar
2 tablespoons catsup
1½ teaspoons cornstarch
1 tablespoon water
½ teaspoon salt
¼ teaspoon soy sauce
dash sesame oil

Combine all of the ingredients in a saucepan. Cook, stirring until the sauce thickens slightly. Set aside.

GLOBAL BITS

Szechwan Beef
Serves 4

2 tablespoons sherry
3 tablespoons soy sauce
1 pound top round beef,
	thinly sliced
2 tablespoons peanut oil
3 green onions, cut into
	one-inch slices
1 tablespoon minced fresh ginger
1 tablespoon chili paste with garlic
2 teaspoons sugar
½ teaspoon white vinegar
1 teaspoon cornstarch dissolved in
	¼ cup cold water
1 teaspoon sesame oil
1 package frozen pea pods, thawed

Mix together the sherry and the soy sauce. Add this mixture to the meat in a large bowl and marinate at room temperature for several hours.

Heat the oil in a wok or a frying pan. Add the meat and stir-fry until it is no longer red.

Add the green onions, ginger, chili paste, sugar, vinegar and cornstarch dissolved in water. Stir the ingredients together and cook for 2-3 minutes.

Add the sesame oil and the pea pods. Stir well.

Cook for 2 minutes more.

Chinese Chews
16 Squares

1 cup flour
1 teaspoon baking powder
½ teaspoon salt
4 tablespoons butter <u>or</u> margarine,
	softened
1 cup sugar
2 eggs
1 teaspoon vanilla
1 cup chopped dates
1 cup chopped walnuts
powdered sugar

Preheat the oven to 375° F.

Combine the flour, baking powder and salt. Set aside.

Cream the butter and the sugar. Add the eggs, one at a time, mixing well after each addition. Add the vanilla.

Fold in the dry ingredients and then the dates and the nuts.

Pour the batter into a greased 8"x8" pan.

Bake for 40 minutes.

When cooled, sprinkle the chews with the powdered sugar and cut them into squares or diamonds.

Chinese Fried Cookies
60-70 Cookies

1 cup shredded coconut,
	chopped
1 cup roasted peanuts,
	finely chopped
½ cup sugar
2 tablespoons sesame seeds,
	toasted
1 pound round wonton skins
1 egg, beaten
oil for frying

Mix the coconut, peanuts, sugar and sesame seeds thoroughly.

Place one teaspoon of the filling in the center of a wonton skin. Brush the edges of the skin with the beaten egg. Fold the skin so that the two rounded edges meet. Press to seal.

If square wontons are used, cut the two opposite corners of the skins off to make them round.

Continue the procedure with the remaining cookies.

Preheat the oil to 375° F. Deep fry the cookies until they are golden brown.

Remove the cookies from the oil and drain on paper towels.

French Dinner

Cream of Sorrel Soup

Crudités

Tournedos of Beef with Roquefort Sauce
Brussels Sprouts with Chestnuts
French Bread

Apple Tart

Cream of Sorrel Soup *Serves 6*

4 tablespoons butter
1 pound fresh sorrel, washed with stems removed
5 cups chicken broth
6 egg yolks
1 cup heavy cream
salt to taste

Melt the butter in a large saucepan.

Stack the sorrel leaves and slice them into thin shreds.

Add the shredded sorrel to the butter and sauté over moderate heat for 3-4 minutes, stirring constantly.

When the sorrel has wilted, slowly add the chicken broth and bring the liquid to a simmer.

Combine the egg yolks and cream and beat with a wire whisk.

Remove the saucepan from the heat. Then, whisking constantly, pour the cream and egg mixture into the stock in a slow thin stream.

Return the soup to the heat and cook, stirring constantly, until it thickens slightly. Do not allow the soup to boil.

Season the soup with the salt. Serve hot.

GLOBAL BITS

Crudités

Crudités are an assortment of seasoned, fresh vegetables. They are served on a large divided platter instead of a salad.

Grated Carrots   Serves 4-6

5 carrots, peeled and finely grated
2 tablespoons finely chopped parsley

Mix the carrots and the parsley together.

Add the dressing to the carrots and toss.

Season with the salt and the pepper.

Dressing:
¾ teaspoon Dijon mustard
1 tablespoon white tarragon vinegar
3 tablespoons oil
1-2 scallions, chopped or
  1 tablespoon chopped chives, optional
salt and pepper to taste

To prepare the dressing, combine the remaining ingredients together.

Tomato Salad   Serves 4-6

3 very ripe tomatoes, cut in half, seeded and sliced
1 tablespoon very finely chopped fresh chives or fresh basil

Arrange the tomato slices on a dish.

Sprinkle the tomatoes with the chives or the basil.

Spoon the dressing over the tomato slices.

Dressing:
1 teaspoon Dijon mustard
1 tablespoon red wine vinegar
3 tablespoons oil
salt and pepper

Combine the dressing ingredients and mix well.

Cucumbers in Cream

Serves 4-6

2 cucumbers
salt

Peel the cucumbers and cut them in half lengthwise. Remove the seeds with a spoon. Slice the cucumbers thinly.

Put the slices in a colander and sprinkle very lightly with salt. Let them stand for 15 minutes.

Remove the cucumber slices from the colander and squeeze them well to drain off the juice.

Toss the slices with the cream dressing. Chill well.

Dressing:
1 teaspoon Dijon mustard
3-4 tablespoons heavy cream
few drops vinegar
pepper
½ teaspoon dried tarragon

In a small bowl combine the mustard, cream and vinegar. Beat until smooth.

Add the tarragon and the pepper. Mix well.

Tournedos of Beef with Roquefort Sauce

Serves 6

2 tablespoons minced shallots
3 tablespoons butter
½ cup dry white wine
2 cups heavy cream
6 6-ounce tournedos of beef cut 1½ inches thick
oil
salt and pepper to taste
7 ounces Roquefort cheese, crumbled

Sauté the shallots in the butter.

Add the wine and reduce the mixture, over medium heat, to about 2 tablespoons.

Add the heavy cream and reduce the mixture to one cup. Keep the sauce warm.

Lightly brush the tournedos with the oil. Grill them in a heavy skillet for 3-4 minutes on each side, or to taste.

Season the tournedos with the salt and pepper and keep them warm on a serving platter.

Add the cheese to the sauce, using a whisk, until just heated through.

Serve immediately with a portion of the sauce over the tournedos. Pass the remaining sauce.

Brussels Sprouts with Chestnuts

Serves 6

1 11-ounce can chestnuts, drained and quartered
5 tablespoons butter
1 pound Brussels sprouts, cooked and drained

In a large saucepan, sauté the chestnuts for about 5 minutes.

Add the Brussels sprouts and stir gently until well heated.

Serve at once.

GLOBAL BITS

1 cup sugar
½ cup butter
8 medium apples, pared,
    quartered and cored
1 tablespoon lemon juice
1 teaspoon grated lemon zest
1 stick pie crust mix
whipped cream

Apple Tart *Serves 6-8*

Preheat the oven to 450° F.

Place the sugar in a heavy, 10-inch skillet which is ovenproof. Cook the sugar over medium heat until it melts and becomes a light brown syrup. Remove from the heat and add the butter, stirring until melted.

Arrange the apples in a layer, rounded side down, in the sugar syrup. Make a second layer, rounded side up, fitting the pieces between the pieces in the first layer. Fill any remaining spaces with apple slices.

Mix together the lemon juice and grated zest. Sprinkle it over the apples.

Prepare the pie crust mix according to package directions. On a lightly floured surface, roll the pastry to make a 10-inch circle. Place the pastry circle over the apples.

Bake for 25-30 minutes, or until the crust is golden brown.

Invert the tart onto a shallow serving dish. Serve warm and garnish with whipped cream.

Indian Dinner

Lamb with Apricots
Chicken Curry
Fresh Mint Chutney
Fresh Banana Chutney
Cucumber Salad
Boiled Rice

Spice Cake

Lamb with Apricots
Serves 4

1 cup dried apricots
6 garlic cloves
1¾-inch piece fresh ginger, peeled and grated
1 pound boneless lean lamb, cut into ½-inch cubes
2 tablespoons oil
1 bunch green onions, chopped
1 2-inch stick cinnamon
3 cups warm water
1 tablespoon sugar

Cover the apricots with water and soak for at least 4 hours.

In a small bowl, mash the garlic with the grated ginger. Set aside.

In a heavy pot, sauté the lamb in the oil until all of the liquid has evaporated.

Add the green onions and the garlic-ginger paste. Cook for several minutes.

Add the cinnamon and the water. Cover the mixture and simmer until the meat is tender and only about ½ cup of the liquid remains, about 1½ hours.

Place the sugar in a skillet over medium heat. Stir until the sugar browns. Add the water used to soak the apricots. Stir over low heat until the sugar has dissolved. Add the apricots and cook for 10 minutes more.

Add the apricots with their syrup to the meat.

Heat the mixture and serve.

GLOBAL BITS

Chicken Curry
Serves 6

The flavor of this recipe is improved if it is made the day before serving. Chicken Curry also freezes well.

1 3-4 pound chicken, cut into pieces
10 peppercorns
1 carrot
1 stalk celery
1 onion, quartered
¼ cup butter
3 onions, sliced
3 cloves garlic, mashed
1 tablespoon ground ginger
1 tablespoon turmeric
1 tablespoon coriander
1 tablespoon chili powder
1 tablespoon paprika
2 tablespoons cumin
2 tablespoons curry powder
1 tart apple, cored and chopped
1 pint plain yogurt
salt and pepper to taste
2 teaspoons Garam Masala
Fresh Mint Chutney
Fresh Banana Chutney
preserved chutney
chopped green onions
currants
roasted peanuts
flaked coconut

In a large pot, add the chicken, peppercorns, carrot, celery and onion. Cover the chicken with water and simmer, covered, for 30-40 minutes.

In a large skillet, melt the butter. Add the onions and the garlic and cook until the onions are transparent.

Add the spices and cook, stirring, for 5 minutes over low heat.

Add the apple and cook for 5 minutes more. Remove from the heat.

Remove the cooked chicken from the bones and add to the skillet. Return to low heat.

Season with the salt and the pepper.

Add the yogurt and stir to coat the chicken.

Add the Garam Masala just before serving.

Serve with the chutneys, chopped green onions, currants, roasted peanuts, and flaked coconut.

Garam Masala
3 Tablespoons

1 tablespoon cardamom seeds
½-inch cinnamon stick
1 teaspoon cumin seeds
1 teaspoon ground cloves
1 teaspoon peppercorns
¼ whole nutmeg

Add all of the ingredients to a blender or food processor and process until powdered.

Fresh Mint Chutney

This should be served on the day it is prepared as an accompaniment to curries.

¼ pound fresh mint leaves
1 fresh green chili
1 small onion
1 teaspoon sugar
¼ teaspoon salt
juice of ¼ lemon

Mince the mint leaves, chili and onion. Mix together thoroughly.

Add the sugar, salt and lemon juice, mixing well.

Let the chutney stand for a few hours before serving.

Fresh Banana Chutney

Serve this fresh chutney on the same day it is prepared.

1 cup chopped banana
1 cup chopped tomato
1 fresh green chili, minced
salt to taste
¼ teaspoon Worcestershire sauce

Combine the banana, tomato and chili.

Add the salt and Worcestershire sauce. Mix well.

Cucumber Salad *Serves 4*

1 cucumber, peeled
½ teaspoon ground cumin
1 tablespoon finely chopped onion
1 small tomato, cut into ½-inch cubes
1 tablespoon chopped fresh coriander
½ cup plain yogurt
salt to taste

Slice the cucumber in half lengthwise. Scoop out and discard the seeds. Slice the cucumber again lengthwise into ⅛-inch slices. Slice crosswise into ½-inch pieces.

Toast the cumin in a skillet over low heat for 30 seconds.

In a bowl, combine all of the ingredients. Stir to blend.

Chill the salad and serve cold.

GLOBAL BITS

Spice Cake *One Cake*

½ pound butter, softened
1 cup superfine sugar
4 eggs, separated
¾ cup semolina
½ cup flour, sifted
½ teaspoon baking powder
1 small nutmeg, grated
¼ teaspoon caraway seeds
¼ teaspoon ground cinnamon
¼ teaspoon ground ginger
2 cups flaked coconut
¼ cup coconut milk
powdered sugar

Preheat the oven to 350° F.

Grease and flour one 9-inch cake pan.

Cream the butter and the sugar thoroughly. Add the egg yolks, one at a time.

Beat the egg whites until stiff. Add them to the creamed mixture.

Add the semolina.

Combine the flour, baking powder, nutmeg, caraway, cinnamon and ginger. Gradually add the dry mixture to the liquid mixture, beating thoroughly.

Add the coconut and the coconut milk. Stir to blend.

Pour the batter into the prepared pan.

Bake for 20 minutes, or until a toothpick inserted in the center comes out clean.

Dust the top of the cake with the powdered sugar.

Italian Dinner

Eggplant Caponata

Florentine Soup

Pasta with Pesto

Veal with Red Pepper Sauce

Mixed Green Salad

Cheesecake or
Sweet Vermicelli Cake

Eggplant Caponata *4 Cups*

¾ cup olive oil
2 cloves garlic, crushed
1 large eggplant, peeled and cubed, about 3 cups
½ cup chopped green pepper
½ cup chopped onion
¼ cup minced parsley
1 tablespoon sugar
½ teaspoon oregano, crushed
¼ teaspoon basil, crushed
1 teaspoon seasoned salt
freshly ground pepper to taste
1 cup tomato paste
¼ cup water
3 tablespoons red wine vinegar
1 4-ounce can mushroom stems and pieces, undrained
½ cup small pimiento-stuffed olives

Heat the oil and the garlic in a heavy skillet. Add the eggplant, green pepper, onion and parsley to the skillet, stirring well.

Cover and cook the mixture over low heat for 10 minutes.

In a small bowl, blend the sugar, oregano, basil, seasoned salt and pepper. Add the tomato paste, water and wine vinegar. Mix well.

Add the tomato mixture to the skillet. Then, stir in the mushrooms and the olives.

Cover and simmer over low heat until the eggplant is just tender, but not too soft.

Turn the eggplant relish into a bowl. Cover and refrigerate it overnight.

Serve with crackers.

GLOBAL BITS

Florentine Soup
Serves 6

1 10-ounce package frozen chopped spinach
1 cup canned cannellini beans
2 14½-ounce cans chicken broth
¼ teaspoon thyme
¼ teaspoon dill weed
salt to taste
1 bay leaf
2 egg yolks
2 tablespoons lemon juice
1 cup cooked rice
grated Parmesan cheese to taste

Cook the spinach as directed on the package. Do not drain.

In a blender or a food processor, purée the cannellini beans in their liquid with one can of the chicken broth.

In a large pot, add the second can of chicken broth, thyme, dill weed, salt and bay leaf.

Add the spinach and the puréed beans.

Bring the mixture to a boil and simmer for 30 minutes.

Beat the egg yolks with the lemon juice. Slowly add the egg-lemon mixture to the simmering soup, stirring constantly. Do not allow the soup to boil.

Add the cooked rice.

Serve this soup hot or cold with the grated Parmesan cheese sprinkled on top.

Pasta with Pesto Sauce
Serves 6

1 cup fresh sweet basil, chopped
½ cup extra virgin olive oil
3 cloves garlic, minced
1¼ cups freshly grated Romano cheese
1½ cups heavy cream
3 teaspoons oregano
3 tablespoons minced parsley
⅔ cup chopped pine nuts
salt to taste
1 pound capellini

Combine all of the ingredients, except the pasta, in a medium bowl. Stir to blend well.

Cook the capellini according to the package directions and drain.

Toss the hot capellini with the pesto sauce and serve immediately.

Veal with Red Pepper Sauce
Serves 6

1 tablespoon chopped parsley
1 clove garlic, minced
3 tablespoons olive oil
1 28-ounce can crushed tomatoes with added purée
2 large sweet red peppers
salt to taste

1½ pounds bottom round of veal or beef, cut into ⅛-inch slices
½ cup flour
3 eggs, beaten
1 cup sifted bread crumbs
2 tablespoons butter
2 tablespoons olive oil
salt to taste

Mince the parsley and the garlic together.

Sauté the mixture in the olive oil in a medium saucepan.

Add the tomatoes and simmer for about 10 minutes.

Peel the peppers by blanching them in boiling water for 20 minutes and stripping off the thin outer skin with a paring knife.

Coarsely chop the peppers and add them to the sauce.

Simmer the sauce for another 5 minutes.

Season with the salt.

Pound the slices of veal with a meat cleaver to tenderize them.

Dip the slices in the flour and pat the flour on the slices.

Dip the slices in the egg and then in the bread crumbs. Pat on as many crumbs as will adhere. Let the slices sit for 5 minutes.

Heat the butter and the oil in a skillet over medium heat.

Sauté the slices on both sides until golden, approximately 5 minutes total time.

Season with the salt.

Serve hot with the sauce.

GLOBAL BITS

2 8-ounce packages cream cheese, softened
1 pound ricotta cheese
1½ cups sugar
4 eggs
3 tablespoons cornstarch
3 tablespoons flour
1½ tablespoons lemon juice
1 teaspoon vanilla
½ cup butter, melted
1 pint sour cream
3-4 graham crackers, crushed
fresh berries, optional

Cheesecake *Serves 12-15*

Preheat the oven to 350° F.

With an electric mixer at high speed, beat together the cream cheese, ricotta and sugar.

At low speed, beat in the eggs. Then, add the cornstarch, flour, lemon juice and vanilla. Add the butter and the sour cream. Beat the mixture until smooth.

Butter the bottom and sides of a 9-inch springform pan. Dust the pan with the crushed graham crackers. Pour the batter into the pan.

Bake for 1 hour and 10 minutes, or until the cake is firm around the edges. Turn off the oven and let the cake remain there for 2 hours more.

Cool the cake completely. Then, refrigerate it for several hours.

Loosen the cake with a spatula and remove the sides of the pan.

Garnish with the fresh berries.

1 cup golden raisins
½ pound vermicelli
2 eggs, beaten
1 cup milk
2 tablespoons sugar
4 tablespoons honey
1½ cups chopped walnuts
butter
3-4 tablespoons unseasoned bread crumbs
cinnamon
powdered sugar

Sweet Vermicelli Cake *Serves 12*

Soak the raisins in warm water to plump them. Drain the raisins.

Soften the vermicelli in salted boiling water for 3 minutes. Do not cook through. Drain the vermicelli.

Combine the milk and the sugar in a medium saucepan and bring to a boil over medium heat. Add the semi-cooked vermicelli and continue to cook, stirring occasionally, until the pasta is cooked *al dente*. If all of the milk has not been absorbed by this time, drain the vermicelli.

Add the beaten eggs to the saucepan, stirring quickly to cook the eggs. Add the honey, raisins and chopped nuts and mix well.

Butter a 9 or 10-inch springform pan and dust it with the bread crumbs. Spoon in the vermicelli mixture.

Bake for 30-40 minutes, or until the top is golden brown.

Remove the cake from the oven. Sprinkle with cinnamon and powdered sugar.

Japanese Dinner

Yakitori

Bean Sprout and Carrot Salad

Sea Scallops with Sake Sauce

Stir Fried Spinach

Rice

Sesame Pound Cake

Yakitori *Serves 6*

Pork or veal may be substituted for the chicken.

4 chicken breasts, boned, skinned and cut into 1½-inch strips
10 large green onions, cut into 2-inch lengths, tops included
¾ cup soy sauce
¼ cup honey
¾ cup sweet sake
soy sauce
cayenne pepper to taste

Alternate pieces of the chicken and the green onion on 6-inch skewers.

Mix together the soy sauce, honey and sake in a flat, rectangular dish. Marinate the chicken kabobs for 30 minutes or more.

Broil the chicken, basting 3-4 times until the meat is white throughout.

Serve Yakitori hot, sprinkled with the soy sauce and the cayenne pepper.

Bean Sprout and Carrot Salad *Serves 6*

1 pound fresh bean sprouts
2 carrots, peeled and shredded
2 tablespoons sesame seeds
2 tablespoons vegetable oil
3 tablespoons sugar
8 teaspoons rice wine vinegar
¼ teaspoon salt

Combine the sprouts and the carrots in a bowl. Chill well.

Heat the sesame seeds and the oil in a skillet until the seeds are light brown. Remove from the heat and cool.

Combine the sugar, vinegar and salt with the cooled oil and seeds, stirring to blend.

Pour the dressing over the salad and serve within 1-2 hours.

GLOBAL BITS

Sea Scallops with Sake Sauce
Serves 6

2 tablespoons soy sauce
4 tablespoons sake
4 tablespoons dry sherry
2 teaspoons sugar
½ teaspoon finely minced fresh ginger
1 cup water
⅓ cup clam juice
1½ teaspoons cornstarch
1 tablespoon cold water

1½-2 pounds sea scallops, washed and drained
1 cup cornstarch
6 tablespoons vegetable oil

In a medium saucepan, combine the soy sauce, sake, sherry, sugar, ginger, water and clam juice. Boil the mixture until it is reduced to one cup.

In a small bowl, blend the cornstarch and the cold water. Pour one third of the sauce into the bowl, stirring constantly.

Pour this mixture back into the saucepan, stirring constantly, until the sauce becomes transparent and thickens. Set the sauce aside and keep warm.

Dredge the scallops in the cornstarch. Shake off any excess cornstarch.

Heat the oil in a large skillet over medium heat. Fry the scallops for 2 minutes. Carefully turn them over and fry for 2 minutes more. Do not overcook the scallops.

Divide the scallops among warm serving dishes and pour the sauce over each serving of the scallops.

Serve with steamed Japanese rice.

Stir-Fried Spinach
Serves 6

3 tablespoons oil
½ cup sliced bamboo shoots, drained
1½ pounds fresh spinach, washed with stems removed
2 teaspoons sugar
1 teaspoon soy sauce
1 tablespoon sesame seeds

Heat the oil over moderately high heat in a skillet or a wok.

Add the bamboo shoots and stir-fry for 30 seconds.

Add the spinach and cook just until it is wilted, stirring constantly. Add the sugar and the soy sauce. Stir just to dissolve the sugar.

Remove the wok from the heat and garnish the spinach with the sesame seeds. Serve the spinach immediately, or keep it warm until serving time.

Sesame Pound Cake
One Cake

¼ cup sesame seeds
¾ cup butter
1 cup sugar
4 eggs
1 tablespoon grated lemon zest
1½ teaspoons vanilla
¾ teaspoon sesame oil
2 cups flour
¼ teaspoon salt
1 teaspoon baking powder
½ cup milk

Preheat the oven to 300° F.

Spread the sesame seeds on a cookie sheet and toast them in the oven until they are brown.

Reserve one tablespoon of the seeds.

Increase the oven temperature to 350° F.

Cream the butter and the sugar. Add the eggs, one at a time, beating well after each addition.

Add the lemon zest, vanilla and sesame oil, mixing well.

Sift together the flour, salt and baking powder. Add the sesame seeds.

Add the flour mixture and the milk alternately to the egg batter.

Pour the batter into a greased and floured 5"x9" loaf pan. Sprinkle the top with the reserved sesame seeds.

Bake for 50-60 minutes, or until a toothpick inserted in the center comes out clean.

Cool the cake in the pan for 10 minutes. Remove it from the pan and cool on a wire rack.

GLOBAL BITS

Jewish Family Dinner

Chicken Soup with Matzoh Balls

Brisket of Beef with Barbecue Sauce
Noodle Kugel
Potato Latkes
Israeli Salad

Walnut and Almond Torte

Chicken Soup with Matzoh Balls *Serves 8*

This delicious soup must be prepared one day in advance.

1 3-pound chicken
water to cover, about 5 cups
6 carrots, sliced
2 stalks celery
5 sprigs fresh parsley
1 whole onion, peeled
5 sprigs fresh dill <u>or</u>
**   2 teaspoons dried dill**
2 parsnips, peeled
2 tablespoons salt
pepper to taste

Place the chicken in a pot or a slow cooker and cover it with the water.

Add the carrots, celery, parsley, onion, dill, parsnips, salt and pepper. Simmer the ingredients uncovered for several hours.

Remove the celery, parsnips, onion and chicken.

Refrigerate the broth overnight.

Before serving, skim off the top layer of fat. Heat the broth and add the cooked Matzoh Balls. Serve hot.

Matzoh Balls

3 eggs, beaten
1 cup matzoh meal
½ cup club soda
salt and pepper to taste
1 tablespoon chicken fat*

Combine the eggs, matzoh meal, club soda, salt, pepper and chicken fat. Mix well with a wire whisk.

Cover and refrigerate the mixture overnight.

Form the mixture into 1½" balls.

Bring a large pot of water to a boil and drop in the matzoh balls. Boil until each ball rises to the surface, approximately 10 minutes.

Add the cooked matzoh balls to the soup and heat through.

*To render the chicken fat, remove a piece of fat from inside the chicken. Place it in a small heavy skillet over low heat. Cook the fat until it has liquefied.

Brisket of Beef with Barbecue Sauce
Serves 8

3 tablespoons liquid smoke
1½ teaspoons garlic salt
3 tablespoons Worcestershire sauce
3 teaspoons celery seed
5-8 pounds brisket of beef

Barbecue Sauce:
1½ cups catsup
¾ cup chili sauce
¾ cup wine vinegar
¾ cup water
½ cup lemon juice
¼ cup A-1 sauce
¼ cup prepared mustard
¾ cup brown sugar
1 tablespoon celery seeds
2 tablespoons Worcestershire sauce
1 tablespoon soy sauce
1 clove garlic, minced
1 dash Tabasco sauce

Combine the liquid smoke, garlic salt, Worcestershire sauce and celery seed to make the marinade.

Trim the fat off the brisket of beef.

Marinate the brisket overnight in the refrigerator.

Preheat the oven to 325° F.

Place the brisket and the marinade in a large Dutch oven. Cover and cook for 3½-4 hours.

In a large saucepan, combine all of the ingredients for the barbecue sauce. Simmer for 30 minutes.

Add the cooking liquid from the brisket to the sauce and pour over the sliced brisket.

Return the meat to the oven, covered. Cook for one hour more.

Noodle Kugel
Serves 8-10

1 8-ounce package fine noodles, cooked and drained
1½ cups butter
1 8-ounce package cream cheese
6 heaping tablespoons sugar
1 pint sour cream
4 large eggs
2 teaspoons lemon juice
½ teaspoon salt
cinnamon to taste
sugar to taste
sliced almonds to taste

This recipe may be made in advance and frozen.

Preheat the oven to 350° F.

Grease a 9"x13"x1¾" baking dish with one tablespoon of the butter.

Cream together the remaining butter, cream cheese and sugar. Add the sour cream and blend well.

Beat the eggs into the mixture, one at a time. Add the lemon juice, salt and the cooked noodles. Stir to mix well.

Pour the noodles into the prepared baking dish. Sprinkle the top with the cinnamon, sugar and sliced almonds.

Bake for one hour.

GLOBAL BITS

Potato Latkes — *Serves 8*

3 eggs beaten
4½ cups grated potatoes, drained
6 tablespoons grated onion
1½ teaspoons salt
¼ teaspoon pepper
3 tablespoons cracker meal
¾ cup butter <u>or</u> oil
sour cream
applesauce

Combine the eggs, potatoes, onion, salt, pepper and cracker meal. Mix well.

Heat the butter or oil in a heavy skillet. Drop the potato mixture by tablespoons into the butter and flatten. When well browned on one side, turn the latkes over and brown on the other side. Add more butter or oil as needed.

Serve the latkes with the sour cream or the applesauce.

Israeli Salad — *Serves 6-8*

2 large tomatoes, cubed
1 large cucumber, peeled, seeded and cubed
1 bunch radishes, sliced
1 bunch scallions, sliced
2 stalks celery, sliced
1 dill pickle, chopped
¼ cup olive oil
¼ cup chopped parsley
2 tablespoons lemon juice
salt and pepper to taste
2 cloves garlic, finely minced
½ teaspoon crushed hot red pepper flakes

In a large salad bowl, combine the tomatoes, cucumber, radishes, scallions, celery and pickle.

Add the olive oil and the parsley

In a separate bowl, mix together the lemon juice, salt, pepper, garlic and red pepper flakes.

Pour the mixture over the salad. Toss and serve at once.

Walnut and Almond Torte — *Serves 8*

6 eggs, separated
1 cup sugar
1 tablespoon lemon juice
2 tablespoons orange juice
1 tablespoon grated orange rind
⅔ cup matzoh meal
½ teaspoon salt
½ cup walnuts, finely chopped
½ cup almonds, finely chopped
powdered sugar

Preheat the oven to 350° F.

Beat the egg yolks.

Add the sugar gradually, beating until the mixture is light in color.

Add the lemon juice, orange juice and orange rind. Mix in the matzoh meal, salt and chopped nuts.

Beat the egg whites until they are stiff but not dry. Fold them into the nut mixture.

Pour the batter into an ungreased 10-inch springform pan.

Bake for 35-40 minutes, or until a toothpick inserted in the center comes out clean.

Sprinkle powdered sugar on the top of the torte.

Mexican Dinner

Cream of Salsa Soup

**Mexican Chicken or
Green Chile Stew**

Avocado and Papaya Salad

Flan

Cream of Salsa Soup   *Serves 6*

3 tablespoons butter
2 cups chopped onion
2 cloves garlic, minced
1 teaspoon ground cumin
pinch of white pepper
1-1½ cups picante sauce
 <u>or</u> other salsa
1 quart half and half
1 cup grated Cheddar cheese

In a heavy 3-quart saucepan, melt the butter over medium heat.

Add the onion and the garlic and cook, stirring occasionally, for about 10 minutes.

Stir in the cumin and the pepper.

Add the picante sauce and heat the mixture. Slowly stir in the cream. Heat the soup thoroughly, but do not boil.

In each soup bowl, place about one tablespoon of the cheese. Ladle the soup into the bowls and sprinkle with additional cheese.

Serve immediately.

Mexican Chicken   *Serves 8*

1 3½ pound chicken
1 onion, chopped
4 tablespoons butter
3 tablespoons flour
1 cup chicken broth
2 cups milk
1 4-ounce can diced green chiles, drained
1 16-ounce can tomatoes, drained and chopped
¾ cup sliced black olives
½ teaspoon salt <u>or</u> to taste
½ teaspoon pepper <u>or</u> to taste
12 ounces Cheddar cheese, grated
10-12 tostada shells
sliced almonds

Cook the chicken in boiling water until it is tender. Bone the chicken and cut it into large pieces.

Preheat the oven to 350° F.

Sauté the onion in the butter.

Stir in the flour and cook for 3-4 minutes. Slowly add the chicken broth and the milk, stirring constantly.

Add the chiles, tomatoes, olives, salt and pepper.

In an ungreased 3-quart casserole, assemble the ingredients in layers of chicken, sauce, cheese and tostada shells. Repeat the layers, ending with a cheese layer.

Top the cheese with the sliced almonds.

Bake for 30-45 minutes, or until bubbly.

GLOBAL BITS

Green Chile Stew
Serves 6-8

4 pounds boneless beef chuck roast, cut into one-inch cubes
2 tablespoons vegetable oil
1 28-ounce can peeled tomatoes
4 cups chopped onions
2 4-ounce cans diced green chiles
2 green peppers, chopped
3 cloves garlic, minced
salt to taste
1¼ teaspoons cumin
½ teaspoon oregano
½ pound mushrooms, chopped
sour cream

Preheat the oven to 350° F.

Heat the oil in a large Dutch oven. Add the beef cubes and brown.

Chop the tomatoes into quarters. Add them with their juice to the meat. Then, add the onions, chiles, peppers, garlic, salt, cumin and oregano. Mix the ingredients well.

Cover the stew and bake for 3 hours.

Add the mushrooms about 10 minutes before serving.

Serve the stew in large bowls with a garnish of sour cream.

Avocado and Papaya Salad
Serves 6

1 large papaya, peeled, seeded and cut into cubes
2 avocados, peeled, seeded and cut into cubes
3 tablespoons olive oil
1 tablespoon red wine vinegar
salt and pepper to taste
1 tablespoon chopped parsley
lettuce

In a medium bowl, place the papaya and avocado cubes.

In a small bowl, whisk together the oil, vinegar, salt, pepper and parsley.

Pour the dressing over the papaya and avocado cubes. Toss gently and serve on a bed of lettuce.

1⅓ cups sugar
4 cups light cream
2¼ teaspoons vanilla
12 egg yolks

Flan
Serves 8

Preheat the oven to 325° F. Place the rack in the center of the oven.

Place one cup of the sugar in a heavy skillet over moderately high heat. Stir it occasionally with a wooden spoon until the sugar starts to melt. Then, stir it constantly until it melts to a smooth caramel consistency. It should be a rich brown but not dark brown.

Immediately pour the caramelized sugar into a warmed 2-quart round baking dish. Tilt the dish to cover the bottom and the sides.

Scald the cream in a heavy saucepan. Add the vanilla and the remaining ⅓ cup of sugar. Stir to dissolve the sugar.

In a large mixing bowl, stir the eggs just to mix. Add the eggs to the cream, stirring constantly. Pour the custard into the caramelized dish.

Place the dish in a large pan. Pour 1-2 inches of hot water into the pan. Cover the custard dish loosely with foil.

Bake 1¼ hours, or until a knife inserted in the center comes out clean.

Remove the dish from the water. Uncover and cool. Refrigerate 10-24 hours.

To serve the flan, loosen the edge with a sharp knife. Unmold the flan on a serving platter. Serve cold.

GLOBAL BITS

Mexican Brunch

<u>Mexican Pinwheels</u>
<u>Zucchini Tostadas</u>
<u>Chile Relleno Casserole</u>
<u>Chicken Enchiladas</u>
Baked Pineapple with Sauce Natillas
<u>Easy Sopaipillas</u>

Mexican Pinwheels *48 Pinwheels*

12 ounces cream cheese, softened
1 4-ounce can diced green chiles, drained
2 2¼-ounce cans chopped black olives, drained
5 tablespoons chopped walnuts
3 tablespoons chopped green onions
garlic powder to taste
6 8-inch flour tortillas
sliced black olives
parsley

In a large bowl, cream together the first 6 ingredients.

Spread the mixture on the tortillas to the edges.

Roll up the tortillas and cover them with plastic wrap. Chill the tortillas thoroughly.

Slice the tortilla rolls into one-inch slices. Arrange the pinwheels on a serving platter. Garnish each pinwheel with a slice of black olive or a leaf of parsley.

Zucchini Tostadas *Serves 8*

3 small zucchini <u>or</u> yellow squash thinly sliced
1 medium onion, thinly sliced
2 tablespoons oil
1 small can mushrooms, drained
1 mild <u>or</u> hot green chile, seeded and diced
8 tostada shells
1 cup grated Cheddar cheese
1 cup sour cream
1 cup chopped fresh tomatoes

Sauté the zucchini and the onion in the oil only until slightly tender.

Add the mushrooms and the chile. Continue cooking to heat thoroughly.

Spread the mixture on the tostada shells. Top with the cheese.

Broil briefly to melt the cheese layer.

Top the tostadas with the sour cream and the tomatoes.

Serve immediately.

Chile Relleno Casserole
Serves 8-10

3-4 7-ounce cans whole green chiles
1 pound Muenster or Cheddar cheese, grated
1 pound Monterey Jack cheese, grated
4 eggs
1 13-ounce can evaporated milk
3 tablespoons flour
1 teaspoon salt
1 16-ounce can tomato sauce or 1 16-ounce can peeled tomatoes, chopped

Preheat the oven to 375° F.

Wash the chiles and carefully remove the seeds. Drain them well.

In a large casserole dish, form layers by placing the chiles flat. Then, add both kinds of cheese. Repeat the chile and cheese layers.

Separate the eggs. Beat the egg yolks and add the evaporated milk, flour and salt.

In a clean bowl, beat the egg whites until stiff. Fold them into the egg yolk mixture.

Pour the ingredients over the chile and cheese layers.

Bake for 45 minutes.

Pour the tomato sauce or the tomatoes over the casserole and continue to bake 25-30 minutes longer.

Chicken Enchiladas
Serves 6-8

1 clove garlic, minced
4 tablespoons olive oil
1½ cups frozen green chiles, seeded and chopped
5 ripe tomatoes, peeled, seeded and chopped
2 medium onions, finely chopped
1 pinch oregano
pinch of salt
water
½ pound Cheddar cheese, grated
1 pint sour cream
½ teaspoon cumin
1 pound chicken breasts, cooked, boned and shredded
12 blue corn tortillas
shortening or lard for frying
chopped lettuce

Preheat the oven to 350° F.

Fry the garlic lightly in the olive oil, and add the chiles, tomatoes, onions, oregano and salt. Add water to cover and cook over low heat until thick.

Combine the grated cheese, sour cream, cumin and chicken, mixing thoroughly.

Fry the tortillas in hot fat for a few seconds, or until soft.

Dip each tortilla in the chile sauce. Fill with the chicken mixture and roll. Place the rolls in a flat casserole dish and cover with the remaining green chile sauce.

Bake for 20-25 minutes, or until thoroughly heated.

Garnish with chopped lettuce.

GLOBAL BITS

Baked Pineapple with Sauce Natillas
Serves 6

1 large pineapple
4 tablespoons rum
¼ cup sugar
butter

Preheat the oven to 350° F.

Cut off a slice from the side of the pineapple to form a pineapple boat. Do not include the green top in the slice. Reserve the slice.

Scoop out the insides of the pineapple. Discard the core and cut the fruit into cubes.

Mix the cubes of pineapple with the rum and the sugar. Return them to the pineapple shell.

Dot the cubes of pineapple with the butter. Cover the pineapple and its green top with aluminum foil.

Bake for 20 minutes, or until warm.

Cover the baked pineapple cubes with the reserved pineapple slice before bringing the pineapple to the table.

Serve with Sauce Natillas.

Sauce Natillas

1 pint light cream
¼ cup sugar
1 whole egg
2 egg yolks
1 teaspoon cornstarch
1 teaspoon vanilla

Scald the cream. Cool it slightly.

Beat the sugar and the whole egg together. Add the egg yolks, cornstarch and vanilla, beating well.

Cook the mixture in a double boiler over hot water, stirring constantly, until smooth and thickened.

Chill the sauce before serving.

Easy Sopaipillas
Serves 8

2 cans refrigerated crescent rolls
1 quart vegetable oil
honey
cinnamon
sugar

Separate the crescent rolls into individual triangles.

Heat the oil in a deep heavy pan. Drop one triangle of dough into the hot oil until it puffs up and turns golden, turning once. Remove the triangle and drain on paper towels.

Repeat the process with the remaining triangles.

Serve the sopaipillas with honey or roll them in cinnamon-sugar.

PORTABLE BITS

Picnics have become an integral part of American family life. Whether transported to an outdoor concert in the mountains or simply to the patio in the backyard, picnic foods always taste better because they are eaten in the open air. In Portable Bits, there are casual and delicious menus and recipes for a variety of picnic occasions. This chapter also presents recipes for brown bag sandwiches and all-purpose salads.

PORTABLE BITS

Boulder Tailgate Picnic

Hot Apple Wine

Baked Cheese and Ham Sandwiches or
Here's The Beef Sandwiches

Norwegian Slaw

Toffee Bars

Hot Apple Wine
Serves 4

1 cup apple cider
¼ cup sugar
1 3-inch cinnamon stick
6 cloves
peel of ¼ lemon
4/5 quart dry white wine
2 tablespoons lemon juice
lemon slices

In a 3-quart saucepan, combine the cider, sugar, cinnamon stick, cloves and lemon peel.

Bring the ingredients to a boil and stir until the sugar dissolves. Simmer uncovered for 15 minutes.

Remove the cinnamon stick, cloves and lemon peel. Stir in the wine and the lemon juice. Heat the mixture, but do not boil.

Carry the wine to the picnic site in a thermos.

Serve the hot wine in mugs garnished with a slice of lemon.

Baked Cheese and Ham Sandwiches
Serves 8

½ cup butter, softened
¼ cup horseradish mustard
¼ cup chopped onion
2 teaspoons poppy seeds
8 crusty buns, split
8 slices Swiss cheese
8 slices boiled ham
8 slices Muenster cheese

Preheat the oven to 350° F.

Combine the first four ingredients in a medium bowl.

Spread the mixture on the bun halves.

Fill each bun with a slice of Swiss cheese, a folded slice of ham and a slice of Muenster cheese.

Wrap each sandwich in foil and bake for 30 minutes.

Wrap the sandwiches in a heavy towel or newspaper to keep them warm.

Here's The Beef Sandwiches
3 Sandwiches

1 tablespoon Dijon mustard
¼ cup mayonnaise
2 teaspoons white vinegar
2 teaspoons fresh dill or
    ½ teaspoon dried dill
1 teaspoon prepared horseradish
¼ teaspoon sugar
freshly ground pepper to taste
6 slices bread
6 Boston lettuce leaves
6 ounces rare roast beef, thinly sliced
salt and pepper to taste
1 small cucumber, sliced

In a bowl, blend the mustard, mayonnaise, vinegar, dill, horseradish, sugar and pepper.

Spread the bread slices with the mayonnaise mixture.

Line half of the bread slices with lettuce leaves. Add the roast beef slices and season with the salt and pepper. Add the cucumber slices and top with the second slice of bread.

Norwegian Slaw
Serves 8

½ cup sugar
½ cup cider vinegar
½ cup vegetable oil
1 teaspoon celery seeds
1 red pepper, chopped
1 green pepper, chopped
1 medium onion, chopped
1 medium head cabbage, shredded

This salad will stay crisp and will keep for up to 2 weeks in the refrigerator.

Mix together the sugar, vinegar, oil, and celery seeds in a small saucepan.

Bring the mixture to a boil and simmer for 2 minutes. Set the mixture aside and let it cool for 5 minutes.

In a large bowl, add the peppers and the onion to the shredded cabbage.

Pour the dressing over the slaw and refrigerate for 24 hours.

Toffee Bars
24 Bars

½ pound unsalted butter
1 cup brown sugar
1 egg yolk
2 cups flour
1 teaspoon vanilla

12 ounces semi-sweet chocolate chips
1 cup walnuts or pecans, chopped

Preheat the oven to 350° F.

Cream the butter and the sugar. Add the egg yolk and beat well.

Add the flour and the vanilla, mixing well.

Spread the batter into a greased 9" x 12" x 1¾" pan.

Bake for 25 minutes.

Remove the pan from the oven and cover the layer with chocolate chips. Return the pan to the oven for 3-4 minutes more.

Remove the pan from the oven and spread the melted chocolate evenly over the top.

Press the nuts into the chocolate layer.

Cool the bars completely in the pan before cutting.

PORTABLE BITS

Bronco Tailgate Picnic

Country Lane Hot Chocolate

Scotch Eggs
Western Baked Beans
Soda Bread Sandwiches
Fruit Salad With Pecan Dressing

Blueberry Cake

Country Lane Hot Chocolate   *Serves 8*

6 cups chocolate milk
2 cups light rum
¼ cup Scotch whiskey
½ teaspoon nutmeg

Combine all of the ingredients in a large saucepan. Heat the mixture.

Pour the drink into a ½-gallon thermos container and transport it to the picnic site.

Scotch Eggs   *Serves 8*

8 hard-boiled eggs, peeled
flour
1 pound bulk pork sausage
¾ cup bread crumbs
½ teaspoon sage
¼ teaspoon salt
dash of pepper
2 eggs, well beaten
vegetable oil

Roll each hard-boiled egg in the flour.

Form a large, flat patty out of 2 ounces of the sausage. Carefully work the sausage around one of the floured eggs. Repeat this procedure with the remaining eggs.

In a shallow bowl, mix together the bread crumbs, sage, salt and pepper.

Dip each sausage egg in the beaten egg and roll it in the bread crumb mixture.

Heat 1-2 inches of vegetable oil in a 3-quart saucepan to 360°F.

Fry the eggs in the oil for 4-6 minutes.

Serve the eggs hot or at room temperature.

Western Baked Beans
Serves 8

**1 16-ounce can pork and beans
1 16-ounce can kidney beans, drained
½ cup catsup
⅓ cup brown sugar
1 onion, chopped
1 teaspoon chili powder
¼ teaspoon cumin
1 cup grated Cheddar cheese**

Preheat the oven to 400° F.

Mix together all of the ingredients except the cheese.

Bake uncovered in a 1½-quart casserole for 40 minutes.

Top the beans with the cheese and bake uncovered for an additional 15 minutes.

Soda Bread Sandwiches
8 Sandwiches

**3 cups whole-wheat flour
1 cup unbleached flour
1 teaspoon baking soda
¾ teaspoon baking powder
1 tablespoon salt
1½-2 cups buttermilk**

Preheat the oven to 375° F.

In a large bowl, mix together all of the dry ingredients.

Add enough buttermilk to make a soft dough which is firm enough to hold its shape.

Knead the dough on a lightly floured surface for several minutes, or until the texture is very smooth.

Form the dough into a round loaf.

Place it in a greased 8-inch round cake pan. Cut a cross on the top of the loaf with a sharp knife.

Bake for 35-40 minutes, or until the loaf sounds hollow when tapped.

Cool the loaf on a wire rack.

**butter, softened
tangerine marmalade
ginger marmalade**

Slice the soda bread very thin. Generously spread the slices with the butter and the marmalade to make sandwiches.

PORTABLE BITS

1 cup cubed pineapple, fresh <u>or</u> canned
2 bananas, sliced
1 cup seedless Thompson grapes
2 red apples, diced

Fruit Salad with Pecan Dressing   *Serves 6-8*

Combine the fruits. Add the Pecan Dressing and toss lightly.

¼ cup salad oil
¼ cup orange juice
1 tablespoon lemon juice
1 teaspoon sugar
¼ teaspoon salt
¼ cup finely chopped pecans, toasted

Pecan Dressing

Pour the salad oil and the orange juice into a one-pint jar. Add the lemon juice, sugar, salt and chopped nuts.

Cover the jar tightly and shake it until the dressing is thoroughly mixed.

½ cup butter
1 cup sugar
3 eggs
1 teaspoon vanilla
1 cup sour cream
2 cups flour
dash of salt
1 teaspoon baking powder
1 teaspoon baking soda
1 20-ounce can blueberry pie filling

Topping:
4 tablespoons flour
3 tablespoons butter, melted
½ cup brown sugar
½ cup chopped pecans

Blueberry Cake   *Serves 8*

Preheat the oven to 350° F.

Grease and flour a 9" x 9" cake pan.

Cream the butter and the sugar until they are well blended. Add the eggs, vanilla and sour cream and mix well.

In a separate bowl, mix together the flour, salt, baking powder and baking soda. Add the dry ingredients to the butter mixture and blend well.

Pour half of the batter into the prepared pan. Place the blueberry pie filling over the batter. Then, pour the remainder of the batter over the pie filling.

Combine the flour, butter, brown sugar and pecans. Sprinkle the mixture over the top of the cake.

Bake for one hour.

If nuts are toasted on a baking sheet in a moderate oven for about 10 minutes, they will be more crisp and flavorful.

Ranch Barbecue

Melon Balls Melba

Lemon Sirloin Steak
Cañon Salad
Filled Corn Muffins

Brownie Torte

Melon Balls Melba
Serves 6

1 tablespoon water
1 tablespoon cornstarch
¼ cup currant jelly
¼ cup rosé wine
6 drops almond flavoring
1 cup fresh raspberries, lightly sugared
3 cups cantaloupe balls
6 sprigs fresh mint

In a saucepan, blend the water and the cornstarch. Stir in the jelly and cook over medium heat until the jelly melts and the mixture comes to a boil.

Remove the sauce from the heat and add the wine, almond flavoring and raspberries.

Cool the mixture.

Spoon the melon balls into plastic glasses. Add the sauce and garnish each glass with a sprig of mint.

Cover the glasses with plastic wrap and transport them to the picnic site.

Lemon Sirloin Steak
Serves 6

1 4-pound sirloin steak, cut 1½"-2" thick
2 teaspoons grated lemon zest
½ cup lemon juice
⅓ cup vegetable oil
1 teaspoon salt
¼ teaspoon pepper
1 teaspoon Worcestershire sauce
1 teaspoon prepared mustard
1 clove garlic, minced
2 green onion tops, sliced
sliced green onions

Score the fat on the edges of the steak and place the meat in a non-metal dish.

Combine the remaining ingredients and pour them over the steak.

Cover and marinate the steak at room temperature for 30 minutes, turning occasionally, or marinate for 3-6 hours in the refrigerator.

Remove the meat from the marinade and pat dry.

Grill the steak 5 inches from hot coals, brushing frequently with the marinade. Allow 12 minutes on each side for rare meat.

Garnish the steak with green onions and serve hot.

Cañon Salad
Serves 6

- 1 head red or green leaf lettuce, washed and chilled
- 1 10-ounce package frozen peas, blanched and chilled
- 1 10-ounce package frozen cut green beans, blanched and chilled
- 1 4-ounce package alfalfa sprouts
- 1 15-ounce can artichoke hearts, quartered
- 1 large cucumber, peeled and sliced

Line a shallow salad bowl with the leaf lettuce. Arrange the peas, beans, alfalfa sprouts, artichoke hearts and cucumbers in a geometric pattern on top of the lettuce.

Serve the salad with Avocado Dressing.

Avocado Dressing

- 1½ ripe avocados, peeled and pitted
- 1 small onion, sliced
- ⅔ cup milk
- 2 tablespoons olive oil
- ½ teaspoon curry powder
- 1 teaspoon lemon juice
- ¼ teaspoon salt

Combine the avocados, onion, milk, olive oil, curry powder, lemon juice and salt in a blender and blend until the mixture is smooth.

Cover the dressing and store it in the refrigerator until it is needed.

Filled Corn Muffins
12 Muffins

- 1 cup corn meal
- 1 cup unbleached flour
- ¼ cup sugar
- 2½ teaspoons baking powder
- ¼ teaspoon salt
- 1 cup buttermilk
- 6 tablespoons melted butter or margarine
- 1 egg, slightly beaten
- berry preserves or sweet chutney

Preheat the oven to 400° F.

Stir together the corn meal, flour, sugar, baking powder and salt.

Add the buttermilk, butter and egg to the dry mixture.

Divide half of the batter evenly among buttered muffin tins. Make a shallow depression in the batter and spoon in the berry preserves or chutney. Top each muffin with the remaining batter.

Bake for 25-30 minutes.

Pastry:
1 cup flour
¼ cup brown sugar, firmly packed
1 ounce unsweetened chocolate, grated
½ cup butter, chilled and cut into pieces
2 tablespoons milk
1½ teaspoons vanilla

Filling:
3 ounces unsweetened chocolate
3 ounces semi-sweet chocolate
½ cup unsalted butter, softened and cut into pieces
1½ cups sugar
3 eggs, beaten separately
2 teaspoons vanilla
½ cup chopped pecans
¾ cup flour

Icing:
4 ounces semi-sweet chocolate
¼ cup unsalted butter
2 teaspoons vegetable oil

Brownie Torte *Serves 10-12*

This chocolate-lovers delight freezes beautifully.

Preheat the oven to 350° F.

Combine the flour, brown sugar and grated chocolate in a large bowl or food processor.

Cut in the butter until the mixture resembles coarse meal.

Mix in the milk and the vanilla with a fork until just blended. If using a food processor, process just until a ball is formed in the work bowl.

Pat the pastry dough onto the bottom and the sides of a greased 11" tart pan with a removable bottom. Refrigerate the pastry for 30 minutes if the mixture becomes too sticky to handle.

For the filling, melt the chocolates in the top of a double boiler or in a microwave. Remove from the heat and stir in the butter, one piece at a time.

Transfer the mixture to a large bowl. Add the sugar and blend well. The mixture will be granular.

Add the beaten eggs, one at a time, blending well after each addition. Add the vanilla and the nuts and mix well.

Gradually add the flour, blending well after each addition.

Pour the filling into the prepared pastry shell.

Bake for 25-30 minutes, or until a cake tester inserted in the center comes out clean.

Cool the torte on a wire rack before frosting.

To prepare the icing, combine the chocolate, butter and oil in the top of a double boiler over medium heat. Stir to blend well.

Cool the icing to a soft consistency and spread it over the top of the torte.

Let the icing stand until it becomes firm.

To freeze the torte, place it uncovered in the freezer until the icing is frozen. Then, wrap it and store in the freezer. Unwrap the torte before thawing it.

PORTABLE BITS

Red Rocks Concert Picnic

Chicken in a Basket

Stuffed Tomato Salad with Italian Green Bean Filling or Creamy Cucumber and Dill Filling

Marmalade Mélange

Chocolate Pots de Crème

Chicken in a Basket *Serves 4*

½ cup flour
1½ tablespoons sesame seeds
1½ teaspoons thyme
¾ teaspoon tarragon
½ tablespoon poppy seeds
½ teaspoon salt
1 teaspoon freshly ground pepper
8 chicken thighs <u>or</u> legs
2 egg whites, beaten
4 tablespoons butter <u>or</u> margarine

Preheat the oven to 350° F.

Combine the first 7 ingredients in a bag and mix well.

Dip the chicken in the beaten egg whites. Then, shake the chicken pieces inside the bag, one at a time.

Melt the butter or margarine in a large skillet. Brown the chicken on all sides. Transfer the browned chicken to a baking dish.

Bake uncovered for 40 minutes.

1 loaf round Shepherd's bread
4 tablespoons butter
3 tablespoons sesame seeds
1 tablespoon thyme
1½ teaspoons tarragon
1 tablespoon poppy seeds

Slice a lid from the top of the loaf and hollow out the soft inside of the bread. Mix together the remaining 5 ingredients and spread over the inside of the loaf.

Fill the loaf with the baked chicken and replace the lid. Place the filled loaf on a cookie sheet and return it to the oven for 10 minutes.

Wrap the loaf in foil and seal the edges. Then, wrap the loaf in several layers of newspaper and transport it to the picnic site.

Stuffed Tomato Salad *Serves 6*

6 medium tomatoes, ripened
1 recipe Italian Green Bean Filling <u>or</u> Creamy Cucumber and Dill Filling
4 slices bacon, cooked, drained and crumbled

Cut the tops off the tomatoes and scoop out the pulp. Invert them and drain well. Cover the tomatoes and chill.

Stuff the tomatoes with Italian Green Bean Filling or Creamy Cucumber and Dill Filling.

Sprinkle the bacon over the top of each stuffed tomato.

Italian Green Bean Filling

3 tablespoons olive oil
1 tablespoon vinegar
2 teaspoons lemon juice
¼ teaspoon salt
¼ teaspoon dry mustard
¼ teaspoon oregano
½ teaspoon paprika
1 teaspoon minced parsley
dash of thyme
¼ pound small mushrooms, thinly sliced
½ cup thinly sliced green onions
1 10-ounce package frozen Italian green beans, thawed and drained

In a small bowl, combine the olive oil, vinegar, lemon juice, salt, dry mustard, oregano, paprika, parsley and thyme.

In a large bowl, combine the mushrooms, green onions, and Italian green beans. Add the oil and vinegar mixture and toss gently.

Chill for 2-3 hours.

Use this filling to stuff tomatoes.

Creamy Cucumber and Dill Filling

2 large cucumbers
1 teaspoon salt
1 cup sour cream
1 tablespoon vinegar
½ teaspoon sugar
½ teaspoon dill seed

Peel the cucumbers and cut them lengthwise into quarters. Then, slice the quarter into ⅛-inch slices.

Place the cucumbers in a bowl and sprinkle them with the salt. Let them stand for 30 minutes.

Rinse and drain the cucumbers. Pat them dry with paper towel.

In a small bowl, combine the sour cream, vinegar, sugar and dill seed. Pour over the cucumbers and toss gently.

Use this filling to stuff tomatoes.

PORTABLE BITS

Marmalade Mélange
Serves 6

1 15¼-ounce can unsweetened pineapple chunks, drained
3 cups cantaloupe balls
1 cup halved strawberries
¼ cup orange marmalade
2 tablespoons orange liqueur
fresh mint sprigs

Combine the pineapple chunks, melon balls and strawberries.

Mix together the marmalade and the orange liqueur. Pour over the fruit.

Chill the ingredients 1-2 hours, stirring occasionally.

Garnish the fruit with mint sprigs.

Chocolate Pots de Crème
Serves 8

1 cup half and half
1 12-ounce package semi-sweet chocolate chips
2 eggs
whipped cream

Heat the half and half over medium heat.

Combine the hot cream, chocolate chips and eggs in a blender and blend until smooth.

Pour the mixture into 4-ounce plastic wine glasses.

Chill for 2-3 hours.

Garnish the dessert with whipped cream. Cover with plastic wrap and carry to the picnic site.

Concert in the Park Picnic

Colorado Corn Soup

Peachy Chicken Salad
Green Beans with Walnuts and Feta
French Bread

German Chocolate Brownies

Colorado Corn Soup *Serves 8*

2 tablespoons butter or margarine
¼ cup finely chopped onion
2 10-ounce packages frozen corn
3½ cups light cream
1 egg, beaten
¾ teaspoon salt
½ teaspoon white pepper

In a large saucepan, melt the butter. Sauté the onions in the butter until they are soft but not brown. Add the corn and cook for 5 minutes more.

Add the cream and the beaten egg. Cook the mixture until it begins to boil, stirring constantly. Continue to cook for about 3 minutes. Add the seasonings.

Cool the mixture slightly. Then, put it in a blender and blend until creamy.

Strain the soup and chill. Serve it very cold.

Peachy Chicken Salad *Serves 6*

½ cup mayonnaise
2 tablespoons salad oil
1 tablespoon vinegar
½ teaspoon salt
1½ cups sliced fresh peaches
3 cups cubed cooked chicken
1 cup diced celery
½ cup pecan pieces, toasted
peach slices
chopped parsley

In a small bowl, combine the mayonnaise, salad oil, vinegar and salt.

In a large bowl, combine the peaches, chicken and celery. Add the mayonnaise mixture and toss gently.

Just before serving, stir in the pecans.

Garnish the salad with the peach slices and the parsley.

PORTABLE BITS

Green Beans with Walnuts and Feta *Serves 6*

1½ pounds fresh green beans, halved
4 quarts boiling water
1 cup chopped walnuts
1 cup diced red onions
1 cup crumbled Feta cheese

Cook the green beans in the boiling water until crisp, about 4 minutes. Drain the beans and plunge them into ice water. Drain the beans again and pat them dry with paper towels.

When the beans are cool, arrange them in a shallow glass serving bowl. Sprinkle them with the nuts, onions and cheese.

Cover and chill until serving time.

Just before serving, pour the Mint Dressing over the salad and toss thoroughly.

Mint Dressing

¾ cup olive oil
½ cup fresh mint leaves, packed
¼ cup white wine vinegar
¾ teaspoon salt
½ teaspoon minced garlic
¼ teaspoon freshly ground pepper

Combine the olive oil, mint, vinegar, salt, garlic and pepper in a food processor. Blend until smooth.

Chill the dressing until serving time.

German Chocolate Brownies *24 Bars*

1 14-ounce bag caramels
1 cup evaporated milk
1 package German chocolate cake mix
¾ cup margarine

1 cup semi-sweet chocolate chips
1 cup chopped pecans, optional

Preheat the oven to 350° F.

Combine the caramels and ½ cup of the evaporated milk. Melt them together in the top of a double boiler or in a microwave. Keep the mixture warm.

Combine the cake mix, margarine and the other ½ cup of the evaporated milk in a bowl.

Lightly grease a 9" x 13" pan. Spread half of the cake batter in the pan.

Bake the cake for 6 minutes.

Remove the pan from the oven and sprinkle the chips and the nuts over the cake. Then, layer the caramel mixture over the top of the cake.

Drop the remaining cake batter, by tiny spoonfuls, on top of the caramel mixture.

Bake for 5 minutes more. Remove the pan from the oven and spread out the spoonfuls into a uniform layer.

Return the pan to the oven and bake for 15-20 minutes more.

Cool completely and then cut into squares.

17th Street Brown Bag

Cold Beet Soup

The Eggs-ecutive

Honeyed Fruit Marnier

Spiced Pecans

Cold Beet Soup *8 Cups*

2-3 medium beets, with their greens
2 cups beet liquid
2 cups water
1 cucumber, peeled, seeded and finely choped
3 radishes, thinly sliced
2 green onions, finely chopped
3 large sprigs fresh dill, minced
1/8 teaspoon sugar
2 cups sour cream
1 tablespoon lemon juice
3 tablespoons red wine vinegar
salt and pepper to taste

Wash and peel the beets. Cook them, with their greens, in the water for 20 minutes, or until tender. Cube the beets. Reserve the beet cooking liquid.

In a large pot, combine the beets, beet liquid, water, cucumber, radishes, green onions, dill and sugar.

In a medium bowl, combine the sour cream, lemon juice and vinegar and blend. Whisk this mixture into the beet mixture, 1/2 cup at a time.

Chill the soup thoroughly before pouring it into a chilled thermos or chilled bowls.

The Eggs-ecutive *Serves One*

Egg Salad:
1 hard-boiled egg, chopped
1 level tablespoon mayonnaise
1 level teaspoon Dijon mustard

Mix together the egg, mayonnaise and mustard.

Cheese Filling:
2 ounces cream cheese, softened
1 tablespoon milk
1 teaspoon chopped chives

4 thin slices white bread
2 tablespoons butter, softened
2 ounces black whitefish caviar

Blend the cream cheese with the milk. Add the chives and blend.

Butter two slices of the bread with the softened butter.

Arrange the sandwich by spreading the egg salad on a slice of the white bread. Top with a slice of the buttered white bread, with the buttered side away from the egg salad. Spread the caviar on the buttered slice of bread and cover with another slice of buttered bread, with the buttered side facing the caviar. Spread the cheese filling on the last slice of bread and place it face down on the layered sandwich.

Slice and wrap the sandwich.

PORTABLE BITS

Honeyed Fruit Marnier *Serves 6-8*

1 cantaloupe, seeded, skinned and cut into chunks
1 pint strawberries, hulled and sliced
1 pineapple, peeled and cut into chunks
seeds from one pomegranate
½ cup honey
2 ounces Grand Marnier

Combine all of the fruit in a large serving bowl.

Heat the honey over medium heat until bubbles appear. Add the Grand Marnier.

Remove the mixture from the heat and pour it over the fruit.

Chill the fruit at least one hour before serving.

Spiced Pecans *One Pound*

1 egg white
1 tablespoon cold water
¼ teaspoon salt
¼ teaspoon cinnamon
½ cup sugar
1 pound pecan halves

Preheat the oven to 225° F.

Butter an edged cookie sheet.

Beat the egg white until frothy but not stiff. Add the water, salt, cinnamon and sugar. Blend well.

Add the pecan halves and mix until well coated. Pour the nuts on the buttered cookie sheet.

Bake for one hour, stirring the mixture every 15 minutes.

Picnic at the Zoo

Orange-Peanut Butter Sandwiches
Lasagne Chips
Carrot and Celery Curls
Frozen Yogurt
High Energy Punch

Orange-Peanut Butter Sandwiches *2 Sandwiches*

1 orange
¼ teaspoon cinnamon
2 tablespoons brown sugar
⅔ cup peanut butter
4 slices bread

Peel and dice the orange, reserving the juice. Sprinkle the diced section with the cinnamon.

Blend together the orange juice, brown sugar and peanut butter.

Spread the mixture thinly on both pieces of bread to avoid soggy sandwiches.

Place the oranges on one side and cover.

Lasagne Chips *Serves 6-8*

1 16-ounce package lasagne noodles
vegetable oil
seasoned salt to taste

Cook the noodles according to the package directions. Rinse with cold water and drain on paper towels.

Cut the noodles into triangular pieces and fry them in the oil until light brown.

Drain the noodles on paper towels to remove any oil. Sprinkle the noodles with the seasoned salt while still hot.

Serve the chips warm or cold as a snack, or with a dip.

Try some sandwich geometry. Children like the novelty of finding their sandwiches cut into different shapes.

PORTABLE BITS

Carrot and Celery Curls
Serves 2

1 large carrot, washed and peeled
2 large stalks celery, washed and trimmed

Cut 6 ½-inch thick rounds from the large end of the carrot. Cut a hole in the middle of each carrot circle to form a ring.

Cut the celery stalks into 3-inch pieces. Place 1-2 celery sticks through the hole in each carrot ring. Cut slits from each end of the celery stick toward the carrot ring.

Soak the carrot and celery curls in ice water for several hours or overnight until the celery pieces curl at each end.

Frozen Yogurt
Serves 2

2 cartons flavored yogurt

Freeze the yogurt in cartons the night before it is to be used.

Remove the cartons from the freezer in the morning. The yogurt will be an icy-cold dessert which is thawed and ready to eat by lunchtime.

High Energy Punch
Serves 2

2 cups pineapple juice
1 cup apricot nectar
2 wedges fresh lime
ice

Combine the pineapple juice and the apricot nectar in a pitcher.

Squeeze a lime wedge into each of two small thermos containers. Add the ice and pour the punch over it.

SANDWICHES:

BLT Pitas *Serves 8*

12 slices bacon, cooked and crumbled
1¼ cups cubed cooked chicken
10 cherry tomatoes, quartered
1 avocado, peeled, pitted and diced
3 cups shredded lettuce
4 pita pockets, halved
½ cup Thousand Island dressing

In a large bowl, combine the bacon, chicken, tomatoes, avocado and lettuce. Toss gently until thoroughly mixed.

Fill the pita pockets with the mixture. Spoon the Thousand Island dressing over the top.

Any favorite dressing may be substituted for the Thousand Island dressing.

Mediterranean Salad Pitas *Serves 4*

1 6-ounce jar marinated artichoke hearts
1 7-ounce can tuna, flaked
2 cups shredded iceberg lettuce
½ cup Bermuda onion rings
1 2¼-ounce can sliced ripe olives, drained
½ small cucumber, thinly sliced
6 radishes, sliced

Dressing:
artichoke marinade
2 tablespoons lemon juice
¼ teaspoon basil
¼ teaspoon oregano

salt and pepper to taste
4 pita pockets, halved

Drain and slice the artichoke hearts. Reserve the marinade.

In a 2-quart container with a lid, combine the artichoke hearts, tuna, lettuce, onion rings, olives, cucumber and radishes. Cover the mixture and refrigerate.

Combine the artichoke marinade, lemon juice, basil and oregano. Let the mixture stand at room temperature until ready to serve.

Before serving, pour the dressing over the salad and mix well. Season with the salt and pepper.

Fill the pita pockets with the salad mixture.

Shrimp Pitas *Serves 2*

1 cup small shrimp, cooked and cleaned
¼ cup chopped celery
¼ cup grated Monterey Jack cheese
1 tablespoon lemon juice
½ teaspoon horseradish
dash of Worcestershire sauce
2 lettuce leaves
2 slices tomato
2 pita pockets, halved

In a medium bowl, mix together the shrimp, celery, cheese, lemon juice, horseradish and Worcestershire sauce.

Layer the lettuce and the tomato slices in the pita pockets. Add the shrimp mixture.

PORTABLE BITS

Turkey Pitas
Serves 3

1 ripe avocado, peeled and pitted
1½ tablespoons lemon juice
3 tablespoons canned, diced green chiles
3 tablespoons thinly sliced green onions
½ teaspoon garlic salt
4 ounces Boursin cheese
3 pita pockets, halved
½ pound turkey, sliced
1 6-ounce package alfalfa sprouts

In a small bowl, mash the avocado. Mix it with the lemon juice, chiles, green onions and garlic salt.

Spread the cheese inside the pita pockets. Top the cheese with the avocado mixture.

Stuff the pita pockets with the turkey and top with the alfalfa sprouts.

Guacamole-Tortilla Sandwiches
Serves 3

1 ripe avocado, peeled and pitted
1½ tablespoons lemon juice
3 tablespoons canned diced green chiles
¼ cup thinly sliced green onion
½ teaspoon garlic salt
3 flour tortillas
1½ cups grated Monterey Jack cheese
6 tablespoons roasted sunflower seeds
6 tablespoons shredded lettuce

In a medium bowl, mash the avocado. Add the lemon juice, green chiles, green onion and garlic salt.

Spread one side of each tortilla with ⅓ of the avocado filling to within ½ inch of the edge.

Sprinkle each tortilla with ½ cup of the cheese, 2 tablespoons of the sunflower seeds and 2 tablespoons of the lettuce.

Roll up each tortilla and serve whole or in halves.

Salami-Tortilla Roll-Ups
Serves 3

3 flour tortillas
3 tablespoons mayonnaise
3 tablespoons Dijon mustard
6 ounces Genoa salami, thinly sliced
6 ounces provolone cheese, thinly sliced
⅓ cup sliced ripe olives
½ cup alfalfa sprouts

Spread one side of each tortilla with one tablespoon of the mayonnaise and one tablespoon of the mustard.

Arrange the salami, cheese, olives and sprouts to within ½ inch of the edge.

Roll up each tortilla and serve whole or in halves.

Tortilla-Wrapped Flank Steak

Serves 6

Marinade:
¼ cup olive oil
¼ cup white wine vinegar
½ teaspoon oregano
⅛ teaspoon pepper
3 cloves garlic, minced

1 large flank steak, about 1½ pounds

Salsa:
2 medium tomatoes, peeled, seeded and chopped
3 green onions, chopped
2 tablespoons diced green chiles
2 tablespoons fresh coriander, chopped, or ½ teaspoon ground coriander
½ teaspoon salt
1 tablespoon olive oil

12 large flour tortillas, 8-10 inches in diameter
1 ripe avocado, peeled, pitted and diced

In a one-cup container, combine the oil, vinegar, oregano, pepper and garlic. Stir well.

Place the steak in a close-fitting container with a lid or in a heavy plastic bag. Pour the marinade over the meat and cover. Refrigerate for 6 hours or overnight.

In a medium container, combine the tomatoes, green onions, chiles, coriander, salt and olive oil. Mix well and cover. Refrigerate for 6 hours or overnight.

On an outdoor grill, cook the marinated flank steak 4-6 inches above the coals for 5-8 minutes per side. Turn once and cut into diagonal slices.

As the steak is cooking, place the tortillas on the grill. Heat for about 30 seconds on each side. Stack the tortillas and wrap in a dampened cloth or foil to keep warm.

Stir the avocado gently into the salsa.

To serve, place the steak strips down the center of each tortilla. Top with the salsa and roll up.

Tuna Tortillas

Serves 3

½ cup mayonnaise
¾ teaspoon curry powder
¼ teaspoon garlic salt
⅔ cup shredded carrot
¼ cup thinly sliced scallions
¼ cup raisins
1 7-ounce can tuna, drained
3 flour tortillas
alfalfa sprouts

Stir together the mayonnaise, curry powder, garlic salt, carrot, green onion, raisins and tuna.

Spread one side of each tortilla with ⅓ of the tuna filling to within ½ inch of the edge. Sprinkle the alfalfa sprouts over the filling.

Roll up the tortilla and serve.

PORTABLE BITS

Beefy Sandwiches
Serves 2

1 cup cooked ground beef
1 teaspoon prepared horseradish
1½ tablespoons chili sauce
1½ tablespoons mayonnaise
salt and pepper to taste
4 slices pumpernickel bread or
    2 hamburger buns, toasted
lettuce

In a bowl, combine the beef with the horseradish, chili sauce, mayonnaise, salt and pepper.

Serve with lettuce on the pumpernickel bread or toasted hamburger buns.

Curried Egg Salad Sandwiches
Serves 3

2 large stalks celery, sliced
1 tablespoon Dijon mustard
⅓ cup mayonnaise
3 tablespoons mango chutney
8 hard-boiled eggs, chopped
1 teaspoon curry powder
¼ teaspoon cinnamon
salt to taste
⅛ teaspoon ground cardamom
⅛ teaspoon ground cloves
pinch of ground red pepper

6 slices bread
1 large tart apple, halved,
    cored and sliced
3 large lettuce leaves

Combine the celery, mustard, mayonnaise and mango chutney.

Add the eggs, curry powder, cinnamon, salt, cardamom, cloves and ground red pepper. Mix the ingredients together until they are well blended.

Spread the egg salad mixture on 3 slices of the bread. Top the egg salad with the apple slices and the lettuce. Close the sandwiches with the remaining slices of bread.

Cut the sandwiches in half and serve.

Ham Pin Wheel Sandwiches
Serves 8

3 loaves of rye or whole-wheat
    bread, sliced lengthwise at
    the bakery
1 pound boiled ham, cut into
    chunks
1 2½-ounce can ripe sliced
    olives, drained
½ cup pickle relish
1½ teaspoons garlic powder
½ cup mayonnaise
large dill pickles or bread and
    butter pickles

These sandwiches should be prepared one day in advance. They will keep for several days refrigerated.

Remove the crust from the bread slices.

Prepare the ham filling in a food processor by combining the ham, olives, relish, garlic powder and mayonnaise.

Spread the ham filling thinly on each long slice of bread.

Put a dill pickle or some bread and butter pickles at the end of one bread slice. Roll up the bread so that the pickle is in the center.

Repeat the process with each slice of bread.

Wrap each roll securely in foil and refrigerate overnight.

Slice through each roll with an electric knife, making pin wheels of desired thickness.

Mango-Tuna Spread *2 Cups*

1 7-ounce can tuna, flaked
½ cup grated carrots
1 mango, peeled and cubed
¼ cup mayonnaise
freshly ground pepper to taste

In a bowl, mix all of the ingredients together.

Spread on bread slices or use as a salad.

Oriental Tuna Spread *1¼ Cups*

½ tablespoon curry powder
¼ cup mayonnaise
1 7-ounce can tuna, drained
¼ cup water chestnuts
2 tablespoons canned crushed pineapple

Mix the curry powder and the mayonnaise together.

Add the tuna, water chestnuts and pineapple and mix well.

Spread on bread slices or serve as a salad.

SALADS:

Any Season Chicken Salad *Serves 10-12*

5 cups shredded iceberg lettuce
¼ pound bean sprouts
1 8-ounce can water chestnuts, drained, rinsed and sliced
½ cup thinly sliced green onions
1 medium cucumber, thinly sliced
4 cups cubed cooked chicken
2 6-ounce packages frozen pea pods, thawed and patted dry
½ cup Spanish peanuts, toasted
12 cherry tomatoes, halved

Spread the lettuce evenly in a shallow 4-quart serving dish. Top with the bean sprouts, water chestnuts, green onions, cucumbers and chicken. Arrange the pea pods on the top.

Spread the dressing evenly over the pea pods. Cover and refrigerate overnight, or until well chilled.

Just before serving, garnish the salad with the peanuts and the tomato halves.

Dressing:
½ teaspoon salt
2 cups mayonnaise
1 teaspoon curry powder
1 tablespoon sugar
½ teaspoon ground ginger

Combine all of the ingredients and blend well.

PORTABLE BITS

Picnic Chicken Salad
Serves 4

4 cooked chicken breasts,
 boned and cut into chunks
2 tomatoes, diced
2 unpeeled cucumbers, thickly
 sliced

In a large bowl, combine the chicken, tomatoes and cucumbers.

Pour the dressing over the salad and toss gently. Cover and refrigerate.

Serve the salad cold.

Dressing:
½ cup salad oil
¼ cup cider vinegar
1 teaspoon salt
dash of white pepper
1 teaspoon tarragon

Combine all of the ingredients and beat until thick.

Rocky Ford Chicken Salad
Serves 6-8

2 cups diced, cooked chicken
3 tablespoons chopped green onions
2 tablespoons raisins
1 cup cantaloupe balls
1 cup honeydew melon balls
3 tablespoons sliced almonds,
 toasted
2 cups cooked rice, hot <u>or</u> cold

In a large bowl, combine the chicken, green onions and raisins.

Pour one half of the Lime Dressing over the mixture. Toss well.

Chill the chicken mixture for 1-2 hours.

Just before serving, stir in the melon balls, 2 tablespoons of the almonds and the remaining Lime Dressing.

Serve the salad in bowls over the rice.

Garnish with the remaining almonds.

Lime Dressing

¾ cup mayonnaise
6 tablespoons freshly squeezed
 lime juice
1½ teaspoons grated lime peel
1½ teaspoons curry powder
½ teaspoon salt
¼ teaspoon pepper

Combine all of the ingredients and mix well.

Waldorf Chicken Salad

Serves 12

2 stalks celery, cut into ½-inch pieces
4 cooked chicken breasts, boned and cubed
3 Golden Delicious apples, cored and cubed
2 cups walnut pieces

Dressing:
1 package ranch dressing mix
1½ cups mayonnaise

Combine the celery, chicken, apples and walnuts.

Toss them with the dressing and serve.

Prepare the ranch dressing mix using 1½ cups mayonnaise but no milk.

Ham and Orange Salad

Serves 6

2 cups finely cubed cooked ham
1 cup thinly sliced celery
⅓ cup chopped green onion
½ cup chopped walnuts
1 11-ounce can mandarin orange segments, drained
crisp greens

Dressing:
¼ teaspoon minced garlic
¼ teaspoon black pepper
⅓ cup mayonnaise
2 tablespoons light cream
1 tablespoon vinegar
1 tablespoon orange juice

In a large bowl, combine the ham, celery, green onion, walnuts and orange segments. Cover and chill the salad.

Just before serving, pour the dressing over the salad and toss until the ingredients are well coated.

Serve the salad on crisp greens.

Combine all of the ingredients and blend well.

PORTABLE BITS

½ medium head cabbage, shredded
4 green onions, sliced
½ pound small shrimp, cooked
2 tablespoons sesame seeds, toasted
½ cup slivered almonds, toasted
1 3-ounce package chicken-flavored Ramen noodles, dry and crumbled

Dressing:
2 tablespoons sugar
3 tablespoons vinegar
¼ teaspoon pepper
½ cup oil
1 teaspoon salt
1 package chicken-flavored soup base from Ramen noodles

Oriental Shrimp Salad *Serves 4*

In a large bowl, combine the cabbage, onions and shrimp.

In a small bowl, combine all of the dressing ingredients.

Just before serving, add the sesame seeds, almonds and noodles to the cabbage.

Pour the dressing over the salad and toss lightly.

¾ pound fresh mushrooms, coarsely chopped
2 tablespoons salad oil
2 tablespoons fresh lemon juice
½ teaspoon salt
2 cups cooked white rice
1½ cups cooked wild rice
1½ pounds shrimp, cooked and cleaned
3 hard-boiled eggs, coarsely chopped
⅓ cup finely chopped green pepper

Shrimp and Rice Salad *Serves 6-8*

Sauté the mushrooms in the oil. Add the lemon juice and the salt and cook until tender, about 5-10 minutes.

Combine the rice, shrimp, eggs and green pepper. Add the mushrooms and mix gently.

Refrigerate the salad overnight.

Just before serving, toss the salad with the Garlic Mayonnaise.

1 clove garlic, minced
¼ teaspoon paprika
1 teaspoon dry mustard
⅛ teaspoon pepper
1 teaspoon warm water
¾ cup mayonnaise

Garlic Mayonnaise

Combine all of the ingredients and blend well.

Confetti Pasta Salad

Serves 6

1 green pepper, chopped
1 red pepper, chopped
1 medium Bermuda onion, chopped
3 medium firm tomatoes, diced
1 stalk celery, chopped
1 7-ounce package cheese tortellini, cooked and drained

In a large bowl, combine the vegetables with the tortellini.

Add the dressing and toss gently.

Serve the salad at room temperature.

Dressing:
4 tablespoons olive oil
3 tablespoons vinegar
salt and pepper to taste

Combine all of the ingredients and mix well.

Pasta Primavera Salad

Serves 10-12

1 pound capellini pasta
2 tablespoons olive oil
1 10-ounce package frozen tiny peas
1 10-ounce package frozen broccoli spears, cut into small pieces
1 6-ounce can pitted whole black olives, quartered lengthwise
1 8-ounce can sliced water chestnuts, drained and rinsed
3 ounces pine nuts
½ cup minced parsley
salt and pepper to taste

Prepare the pasta according to the package directions. Add the olive oil to keep the pasta from sticking to the pot.

Blanch the peas and the broccoli for 3 minutes in boiling water. Remove them and rinse in cold water.

In a large serving bowl combine the pasta, peas, broccoli, olives, chestnuts, pine nuts, parsley, salt and pepper.

Pesto Sauce:
1½ cups olive oil
½ cup white wine vinegar
2 teaspoons dry mustard
40 fresh basil leaves, shredded
1 cup grated Parmesan cheese
4 cloves garlic
salt to taste
white pepper to taste

Combine the oil, vinegar, mustard, basil, cheese and garlic in a blender or a food processor.

Season with salt and pepper.

Add the pesto sauce to the pasta and toss to mix.

Adjust the seasoning if necessary.

cooked pea pods
spinach leaves
watercress

Serve the salad at room temperature or slightly chilled, on a large platter, garnished with pea pods, spinach leaves or watercress.

PORTABLE BITS

Shrimp and Pasta Salad
Serves 4

1 10-ounce package shell pasta, cooked and drained
1 cup broccoli florets, blanched
8 ounces cooked small shrimp
1 small zucchini, cut into julienne strips
1 6-ounce jar marinated artichoke hearts, drained
5 green onions, sliced on the diagonal

Dressing:
½ cup mayonnaise
2 teaspoons curry powder
1 teaspoon Dijon mustard

In a large bowl, combine all of the ingredients. Add the dressing and toss well.

Chill the salad until ready to serve.

Combine the mayonnaise, curry powder and mustard. Mix well.

Durango Salad
Serves 8

1 package frozen peas, thawed and drained
1 cup Spanish peanuts, salted
1 cup finely chopped celery
dash of salt
dash of Tabasco sauce
juice of ½ lemon
Miracle Whip

In a salad bowl, combine the peas, peanuts, celery, salt, Tabasco sauce and lemon juice. Mix well.

Add enough Miracle Whip to make the salad moist.

Refrigerate the salad until ready to serve.

Marinated Broccoli Salad
Serves 6

1 pound broccoli florets
1 medium sweet onion, sliced
½ pound fresh mushrooms, sliced
6 hard-boiled eggs, diced
½ cup chopped green olives
garlic salt to taste
½ cup cashew nuts

Dressing:
1 cup mayonnaise
2 tablespoons Dijon mustard

In a large bowl, combine the broccoli, onion, mushrooms, eggs, olives and garlic salt.

Pour the dressing over the vegetables. Cover the salad and marinate in the refrigerator for 6 hours.

Garnish the salad with the cashew nuts before serving.

Combine the mayonnaise and the mustard. Mix well.

FAMILY BITS

FAMILY BITS

SOUPS:

Cheese and Herb Soup
Serves 4

¼ cup butter
3 tablespoons flour
1 tablespoon finely chopped chives
1 teaspoon paprika
1¼ teaspoons dry mustard
1 14½-ounce can chicken broth
2 cups half and half
4-5 ounces semi-soft garlic and herb cheese
salt and white pepper to taste
croutons

In a medium saucepan, melt the butter over medium heat.

Add the flour and stir the mixture for 4 minutes. Blend in the chives, paprika and mustard and cook for 1-2 minutes more.

Gradually blend in the broth. Add the cream and the cheese and heat the soup until steaming.

Season with the salt and white pepper.

Ladle the soup into bowls and garnish with the croutons.

Crab Gumbo
Serves 6

1 medium onion, sliced into rings
⅓ cup chopped green pepper
2 tablespoons butter
2 tablespoons flour
1 teaspoon salt
¼ teaspoon pepper
¾ teaspoon ground thyme
2½ cups canned tomatoes with juice
1 14½-ounce can okra
2 6-ounce cans crab
Tabasco sauce to taste
2 cups milk
3 cups cooked rice

In a large saucepan, sauté the onion and the green pepper in the butter.

Add the flour, salt, pepper and thyme, stirring well.

Stir in the tomato, okra, crab and Tabasco sauce.

Simmer the mixture for 20 minutes.

Just before serving, add the milk gradually and heat through. Do not boil.

Place a mound of rice in the center of each soup bowl. Ladle the gumbo around the rice and serve immediately.

Mexican Beef Soup
Serves 6

1 pound ground beef
1 medium onion, chopped
salt and freshly ground pepper to taste
¾ cup chopped celery
1½ cups sliced carrots
1 16-ounce can peeled tomatoes, undrained
1 zucchini, sliced
1 cup water
1 cup fresh or frozen corn kernels
1-2 tablespoons chili powder
1 cube beef bouillon
2 teaspoons cumin

Cook the beef in a large saucepan over medium heat until partially browned. Break the meat into chunks.

Add the onion, salt and pepper and simmer until the meat is cooked through.

Add the remaining ingredients. Increase the cooking temperature and bring the soup to a boil.

Reduce the heat to low and simmer for about 30 minutes, or until the vegetables are tender.

Serve hot.

Hearty Chicken Soup

Serves 10-12

This soup is a meal in itself. It is worth the two hour preparation and cooking time. It makes a large quantity and freezes beautifully.

4 pounds chicken
5 cubes chicken bouillon
2 bay leaves
1 teaspoon salt
1 teaspoon pepper
7 pints water
¼ pound butter
1 tablespoon olive oil
5 stalks celery, chopped
3 medium onions, chopped
12 ounces bulk pork sausage
8 ounces stuffing mix
½ cup water
2 tablespoons sage
1 cup Parmesan cheese
1 tablespoon basil
2 tablespoons parsley
1 teaspoon celery seed
2 pinches rosemary

In a large 8-quart pot, add the chicken, bouillon cubes, bay leaves, salt, pepper and water, making sure the water covers the chicken. Cover the pot and simmer for 2 hours.

In a medium skillet, heat the butter and the olive oil. Sauté the celery and the onion until the onion is transparent. Remove and set aside.

In the same skillet, brown the sausage and drain the fat.

Preheat the oven to 300° F.

Combine the onion, celery, sausage, stuffing mix, water, sage, cheese and basil. Mix well and pour into a greased 9"x13" pan.

Cover and bake the stuffing for 1½ hours.

After the chicken has cooked, strain the broth into another large pot.

Add the parsley, celery seed and rosemary to the broth.

Remove the meat from the bones and cut into bite-sized pieces. Add the meat to the broth.

Add the cooked stuffing mixture to the soup and stir to mix well.

Adjust the seasoning and add more bouillon, if needed.

Serve hot.

Sausage and Bean Chowder

Serves 6

1 pound bulk Italian sausage, browned and drained
2 16-ounce cans kidney beans, with their liquid
2 16-ounce cans tomatoes, chopped
2 cups water
2 medium onions, chopped
1 bay leaf
¾ teaspoon salt
½ teaspoon garlic powder
½ teaspoon thyme
¼ teaspoon pepper
1 cup diced potatoes
¼ cup diced green pepper, optional

Combine all of the ingredients, except the potatoes and the green pepper.

Cover the mixture and cook for 30 minutes.

Add the potatoes and the peppers and cook for another 20-30 minutes.

FAMILY BITS

SALADS:

Also see Portable Bits, pages 139-144.

Pineapple and Cabbage Salad — Serves 8

2 cups shredded fresh cabbage
1 6-ounce can crushed pineapple, in heavy syrup
½ cup raisins
½ cup chopped walnuts
1 11-ounce can mandarin oranges, drained

Dressing:
¼ cup plain yogurt
¼ cup Miracle Whip salad dressing
⅓ cup orange juice

Combine all of the salad ingredients.

Blend all of the dressing ingredients.

Pour the dressing over the salad ingredients. Toss to mix.

Italian Marinated Carrots — Serves 8

1 pound carrots, cut into sticks
2 cloves garlic, minced
½ teaspoon oregano, or more to taste
¾ cup oil
¼ cup red wine vinegar
salt and pepper to taste

Prepare this dish in advance to produce a good blending of flavors.

Cook the carrots for 5-10 minutes, or until slightly crisp.

Rinse the carrots and cool them in a large bowl.

Combine the remaining ingredients in another bowl.

Pour the dressing over the carrots and chill before serving.

Spicy Spinach Salad — Serves 4-6

10 ounces fresh spinach, washed, dried, and torn into bite-sized pieces
12 ounces dry curd cottage cheese
1 cup pecan pieces
1 cup sour cream or plain yogurt
3 tablespoons sugar
3 tablespoons white vinegar
1¼ teaspoons dry mustard
4 teaspoons horseradish
⅛ teaspoon salt

Refrigerate the spinach until ready to serve.

In a medium bowl, combine all of the other ingredients. Stir to blend.

Just before serving, pour the dressing over the spinach and toss well.

Grapefruit juice can be used in place of vinegar in many oil and vinegar dressings.

Red Cabbage Salad — *Serves 6*

1 small head red cabbage, shredded
1 avocado, peeled, seeded and sliced
1 small bunch seedless grapes, red <u>or</u> green
6 green onions, sliced
½ cup Poppy Seed Dressing

In a large salad bowl, combine the cabbage, avocado and grapes.

Pour the Poppy Seed Dressing over the salad and toss.

Poppy Seed Dressing — *3 Cups*

This dressing is very tasty on fresh fruit salads and spinach salads.

⅔ cup white vinegar
½ cup sugar
2 teaspoons dry mustard
2 teaspoons salt
2 cups salad oil
2 tablespoons poppy seeds

In a blender, combine the vinegar, sugar, mustard and salt.

Blend in the oil until the mixture is thick.

Add the poppy seeds and mix well.

Parsnip Slaw — *Serves 6*

2 cups grated parsnips
1 cup thinly sliced celery
½ cup mayonnaise
2 tablespoons lemon juice
2 chopped green onions, optional
salt to taste
freshly ground pepper to taste
3-4 large lettuce leaves

Combine all of the ingredients, except the black pepper and lettuce leaves. Mix gently until well blended.

Mound the slaw on the lettuce leaves and sprinkle with the pepper.

ENTREES:

Broiled Fish with Dill — *Serves 4-6*

1½-2 pounds boneless orange roughy <u>or</u> other fish fillets
2 tablespoons mayonnaise <u>or</u> yogurt
juice of ½ medium lime
1½ teaspoons finely chopped fresh dill <u>or</u> ⅓ teaspoon dried dill
freshly ground pepper to taste
lime wedges
fresh dill

Preheat the broiler to high.

Lightly oil a shallow, flameproof baking dish large enough to hold the fillets in one layer. Place the fish in the dish.

Blend together the mayonnaise, lime juice and dill. Brush the tops of the fillets with the mixture.

Place the fish under the broiler about 12 inches from the heat. If this is not possible, reduce the broiler heat to 400° F. Broil for 10 minutes or until the fish flakes easily.

Serve with the lime wedges and garnish with the fresh dill.

FAMILY BITS

Beer Batter Fried Fish
Serves 6

The beer batter for fried fish improves if it is made at least 6 hours in advance.

Combine all of the ingredients, except the fish, and mix well.

Rinse the fish and wipe it as dry as possible.

Dip the fish into the batter. Fry it in deep hot oil until golden brown.

1 cup beer
1 cup flour
½ teaspoon salt
1 teaspoon baking soda
2 eggs, beaten
½ teaspoon dill weed
2 pounds fish fillets or smelts
oil for deep frying

Baked Stuffed Fish
Serves 4

Preheat the oven to 350° F.

Fry the bacon until crisp. Remove the bacon from the pan and set aside. Pour off all but about one tablespoon of the bacon drippings.

Add the celery and the onions and sauté until tender, but not brown.

Prepare the stuffing mix as directed on the package. Stir in the celery-onion mixture.

Spread the stuffing mixture evenly in a buttered, shallow baking dish.

Arrange the fish fillets on top of the stuffing and sprinkle with the salt and the lemon juice. Crumble the bacon on top of the fish.

Bake uncovered for 25 minutes, or until the fish flakes easily.

Sprinkle with the paprika before serving.

4 slices bacon
1 cup sliced celery
1 medium onion, chopped
1½ cups herb-seasoned stuffing mix
1½ pounds fresh sole or cod fillets
¼ teaspoon salt
1 tablespoon lemon juice
paprika to taste

Steamed Red Snapper
Serves 6

Wash the fish and pat it dry.

In a flat dish, combine the soy sauce and the oil. Marinate the fish for 20-30 minutes. Turn the fish a few times in the marinade.

Place the fish on a steamer rack and top it with the tangerine peel, onion and mushrooms.

Steam the fish, using a guide of 10 minutes per inch for the cooking time. Measure the fish at its thickest part.

Serve the fish on a warmed platter with the tangerine peel, onions, mushrooms and about ½ cup of the steaming broth.

1 2-pound red snapper or red snapper fillets
¼ cup soy sauce
¼ cup oil
peel of 1 tangerine, sliced into small pieces
1 medium onion, thinly sliced
¼ pound mushrooms, sliced

Salmon Florentine
Serves 4

2 10-ounce packages frozen spinach, thawed and well drained
1 17-ounce can red sockeye salmon, flaked, with liquid reserved
¼ cup butter
¼ cup flour
½ teaspoon dry mustard
milk
¼ teaspoon salt
⅓ cup grated Parmesan cheese
1 tablespoon grated Parmesan cheese

Preheat the oven to 425° F.

Place the spinach in a buttered 8"x8" baking dish. Flake the drained salmon over the spinach.

In a medium saucepan, melt the butter. Add the flour and the dry mustard. Blend.

Add enough milk to the salmon mixture to measure 1½ cups when combined. Stir the liquid and the salt into the saucepan.

Bring the mixture to a boil stirring constantly. Add the ⅓ cup Parmesan cheese.

Pour the sauce over the salmon. Sprinkle with the one tablespoon Parmesan cheese.

Bake uncovered for 20-25 minutes, or until bubbly.

Stir-Fry Shrimp and Pineapple
Serves 4

1 pound medium-sized shrimp, shelled and deveined
2 tablespoons vegetable oil
2 large carrots, cut diagonally into thin slices
3 stalks celery, cut diagonally into thin slices
1 green pepper, cut into chunks
1 onion, cut into thin wedges
1 8-ounce can pineapple chunks, drained
¾ cup Stir-Fry Sauce Mix
hot cooked rice

Heat one tablespoon oil in a wok over medium-high heat. Add the shrimp and stir-fry 2 minutes. Remove from the wok.

Heat the remaining one tablespoon of oil and add the carrots, celery, green pepper, and onion. Stir-fry the vegetables until crisp-tender. Add the pineapple chunks and the Stir-Fry Sauce Mix to the wok and cook, stirring, until the mixture thickens.

Serve over hot cooked rice.

Stir-Fry Sauce Mix
3½ Cups

¼ cup cornstarch
1 teaspoon garlic powder
1 teaspoon ground ginger
¼ teaspoon white pepper
¼ cup white vinegar
⅓ cup dry sherry
½ cup soy sauce
½ cup light molasses or dark corn syrup
2 teaspoons powdered beef bouillon
2 cups water

In a one-quart container, combine the dry ingredients. Add the vinegar and sherry and stir until the dry ingredients are dissolved. Add the remaining ingredients and mix well.

Store the sauce in a jar with a tight-fitting lid. Refrigerate for up to four weeks.

Stir well before measuring out the desired amount.

FAMILY BITS

Marinated Salmon Steaks *Serves 8*

Place the salmon steaks in a large dish.

Mix together the remaining ingredients. Pour over the fish. Marinate the fish for at least 30 minutes, or overnight.

Place the salmon steaks on a greased broiler pan. Broil the fish, brushing with the marinade for about 15 minutes, or until the fish flakes easily. Turn the steaks at least once while cooking.

The salmon steaks can also be grilled over coals in foil bundles.

8 salmon steaks
¾ cup dry vermouth
¾ cup olive oil
1½ tablespoons lemon juice
dash of pepper
¼ teaspoon thyme
¼ teaspoon marjoram
⅛ teaspoon sage
1 tablespoon minced parsley

Sauté of Sole with Lemon *Serves 4*

Place the fish fillets in a dish with the milk.

Combine the flour and the pepper, blending well.

In a large skillet, heat half of the oil.

Remove the fish from the milk, but do not dry or drain it. Coat it quickly with the seasoned flour.

When the oil is hot, but not smoking, add 2 or 3 fillets and cook them until they are golden on each side. Turn once. The cooking time will be about 4-5 minutes for each fillet. As the fillets are cooked, transfer them to a warm platter.

Add more oil to the skillet to complete the cooking of the remaining fillets.

Peel the lemon and remove all of the white pith. Cut the pulp into slices and then into cubes. Discard any seeds.

To prepare the sauce, melt the butter in the skillet just until slightly brown. Remove from the heat and add the cubed lemon pulp, stirring once.

Pour the sauce over the fish, sprinkle it with the parsley and serve hot.

1½ pounds fillet of sole
¼ cup milk
½ cup flour
freshly ground pepper to taste
½ cup vegetable oil
2 tablespoons butter
½ small lemon
1 tablespoon minced parsley

Grilled Swordfish *Serves 6-8*

Prick the swordfish all over and place in a shallow glass dish.

Combine all of the remaining ingredients, except the lemon wedges and parsley, and pour over the swordfish.

Marinate the fish for 1-3 hours.

Broil or grill the fish using moderate heat for 5-6 minutes per side, basting with the remaining marinade.

Garnish with lemon wedges and parsley. Serve at once.

4 large swordfish steaks, cut in half
⅓ cup soy sauce
1 teaspoon grated lemon peel
¼ cup fresh lemon juice
1 clove garlic, crushed
2 teaspoons Dijon mustard
½ cup oil
lemon wedges
parsley

Hot Tub Trout
Serves One

1 trout
1 quart boiling water
1 large sprig fresh dill
3 thin lemon slices
lemon pepper
¼-⅓ cup dry white wine

Preheat the oven to 375° F.

Place the trout in a pan in the sink.

Pour the boiling water over the trout. Leave the trout in the boiling water until the skin begins to loosen. Immediately submerge the trout in cold water.

Skin the trout. Place it on a large piece of heavy duty aluminum foil which has no holes or tears.

Arrange the dill and the lemon slices on the fish. Sprinkle with the lemon pepper.

Draw up the foil to form a container around the fish and pour in the wine.

Tightly seal the trout packet by pinching together the foil edges.

Bake for 15-20 minutes, depending on the size of the trout.

Serve the trout in its packet, if desired.

Basic Italian Sauce
12 Cups

2-3 medium onions, chopped
2 large cloves garlic, minced <u>or</u> pressed
6 tablespoons vegetable oil
2 28-ounce cans tomatoes
2 15-ounce cans tomato sauce
1 12-ounce can tomato paste
¾ cup water
4 tablespoons parsley flakes
¼ cup sugar
1 teaspoon seasoned salt
1 teaspoon salt
2 teaspoons basil
½ teaspoon marjoram
½ teaspoon oregano
sliced fresh mushrooms, optional
chopped green pepper, optional
chopped olives, optional
2 pounds lean ground beef, browned, <u>or</u> 2 pounds Italian sausage, browned, optional

This sauce freezes well and can be used in any recipe calling for a basic Italian red sauce.

In a large Dutch oven or soup pot, brown the onion and the garlic in the oil.

Add the remaining ingredients and any of the optional ingredients.

Simmer the sauce for 3-4 hours.

For freezing, cool the sauce and measure into freezer containers. Allow ½ inch head space in the containers for expansion. Freeze and use the sauce within 3 months.

To neutralize the odor of cooking fish, burn some sugar in a disposable aluminum foil pan.

FAMILY BITS

Cabernet Pot Roast
Serves 6-8

1 4-pound chuck roast
salt and pepper to taste
2 tablespoons flour
3 tablespoons oil
1 8-ounce can tomato sauce
1 cup Cabernet Sauvignon <u>or</u> other dry red wine
½ teaspoon dried oregano
½ teaspoon dried rosemary

Season the roast with the salt and the pepper. Dredge it in the flour.

In a large, heavy skillet, heat the oil. Brown the roast on both sides.

Transfer the meat to a slow cooker and add the remaining ingredients.

Simmer on low heat for 6-8 hours.

If desired, the roast may be cooked in a covered roasting pan for 3-4 hours in a 350° F. oven.

Stir-Fry Beef and Vegetables
Serves 4

1 pound top sirloin steak
3 tablespoons vegetable oil
1½ cups carrots, thinly sliced
1½ cups broccoli, sliced
1½ cups zucchini, sliced
4 - 5 green onions, thinly sliced
¾ cup Stir-Fry Sauce Mix, see page 151
hot cooked rice

Trim excess fat from the steak. Cut the meat across the grain in thin, slanting slices.

Heat 2 tablespoons of the oil in a wok over high heat. Add the meat about ¼ pound at a time, stirring until browned, about 2 minutes. Set the meat aside.

Add one tablespoon of the oil to the wok. When it is hot, add the carrots and stir-fry for 2 - 3 minutes. Stir in the broccoli and cook 2 minutes longer. Stir in the zucchini and cook 1 - 2 minutes more.

Return the meat to the wok. Add the Stir-Fry Sauce to the mixture and cook, stirring, until the sauce thickens and coats the meat and vegetables.

Turn into a serving dish and top with the green onions.

Serve with hot cooked rice.

Steak Magnifique
Serves 4

1 cup vegetable oil
¾ cup soy sauce
½ cup fresh lemon juice
¼ cup Worcestershire sauce
⅓ cup Dijon mustard
1 tablespoon freshly ground pepper
salt to taste
3 garlic cloves, minced
1 2-pound flank steak

This marinade recipe is also delicious with beef tenderloin and chicken.

Combine the first 7 ingredients in a large bowl. Whip to blend well.

Pour the desired amount of marinade over the meat and let it marinate at room temperature for at least 30 minutes.

Place the meat on a broiler rack or a hot barbecue grill about 4-5 inches from the source of heat.

Broil about 3-5 minutes on each side. The cooking time will depend on the desired degree of doneness.

Cowgirl Casserole

Serves 6

1 pound ground beef
1 small onion, chopped
1 garlic clove, minced
½ green pepper, chopped
1 16-ounce can tomato sauce
1 tablespoon Worcestershire sauce
1 4-ounce can sliced mushrooms
¼ teaspoon dry mustard
2 cups water
8 ounces macaroni
1 cup grated Monterey Jack cheese

Cowgirl Casserole is a real kid pleaser. It is a good recipe to prepare in large quantities, freeze, thaw and reheat when needed.

Brown the beef, onion, garlic and green pepper. Drain well.

Add all of the other ingredients, except the macaroni, and bring the mixture to a boil. Reduce the heat and cover.

Simmer over low heat for 20 minutes.

Add the macaroni and simmer for another 15 minutes, or until the macaroni is tender.

Preheat the oven to 350° F.

Pour the mixture into a buttered casserole dish and top with the cheese.

Bake for 20-25 minutes or until heated through and the cheese is melted.

For quicker preparation, omit the baking step and serve the Cowgirl Casserole in bowls sprinkled with the cheese.

Taco Pie

One 10-inch Pie

1 pound ground beef
½ cup chopped onion
1 1¼-ounce package taco seasoning mix
1 4-ounce can diced green chiles
1¼ cups milk
¾ cup Master Baking Mix, see page 174 or biscuit mix
3 eggs
2 tomatoes, sliced
1 cup grated Monterey Jack or Cheddar cheese
sour cream
chopped tomatoes
shredded lettuce

Preheat the oven to 400° F.

Brown the beef in a skillet. Drain off the excess fat. Stir in the onion and the taco seasoning mix. Cook for 5 minutes longer.

Spread the meat mixture in a greased 10-inch pie pan. Sprinkle it with the chiles.

Beat together the milk, Mix and eggs until smooth. Pour over the meat.

Bake for 25 minutes.

Remove from the oven and top the pie with the tomatoes and the cheese. Continue to bake for 8-10 minutes more, or until a knife inserted in the center comes out clean.

Cool 5 minutes before cutting.

Serve with the sour cream, chopped tomatoes and shredded lettuce.

Yogurt makes an excellent meat tenderizer. Pour plain yogurt over the meat, cover and refrigerate overnight. Then, wipe the yogurt off before cooking.

FAMILY BITS

Eldorado Beef Casserole
Serves 4-6

1 pound lean ground beef
1 tablespoon minced onion
⅛ teaspoon garlic powder
2 8-ounce cans tomato sauce
2 2¼-ounce cans sliced ripe olives, drained
1 cup plain yogurt **or** sour cream
1 cup small curd cottage cheese
2 4-ounce cans diced green chiles
2 cups grated Monterey Jack cheese
1 6½-ounce package tortilla chips, slightly crumbled

Preheat the oven to 350° F.

Brown the beef in a large skillet. Drain the fat.

Add the onion, garlic powder, tomato sauce and olives. Stir to mix. Remove the skillet from the heat.

Mix the yogurt or sour cream, cottage cheese, green chiles and cheese.

In a 2½-quart casserole dish, layer the tortilla chips, the meat mixture and the cottage cheese mixture. Repeat the layers once and top with tortilla chips.

Bake uncovered for 30 minutes and serve hot.

Flank Steak in Mushroom Sauce
Serves 4-5

1-1½ pounds flank steak
¼ cup sauterne wine
1 tablespoon soy sauce
1 clove garlic, minced
1 10½-ounce can beef broth
1 tablespoon catsup
2 teaspoons Dijon mustard
1 tablespoon instant minced onion **or** ¼ cup chopped onion
¼ pound fresh mushrooms, sliced
2 tablespoons cornstarch
2 tablespoons water

Place the steak in a slow cooker on low heat.

Combine the sauterne, soy sauce, garlic, broth, catsup, mustard, onion and mushrooms. Pour the mixture over the steak.

Cover and cook the steak for 6-8 hours.

Dissolve the cornstarch in the water and stir into the pot.

Turn the heat control to high for 20-30 minutes or until the sauce thickens.

Lemon Chicken and Potatoes
Serves 4

1 chicken, cut into pieces
4 medium potatoes, peeled and quartered
2 medium onions, peeled and sliced into rings
juice of 1½ large lemons
3 tablespoons butter **or** margarine
1 tablespoon dried oregano
salt and pepper to taste

Preheat the oven to 350° F.

Place the chicken pieces, skin side up, in a shallow baking pan. Arrange the potatoes between the pieces and the onion rings on top.

Add ½-inch of water to the bottom of the pan.

Dot the chicken, potatoes and onions with the butter and pour the lemon juice over all.

Season with the oregano, salt and pepper. Cover the pan.

Bake for 30 minutes. Then, uncover the pan and bake for another 30 minutes, basting occasionally.

Serve hot.

Baked Honey Chicken
Serves 4

1 3-pound chicken, cut into serving pieces
½ cup flour
½ teaspoon pepper
4 tablespoons butter
¼ cup honey
¼ cup lemon juice
1 tablespoon soy sauce

Preheat the oven to 350° F.

Wash and drain the chicken pieces.

Combine the flour and the pepper in a paper bag. Shake the chicken pieces in the bag to coat them with the flour.

Melt 2 tablespoons of the butter in a 9"x13"x1¾" pan. Roll the chicken pieces in the butter to coat them. Place them, skin side down, in a single layer in the baking dish.

Bake the chicken for 30 minutes.

Melt the remaining 2 tablespoons of the butter in a small saucepan. Stir in the honey, lemon juice and soy sauce until well mixed.

Turn the chicken. Pour the honey mixture over the top.

Continue to bake the chicken, basting it several times with the sauce. Cook for 30 minutes more, or until the chicken is tender and richly glazed.

Chicken and Artichoke Casserole
Serves 6

½ pound mushrooms, sliced
2 tablespoons butter
1 14½-ounce can chicken broth
4 whole chicken breasts
1 14-ounce can artichoke hearts, drained
¼ cup margarine
¼ cup flour
¼ teaspoon salt
dash of pepper
¾ cup chicken broth
¼ cup half and half
½ cup grated Parmesan cheese
2 tablespoons sherry
½ teaspoon rosemary

Preheat the oven to 350° F.

Sauté the mushrooms in the butter. Set aside.

Simmer the chicken breasts in the broth for 20 minutes. Reserve the broth.

Remove the bones and skin from the chicken. Arrange the meat in an ovenproof casserole in one layer.

Top the chicken with the artichoke hearts.

Melt the margarine and stir in the flour, salt and pepper. Cook, stirring until smooth.

Gradually add the ¾ cup chicken broth and the cream, stirring constantly. Cook the sauce until it boils and thickens.

Blend in the cheese, sherry and rosemary.

Pour the sauce over the chicken and top with the mushrooms.

Bake for 30 minutes.

Mushroom caps slice very easily with an egg slicer.

FAMILY BITS

Chicken Marsala
Serves 4

4 chicken breasts, skinned and boned
salt and white pepper to taste
¼ cup flour
2 tablespoons butter
1 tablespoon olive oil
⅓ cup Marsala wine
½ pound mushrooms, sliced
1 cup chicken broth
½ cup heavy cream
¼ cup minced parsley

Cut the chicken breasts into 8 scallops lengthwise.

Pound each chicken piece between two pieces of wax paper until fairly thin.

Season the chicken with the salt and pepper. Dredge the pieces in the flour.

In a large skillet, heat the butter and the oil. Sauté the chicken over moderately high heat for one minute on each side. Transfer to a heated platter when cooked.

Add the Marsala to the skillet and deglaze the skillet.

Add the mushrooms, chicken broth and cream. Cook for 3 minutes, or until the sauce has thickened.

Pour the sauce over the scallops.

Sprinkle with the parsley and serve hot.

Chicken with Spinach and Linguine
Serves 6-8

½ cup butter <u>or</u> margarine, melted
1 medium onion, thinly sliced
2 cloves garlic, minced
1 tablespoon dry basil
8 chicken thighs
2 10-ounce packages frozen chopped spinach, thawed, moisture removed
8 ounces dry linguine
1 cup grated Parmesan cheese
juice of one orange
1 teaspoon crushed hot red pepper, seeds removed, optional
salt to taste

Preheat the oven to 400° F.

Combine the butter, onion, garlic and basil in a large ovenproof casserole.

Place the chicken thighs, skin side up, on top of the mixture.

Bake uncovered for 45 minutes. The chicken skin should be well browned.

Ten minutes before the chicken is done, cook the linguine according to the package directions.

Remove the cooked chicken from the pan. Add the spinach to the pan and stir to scrape up the browned bits.

Add the cooked linguine, Parmesan cheese, orange juice, hot pepper and salt. Mix to blend the ingredients.

Serve the linguine and spinach with the chicken thighs at the side.

1 3-3½ pound chicken,
    cut into serving pieces
1 cup pancake mix
1 egg
⅓ cup water
1 tablespoon vegetable oil
1 tablespoon soy sauce
salt to taste
⅛ teaspoon pepper
¼ teaspoon garlic powder
¼ teaspoon paprika
¼ teaspoon basil

Oven-Fried Chicken
Serves 4

Preheat the oven to 350° F.

Combine all of the ingredients, except the chicken.

Coat the chicken pieces with the mixture.

Place the chicken in a single layer on a greased baking sheet.

Cook for about 50-60 minutes, or until cooked through.

4 chicken breast halves,
    skinned and boned
3 tablespoons vegetable oil
½ pound fresh pea pods,
    ends removed
¼ pound fresh mushrooms,
    sliced
1 8-ounce can sliced water
    chestnuts, drained
1 cup unsalted cashews
¾ cup Stir-Fry Sauce Mix,
    see page 151
hot cooked rice

Stir-Fry Cashew Chicken
Serves 4

Cut the chicken breasts into thin strips.

Heat 2 tablespoons of the oil in a wok over high heat. Add the chicken to the wok about ⅓ at a time. Stir-fry until cooked, about 3 minutes. Set the meat aside.

Heat one more tablespoon oil in the wok and add the pea pods and mushrooms. Stir-fry only until heated thoroughly.

Return the chicken to the wok with the water chestnuts and the Stir-Fry Sauce Mix. Cook until thickened.

Stir in the cashews.

Serve over hot cooked rice.

½ cup flour
½ teaspoon nutmeg
salt and pepper to taste
2 whole chicken breasts, split,
    skinned and boned
2 eggs, slightly beaten
¾ cup bread crumbs
½ cup grated Swiss cheese
⅓ cup butter, melted
4 lemon wedges

Swiss Chicken
Serves 4

Mix together the flour, nutmeg, salt and pepper.

Dredge the chicken breasts lightly in the flour mixture. Then, dip them in the eggs.

Combine the bread crumbs and the Swiss cheese. Dredge the chicken breasts in this mixture.

Brown the breasts on both sides in the melted butter. Continue to cook over low heat until the chicken is done.

Serve hot with lemon wedges.

FAMILY BITS

Basque Cassoulet — *Serves 8*

½ pound pepperoni, sliced
1 whole chicken breast, skinned and boned
6 green onions, chopped
1-2 cloves garlic, minced
4 medium carrots, sliced
2 cups cabbage, shredded
1 16-ounce can garbanzos, undrained
1 16-ounce can red kidney beans, undrained
1 16-ounce can stewed tomatoes, chopped, undrained
1 teaspoon salt
1½ teaspoons thyme
½ teaspoon pepper

Sauté the pepperoni in a large skillet. Remove it with a slotted spoon.

Cut the chicken breast into one-inch pieces and brown them in the pan drippings. Drain off the excess grease.

Add the remaining ingredients and simmer over low heat for 20-30 minutes. Add a little water if the casserole seems too dry.

Chicken Parmigiana — *Serves 6*

2 eggs, lightly beaten
1 teaspoon salt
4 teaspoons water
⅛ teaspoon pepper
4 large chicken breasts, split, skinned and boned
1 cup Italian bread crumbs
4 tablespoons vegetable oil
3 cups Basic Italian Sauce, see page 153
½ cup freshly grated Parmesan cheese
8 ounces mozzarella cheese, grated

Preheat the oven to 350° F.

Mix together the eggs, salt, water and pepper.

Dip the chicken breasts into the egg mixture and then into the crumbs.

In a heavy skillet, heat the oil and brown the chicken. Remove the chicken and drain on a paper towel.

Arrange the chicken in a baking dish and top with the Basic Italian Sauce. Sprinkle it with the Parmesan cheese.

Bake covered for 30 minutes.

Top with the mozzarella cheese and continue to bake, uncovered, for 10 minutes longer, or until the cheese has melted.

Serve the chicken with cooked pasta.

Blue River Liver
Serves 6

The sugar in this sauce can be omitted for a slightly tart variation.

2 large onions, thinly sliced
2 tablespoons vegetable oil
2 tablespoons unsalted butter
1½ pounds calf liver,
    sliced less than ½ inch thick
seasoned flour
1 tablespoon sugar
1 14½-ounce can chicken broth
¼ cup fresh lemon juice
1 tablespoon flour, dissolved
    in ¼ cup water

In a large stainless steel or enamel skillet, sauté the onions in the oil and butter over moderately high heat. Cook, stirring until the onions are golden. Transfer the onions to a warm platter and cover.

Dredge the liver in the seasoned flour and shake off the excess.

Sauté the liver in the remaining oil over moderately high heat. Cook it on both sides until it is lightly browned on the outside, but still pink inside. Transfer the liver to the platter as it is cooked. Add more oil and butter to the skillet, if necessary.

Pour off all of the fat from the skillet. Stir in the sugar, chicken broth and lemon juice. Reduce the sauce over high heat by about ⅓ of a cup. Stir the sauce occasionally.

Lower the heat. Add the flour and water mixture, stirring constantly until the sauce is thickened only slightly.

Cover the onions and the liver with the sauce and serve immediately.

Lemon Lamb Chops with Rice
Serves 4

2 chicken bouillon cubes
1¼ cups boiling water
1 tablespoon margarine
1 clove garlic, minced
4 shoulder lamb chops
½ cup rice
¾ teaspoon salt
juice of ½ lemon
2 tablespoons chopped parsley
freshly ground pepper to taste

Dissolve the bouillon cubes in the boiling water. Set aside.

In a large skillet, melt the margarine and sauté the garlic. Add the lamb chops and brown them quickly over high heat.

Pour the bouillon into the skillet. Place the rice around the chops.

Sprinkle the salt, lemon juice, parsley and pepper over the chops and rice.

Bring to a boil and cover.

Simmer for 25-30 minutes, or until the liquid is absorbed and the rice is done.

Remove from the heat and let stand, covered, for 5 minutes before serving.

FAMILY BITS

Lamb Patties with Dill Sauce
Serves 6

1½ pounds ground lamb
½ cup quick oats
1 egg, beaten
1 tablespoon minced onion
½ teaspoon salt
¼ teaspoon ground thyme
freshly ground pepper
6 slices bacon
12 ounces yogurt or sour cream,
   at room temperature
1 teaspoon fresh dill

In a large bowl, combine the lamb, oatmeal, egg, onion, salt, thyme and pepper. Mix the ingredients well and shape into 6 patties.

Wrap a slice of bacon around each patty and secure with a toothpick.

Broil the patties 5 inches from the heat for about 5-7 minutes per side, or until done as desired.

To prepare the sauce, combine the yogurt and the dill weed. Stir until smooth.

Serve the lamb patties and pass the sauce.

Orange-Glazed Pork Chops
Serves 4

4 loin pork chops
salt and freshly ground pepper
   to taste
⅔ cup flour
1 tablespoon butter
½ cup fresh orange juice
½ cup dry white wine
2½ tablespoons orange marmalade
orange slices
watercress

Season the pork chops with the salt and the pepper. Dredge the chops lightly in the flour, shaking off any excess.

In a large, heavy skillet, melt the butter over medium heat. Add the chops and cook them for about 3-5 minutes on each side, or until they are golden brown.

Stir in the orange juice, wine and marmalade.

Cover the chops, reduce the heat to low, and simmer the mixture for 20-25 minutes, turning the chops once.

Transfer the chops to a platter and keep them warm.

Continue to cook the sauce until it has thickened, about 4 minutes. Spoon the sauce over the chops.

Garnish the chops with the orange slices and the watercress.

Serve immediately.

Pork Chops and Apples
Serves 4

5 apples, pared, cored and sliced
1 medium onion, peeled and sliced
4 pork chops, with fat trimmed
salt and pepper to taste
3 tablespoons margarine
3 tablespoons flour
1½ cups beer

Preheat the oven to 350° F.

Place the apples and onions in a large, buttered casserole.

Lay the pork chops on top of the apples and onions. Season with the salt and the pepper.

In a small saucepan, melt the margarine. Mix in the flour to form a roux.

Add the beer, all at once, stirring constantly until the sauce thickens.

Pour the beer sauce over the pork chops and apples.

Bake for 1½ hours.

Stir-Fry Pork
Serves 4

¾ pound pork tenderloin
2 3-ounce packages Ramen noodles, pork flavor
3 tablespoons vegetable oil
2 small onions, cut into thin wedges
2 green peppers, cut into one-inch squares
1 8-ounce can pineapple chunks, undrained
¾ cup Stir-Fry Sauce Mix, see page 151
½ teaspoon cornstarch

Cut the meat across the grain in thin, slanting slices.

Cook the noodles according to the directions. Drain them and add the flavor packets. Turn out onto a large rimmed platter, cover and keep warm.

Heat 2 tablespoons of the oil in a wok over medium-high heat. Add the meat, about ¼ pound at a time. Stir-fry until cooked thoroughly, about 5 minutes. Remove the meat from the pan.

Heat one more tablespoon oil in the wok and add the onion and green pepper. Stir-fry until the vegetables are crisp-tender.

Add the pineapple with the syrup and the meat to the vegetables in the wok.

Stir the cornstarch into the Stir-Fry Sauce Mix and add it to the wok. Cook, stirring, until the sauce thickens.

Serve the mixture over the hot cooked noodles.

CHEESE AND EGG DISHES:

Lasagne Pie
One 10-Inch Pie

1 pound ground beef **or** Italian sausage
1 teaspoon oregano
½ teaspoon basil
1 6-ounce can tomato paste
1 cup grated mozzarella cheese
½ cup small curd cottage cheese
¼ cup grated Parmesan cheese
1 cup milk
⅔ cup Master Baking Mix, see page 174 **or** biscuit mix
2 eggs
½ teaspoon salt
pepper to taste

Preheat the oven to 400° F.

In a skillet, brown the beef. Drain off the excess fat.

Stir in the oregano, basil, tomato paste and ½ cup of the mozzarella cheese.

In a greased 10-inch pie pan, layer the cottage cheese and the Parmesan cheese. Spoon the beef mixture over the layers.

Combine the remaining ingredients, except the mozzarella cheese, in a blender. Blend for one minute or until smooth.

Pour the mixture over the layers in the pie pan.

Bake for 30-35 minutes, or until a knife inserted in the center comes out clean.

Sprinkle the top with the remaining cheese.

Cool for 5 minutes before serving.

FAMILY BITS

Brunch Pie   *Serves 6-8*

1 10-ounce package frozen chopped broccoli or spinach <u>or</u> 1 8-ounce package frozen asparagus spears, thawed
1 cup sour cream
1 cup creamed cottage cheese
½ cup Master Baking Mix, see page 174 <u>or</u> biscuit mix
¼ cup butter <u>or</u> margarine, melted
2 eggs
1 tomato, peeled and thinly sliced
¼ cup grated Parmesan cheese

Preheat the oven to 350° F.

Grease a 10-inch pie pan.

Spread the vegetables in the pan.

Beat the sour cream, cottage cheese, Mix, butter and eggs until the mixture is smooth. This will take 15 seconds in a blender on high speed or one minute with a hand beater.

Pour the mixture into the pie pan.

Top the pie with the tomatoes and the Parmesan cheese.

Bake for 30 minutes, or until a knife inserted in the center comes out clean.

Cool the pie for 5 minutes before cutting it.

Cheese Tart   *Serves 4*

paprika
1½ cups grated Swiss cheese
4 slices bacon, cooked and crumbled
3 eggs
⅛ teaspoon salt
¼ teaspoon nutmeg, optional
1½ cups milk
1 teaspoon minced onion
⅓ cup Master Baking Mix, see page 174 <u>or</u> biscuit mix

Preheat the oven to 350° F.

Butter a 9-inch pie pan and sprinkle the bottom and the sides lightly with the paprika.

Layer the cheese and then the bacon in the pan.

In a blender, combine the eggs, salt, nutmeg, milk, onion and Mix. Blend until thoroughly mixed, about one minute. Pour the mixture over the cheese and bacon in the pie pan.

Bake for 30-40 minutes, or until a toothpick inserted in the center comes out clean.

Serve hot.

Tofu Enchiladas   *Serves 4*

8-10 corn tortillas
1 29-ounce can tomato sauce
1 teaspoon garlic powder
1 teaspoon onion powder
¼ teaspoon oregano
¼ teaspoon basil
1¼ teaspoons chili powder <u>or</u> to taste
pepper to taste
16 ounces tofu, squeezed dry
½ pound Cheddar cheese, grated
black olives

Preheat the oven to 350° F.

Mix all of the ingredients together, except the tofu and the cheese, to make the sauce.

Simmer over a medium heat for 15 minutes.

In a 9"x13" baking dish, place ⅓ of the sauce.

Place a strip of tofu in each tortilla and roll up. Place in the baking dish.

Cover all of the tortillas with the rest of the sauce and the grated cheese.

Bake 15-20 minutes.

Garnish with black olives.

Potato Crust Quiche

Serves 6

2 large potatoes, peeled
2 teaspoons lemon juice
¼ cup butter <u>or</u> margarine, melted
1 cup grated <u>hot</u> pepper cheese
1 cup grated Swiss cheese
8 slices cooked bacon, diced <u>or</u>
    1 cup diced cooked ham
¾ cup half and half <u>or</u> ½ cup milk
3 eggs
¼ teaspoon seasoned salt

Preheat the oven to 400° F.

Grease the bottom and sides of a 10-inch pie pan.

Shred the potatoes and add the lemon juice. Toss the potatoes to coat them. Remove any excess moisture from the potatoes with paper towels.

Spread the potatoes over the pie pan. Pat them over the bottom and sides of the pan, trimming any excess. Brush the potatoes with the melted butter.

Bake the potato crust for 20-25 minutes. Remove the crust and reduce the oven to 350° F.

Sprinkle the cheese and meat evenly over the crust.

Beat together the cream, eggs and salt. Pour over the cheese and meat.

Bake uncovered for about 30 minutes, or until a knife inserted in the center comes out clean.

Spinach and Sausage Frittata

Serves 6

½ pound bulk Italian sausage
2 tablespoons olive oil
½ pound fresh mushrooms, sliced
½ cup minced onion
1 10-ounce package frozen chopped
    spinach, thawed and well drained
6 eggs, lightly beaten
1 cup grated Romano cheese
1 cup grated provolone cheese
2 cloves garlic, minced
1 teaspoon dried basil, crushed
½ teaspoon dried marjoram, crushed
freshly ground pepper to taste

In a large skillet, brown the sausage. Remove the sausage from the pan and discard any remaining grease. Drain the sausage well.

Heat the olive oil in the skillet. Stir-fry the mushrooms and the onions over high heat until lightly browned.

Stir in the spinach and cook for 3 minutes. Remove the skillet from the heat.

In a large bowl, combine the eggs, ⅔ cup of the Romano cheese, ⅓ cup of the provolone cheese, garlic, basil, marjoram and pepper.

Stir the sausage and the vegetables into the bowl. Mix well. Pour the mixture into a greased 10-inch pie pan.

Sprinkle with the remaining Romano and provolone cheese.

Bake for 30-40 minutes, or until set. Do not overbake the frittata or it will become dry.

FAMILY BITS

SIDE DISHES AND VEGETABLES:

Breckenridge Pineapple Pudding *Serves 6-8*

This delicious pudding is reminiscent of the old toast, "Here's to the pleasure of living in Colorado".

2 tablespoons flour
½ cup sugar
3 eggs, beaten
1 1-pound, 4-ounce can crushed pineapple, undrained
5 slices bread, cubed
4 tablespoons butter, melted

Preheat the oven to 350° F.

In a large bowl, combine the flour and the sugar.

Add the beaten eggs, pineapple with its juice and bread cubes, reserving ¼ of the bread cubes for the topping.

Pour the mixture into an ungreased 1 ½-quart casserole and sprinkle with the reserved bread crumbs.

Pour the butter over the top.

Bake for one hour.

Serve warm as a side-dish.

Blender Potato Bake *Serves 4*

1 cup milk
3 eggs
½ teaspoon salt
⅛ teaspoon pepper
3 cups cubed, raw potatoes
2 tablespoons butter, softened
½ small onion, cut into pieces
1 cup cubed Cheddar cheese
½ cup grated Cheddar cheese

Preheat the oven to 375° F.

Place all of the ingredients, except for the grated cheese, in a blender. Blend just until all of the potatoes are grated.

Pour the mixture into a greased 8"x8" baking dish. Top with the grated cheese.

Bake for 35-40 minutes.

Lemon Herbed New Potatoes *Serves 6-8*

1-1½ pounds new potatoes, scrubbed and quartered
1 tablespoon butter
juice of ½ lemon
¼ teaspoon dried rosemary, crushed or ¼ teaspoon dried dill weed
salt and pepper to taste

Cook the potatoes in boiling water for about 10 minutes, or until tender. Drain.

Add the butter, lemon juice, rosemary, salt and pepper.

Stir the ingredients very gently over medium heat for about 30 seconds.

Serve immediately.

Oven-Fried Potatoes
Serves 4

1½ pounds potatoes
¼ cup vegetable oil
1 tablespoon grated Parmesan cheese
¼ teaspoon salt
¼ teaspoon garlic powder
¼ teaspoon paprika
⅛ teaspoon pepper

Preheat the oven to 375° F.

Scrub the potatoes and cut them into ½-inch wedges.

Combine the remaining ingredients in a large bowl. Add the potato wedges to the bowl and mix thoroughly to coat.

Place the potatoes in a single layer on a cookie sheet and bake for 40-45 minutes.

Potato Casserole
Serves 8

6 medium potatoes, cooked and mashed
3 cups cottage cheese
½ cup sour cream
1½ teaspoons grated onion
½ cup grated sharp Cheddar cheese

Preheat the oven to 350° F.

Combine all of the ingredients in a large bowl.

Place the mixture in a greased 2-quart casserole and top with the cheese.

Bake for 30 minutes.

A Different Rice
Serves 6

½ medium onion, chopped
2 tablespoons butter or margarine
¼ cup raw lentils
½ teaspoon cinnamon
2½ cups chicken stock or water
1 tablespoon tomato paste
¼ teaspoon salt
½ cup raisins
1 cup rice
¼ cup pine nuts or sunflower seeds or chopped almonds

Sauté the onion in the butter until it is soft.

Combine all of the other ingredients, except for the rice and nuts, and simmer covered for 20 minutes.

Add the rice and the nuts and cook for another 20 minutes.

Lemon Rice
Serves 4-6

1¾ cups chicken broth
1 teaspoon grated lemon zest
¼ cup fresh lemon juice
1 cup long grain white rice
2 tablespoons butter
¼ cup chopped celery
⅓ cup minced onion
¼ pound fresh mushrooms, sliced
½ teaspoon dried fines herbes
salt and white pepper to taste

In a large saucepan, combine the chicken broth, lemon zest and juice. Bring to a boil and add the rice. Reduce the heat to low and simmer covered for 17 minutes.

Melt the butter in a skillet and sauté the celery, onion and mushrooms. Sprinkle with the fines herbes.

Add the vegetable mixture to the rice. Stir and cook 5 minutes more. Add the salt and the pepper.

FAMILY BITS

Sautéed Papaya with Lime Juice *Serves 6*

2 ripe papayas, peeled
3 tablespoons butter or margarine
juice of ½ lime

Halve the papayas crosswise and remove the seeds with a spoon.

Slice the halves into circles ½-inch thick. Sauté the circles in the butter until their color becomes golden. Do not brown.

Transfer the papayas to a warm platter. Squeeze the lime juice over the slices

Serve hot.

Honey-Glazed Carrots *Serves 4*

4 medium carrots, cut into ½-inch thick slices
⅓ cup orange juice
1½ tablespoons butter or margarine
1 tablespoon honey
¼ teaspoon salt

Parboil or steam the carrots for 5 minutes. Drain well.

Add the remaining ingredients and cook for another 5-10 minutes, or until the carrots are crisp, yet tender.

Green Beans with Hazelnuts *Serves 6*

1½ pounds fresh green beans, trimmed
salt to taste
3 tablespoons butter
¼ cup chopped hazelnuts

Steam the green beans until tender, about 8 minutes. Drain the beans and season with the salt.

In the same pan, melt the butter and add the nuts. Sauté for one minute.

Pour the butter and the nuts over the green beans and mix lightly.

Green Pepper-Mushroom Medley *Serves 6*

2 tablespoons butter or margarine
2 tablespoons olive oil
1 clove garlic, minced
3 green peppers, cut into one-inch squares
1 cup mushrooms, sliced
¾ cup dry white wine
1 2-ounce jar chopped pimiento
½ teaspoon salt
¼ teaspoon oregano
¼ teaspoon freshly ground pepper

Heat the butter and the oil in a medium skillet until bubbly.

Cook and stir the garlic, green pepper pieces and mushrooms over a high heat until the pepper skins blister and the mushrooms are golden. This will take about 10 minutes.

Stir in the wine and heat to boiling. Reduce the heat and simmer for 5 minutes.

Stir in the remaining ingredients and simmer another 3 minutes. The peppers should be tender but not soft.

Spinach Soufflé
Serves 6

1 10-ounce package frozen chopped spinach, thawed and drained well
¼ pound sharp Cheddar cheese, cut into ½-inch chunks
1 cup cottage cheese
4 eggs, beaten
2 tablespoons flour
4 tablespoons butter or margarine, melted

Preheat the oven to 350° F.

Grease a medium casserole.

Combine all of the ingredients and pour into the casserole.

Bake for one hour.

Apple-Filled Squash
Serves 6

3 acorn squash
4 tart apples, peeled and sliced
¾ cup brown sugar
1 teaspoon lemon juice
½ teaspoon freshly grated ginger or ¼ teaspoon ground ginger
6 tablespoons butter

Preheat the oven to 350° F.

Halve the squash lengthwise and remove the seeds. Place the squash, cut side down, in a greased baking dish.

Bake for 35 minutes.

In a large bowl, combine the apples, brown sugar, lemon and ginger.

Remove the squash from the oven and turn cut side up.

Fill the squash with the apple mixture. Dot the top of the apples with the butter and return the squash to the oven.

Bake for 25 minutes more.

Serve hot.

Squash Patties
Serves 6

1 pound zucchini, grated
1 cup flour
1 teaspoon baking powder
2 eggs, slightly beaten
⅓ cup grated onion
½ teaspoon salt
¼ cup grated Parmesan cheese
butter for frying
oil for frying

Mix all of the ingredients together.

Shape the mixture into patties.

In a large skillet, heat a mixture of butter and oil for frying.

Fry the patties on both sides until golden brown.

FAMILY BITS

Stuffed Spaghetti Squash
Serves 6

1 2-pound spaghetti squash
4 slices bacon
⅓ pound mushrooms, sliced
¼ teaspoon freshly grated nutmeg
2 tablespoons chopped green onion
salt and pepper to taste
1 cup grated Swiss cheese

Preheat the oven to 350° F.

Place the whole squash in a baking pan. Pierce it in several places with a fork.

Bake for 1-1½ hours, or until the shell gives slightly when pressed.

The squash can be cooked in a microwave oven at full power for 15-20 minutes. Turn the squash over once or twice during the cooking time.

Fry the bacon until crisp. Drain and crumble it.

In a small amount of the bacon fat, sauté the mushrooms and the green onions.

Cut the squash in half lengthwise. Discard the seeds. Pull the strands of pulp from the shell with a fork.

In a medium bowl, combine the squash, bacon, mushrooms, nutmeg, green onions, salt, pepper and cheese.

Mound the mixture in the squash shells or in a shallow 2-quart baking pan.

Bake until heated through and serve hot.

Broiled Sherried Tomatoes
Serves 6

3 large firm tomatoes
2 tablespoons sherry
dried dill weed to taste
salt and pepper to taste
2 tablespoons mayonnaise
⅓ cup grated Swiss cheese

Cut each tomato in half crosswise and pierce the cut edge with a fork in several places. Sprinkle each tomato half with the sherry and season with the dill weed, salt and pepper.

Place the tomatoes on a broiler pan, cut side up, and broil 4-5 minutes, or until heated through.

Combine the mayonnaise and the cheese.

Remove the tomatoes from the oven and spread each half with the mayonnaise-cheese mixture.

Return the pan to the oven and broil 2-3 minutes more, or until browned lightly.

Fried Tomatoes with Parmesan Cheese
Serves 4

4 medium tomatoes, cored
½ cup dried whole-wheat bread crumbs
2 tablespoons grated Parmesan cheese
½ teaspoon dried oregano
4 tablespoons butter or margarine
freshly ground pepper to taste

Cut the tomatoes into ½-inch-thick slices.

Mix the remaining ingredients together. Coat both sides of the tomatoes with the mixture.

Melt one tablespoon of the butter in a large frying pan. Sauté the tomato slices until golden brown on both sides. Remove them to a warm platter.

Repeat the procedure until all of the tomatoes are cooked.

DESSERTS:

Also see Cookie Bits, pages 193 to 210.

Apple Cake
One 8"x8" Cake

¼ pound butter <u>or</u> margarine
¾ cup sugar
1 teaspoon vanilla
2 eggs
1¾ cups flour
½ teaspoon baking powder
4 large apples, peeled, cored and sliced
juice of one lemon
½ cup golden raisins
¼ cup sugar
1 teaspoon cinnamon

Topping:
2 tablespoons butter
2 tablespoons sugar
2 tablespoons flour
1 teaspoon cinnamon

Cream the butter and the sugar. Add the vanilla and the eggs. Beat well.

Blend together the flour and the baking powder and add to the creamed mixture. Stir to mix well. Chill the dough thoroughly.

Preheat the oven to 325° F.

Grease an 8"x8" baking dish.

In a medium bowl, combine the apple slices, lemon juice, raisins, sugar and cinnamon and stir to mix well.

Cut the chilled dough in half. Press half the dough over the bottom of the baking dish. Layer the apples evenly over the dough in the pan.

On a floured piece of waxed paper, press the second half of the dough into an 8"x8" shape. Place the dough over the apples.

In a small bowl, combine the butter, sugar, flour and cinnamon until coarse crumbs are formed. Sprinkle the crumbs over the top of the cake.

Bake the cake for one hour and 5 minutes.

Chocolate Pudding Cake
Serves 8

1½ cups Master Baking Mix, see page 174 <u>or</u> biscuit mix
⅓ cup sugar
2 tablespoons cocoa
¾ cup chopped walnuts
½ cup milk
1 teaspoon vanilla
⅔ cup brown sugar, firmly packed
3 tablespoons cocoa
1½ cups boiling water

Preheat the oven to 350° F.

In an unbuttered 8"x8" baking dish, combine the Mix, sugar, 2 tablespoons cocoa, nuts, milk and vanilla. Blend well.

Combine the brown sugar and the 3 tablespoons cocoa. Sprinkle over the top of the cake mixture.

Gently pour the boiling water over the top of the mixture. Do not stir.

Bake 30-35 minutes, or until the edges separate from the dish.

Cool the cake in the dish for 15 minutes before serving.

FAMILY BITS

¾ cup sugar
½ cup Master Baking Mix,
    see page 174 or biscuit mix
2 tablespoons butter or margarine
1 13-ounce can evaporated milk
2 eggs
1 16-ounce can pumpkin
2 teaspoons pumpkin pie spice
1½ teaspoons vanilla
½ cup chopped pecans

Crustless Pumpkin Pie — *Serves 8*

Preheat the oven to 375° F.

Place all of the ingredients except the pecans in a blender. Blend until smooth, about one minute.

Pour into a greased 10-inch pie pan. Sprinkle with the pecans.

Bake for 45-50 minutes, or until the pie is golden brown and a knife inserted in the center comes out clean.

4 egg whites
¾ cup sugar
½ teaspoon vanilla
½ teaspoon vinegar
3 cups fresh strawberries, sliced or
    fresh peaches, peeled and sliced
whipped cream for garnish

High Strawberry Pie — *Serves 6*

Preheat the oven to 325° F.

Beat the egg whites until they will hold soft peaks.

Gradually add the sugar, vanilla and vinegar. Continue to beat the egg whites for another 30 seconds or until they hold stiff peaks.

Spread the mixture in a buttered 11-inch pie plate.

Bake for 45 minutes.

Layer the sliced strawberries on the cooled pie top. Garnish the pie with the whipped cream, if desired.

1 cup flour
½ cup butter, softened
⅛ teaspoon salt
2-3 tablespoons water

100-Watt Pie Crust — *One 9-Inch Crust*

In a medium bowl, combine the flour and the butter with a pastry blender until crumbly.

Add small amounts of water until the pastry holds together.

Flour your hands and shape the pastry into a ball. Press the pastry into the pie pan and form a rim around the top edge.

½ cup flour
¾ cup sugar
1 teaspoon baking powder
½ cup chopped pecans or walnuts
1 egg
1 teaspoon vanilla
1 cup diced rhubarb or apples

Fast Rhubarb Pie — *Serves 6*

Preheat the oven to 350° F.

Mix all of the ingredients together. Place them in a greased 9-inch pie pan.

Bake for 25 minutes.

Serve with ice cream or whipped cream.

Sunny Side Up Peach Pie *One 9-Inch Pie*

4-5 ripe peaches, peeled, pitted and halved
1 cup sugar
2 tablespoons flour
⅓ cup butter, melted
½ teaspoon vanilla
1 egg, beaten

Preheat the oven to 400° F.

Place the peaches, cut side down, on an unbaked 9-inch pie crust.

In a medium bowl, combine the sugar, flour, melted butter, vanilla and egg. Stir to blend well.

Pour the mixture evenly over the peaches.

Bake for 15 minutes at 400° F. Lower the oven to 300° F. and bake 50 minutes more.

Reversible Cobbler *Serves 8*

This dessert "reverses" itself so that the fruit is on the bottom, topped with crispy cobbler.

1 cup flour
2 teaspoons baking powder
⅛ teaspoon salt
¼ cup butter, softened
½ cup sugar
½ cup milk
1 16-ounce can cherries, blueberries or raspberries, undrained
¼ cup sugar

Preheat the oven to 375° F.

Mix together the flour, baking powder and salt.

In a 2-quart bowl, beat the butter and ½ cup sugar with an electric mixer. Add the dry ingredients and the milk, beating until smooth.

Spread the batter in a buttered 8"x8" baking dish.

Pour the fruit with its juice on top of the cake mixture. Do not stir. Sprinkle with ¼ cup sugar.

Bake for 45 minutes.

BREADS AND BREAKFAST:

Pancakes or Waffles *4-6 Pancakes or 3-4 Waffles*

1 egg
1 cup Master Baking Mix, see page 174
¾ cup milk **or** ½ milk and ½ yogurt

In a blender, add the egg, Mix and milk. Blend for one minute on medium to high speed, or until all of the ingredients are thoroughly combined. Allow the batter to stand for 5 minutes.

The consistency of the batter can be corrected with the addition of milk or Mix.

Cook on a hot griddle or in a preheated waffle iron.

If you have mixed more waffle batter than needed, prepare the waffles, let them cool, wrap and freeze. To reheat the waffles, put them directly in the toaster without thawing.

Pumpkin Pancakes with Sautéed Apples
Serves 4

2 small apples, peeled and thinly sliced
1 tablespoon butter
½ cup yellow corn meal
1 cup boiling water
1 cup milk
½ cup canned pumpkin
1 large egg, beaten lightly
1 cup flour
1 tablespoon sugar
2½ teaspoons baking powder
1 teaspoon ground allspice
½ teaspoon salt
maple syrup

In a skillet, sauté the apple slices in the butter for 3 minutes, or until they are softened. Keep the apple slices warm.

In a large bowl, combine the corn meal and the boiling water. Let stand for 5 minutes.

Stir in the milk, pumpkin and egg, mixing well.

Sift together the flour, sugar, baking powder, allspice and salt.

Add the dry ingredients to the pumpkin mixture and blend well.

Pour a scant ¼ cup of batter onto a hot, oiled griddle for each pancake. Cook the pancakes until they are golden brown, turning once.

Top the pancakes with the sautéed apples and serve with the maple syrup.

Master Baking Mix
12 Cups

9 cups flour, which can include up to 4¼ cups whole-wheat or other type flour
⅓ cup baking powder minus 1 tablespoon
1 tablespoon salt
2 teaspoons cream of tartar
¼ cup sugar
1 16-ounce can vegetable shortening

In an extra-large bowl, combine the flour, baking powder, salt, cream of tartar and sugar. Stir to mix evenly.

Cut the shortening into the flour mixture until the Mix has the consistency of corn meal.

Store in a tightly covered container and keep in a cool, dry place. The Mix does not require refrigeration. It should be used within 3-6 months.

To measure the Mix, pile it into a dry measuring cup and level it off with the straight edge of a knife. Do not pack tightly.

The Master Baking Mix has been adjusted for 5,000 feet above sea level.

At sea level, change the baking powder to ⅓ cup.

At 3,000 feet, change the baking powder to ⅓ cup minus 1½ teaspoons.

At 7,000 feet, change the baking powder to 4 tablespoons.

Coffee Cake
One Cake

¼ cup brown sugar <u>or</u> honey
1 egg
⅔ cup milk
2-3 tablespoons melted butter <u>or</u>
   vegetable oil
2 cups Master Baking Mix, see
   page 174

Topping:
2 tablespoons brown sugar
¼ cup Master Baking Mix, see
   page 174
1 teaspoon cinnamon
1 tablespoon butter
½ cup chopped nuts, optional

Preheat the oven to 400° F.

Beat together the first 4 ingredients. Add them to the Mix, stirring just enough to moisten.

Spread the batter into a greased 8-inch or 9-inch pie pan.

In a small bowl, mix the topping ingredients until they are crumbly. Sprinkle over the batter.

Bake for 20-25 minutes.

Muffins
18 Muffins

3-4 tablespoons sugar, white
   <u>or</u> brown
1 cup milk
1 egg
3-4 tablespoons melted butter <u>or</u>
   vegetable oil
3 cups Master Baking Mix, see
   page 174
1 cup fresh fruit <u>or</u> canned fruit,
   drained, optional
½ cup chopped nuts, optional
1 tablespoon cinnamon, optional

Preheat the oven to 425° F.

Beat together the first 4 ingredients.

Stir in the Mix just enough to moisten.

Fold in the fruit, nuts or cinnamon, if used.

Fill lined or greased muffin cups ½-⅔ full.

Bake for 12-18 minutes.

Corn Pone Piggies
12 Muffins

1 15-ounce package corn bread mix
½ pound bulk sausage, cooked,
   crumbled and drained
1 apple, peeled and chopped
   into small pieces
3 tablespoons brown sugar

Prepare the cornbread batter as directed on the package.

Pour ½ of the batter into 12 greased muffin molds. Place some sausage, some apple chunks, and a sprinkle of brown sugar in each mold over the batter. Top each mold with the remaining batter.

Bake for 20 minutes, or until lightly browned.

FAMILY BITS

Pumpkin Bread *One Loaf*

2 cups Master Baking Mix, see page 174
¼ teaspoon soda
¾-1 cup sugar
½ teaspoon cinnamon
½ teaspoon allspice
¼ teaspoon ground cloves
½ teaspoon nutmeg
2 eggs, well beaten
1½ cups canned pumpkin
¼ cup milk
1 teaspoon vanilla
½ cup chopped nuts, optional

Preheat the oven to 350° F.

Stir together the first 7 ingredients.

Combine the eggs, pumpkin, milk and vanilla, stirring until blended.

Stir the liquid mixture into the dry ingredients until well blended.

Stir in the nuts, if desired.

Bake in a greased loaf pan for 50-60 minutes.

Easy Crepes *12 Crepes*

3 eggs
1 cup milk
¾ cup Master Baking Mix, see page 174
2 tablespoons vegetable oil

Crêpes may be wrapped securely and frozen for up to 3 months. Thaw overnight in the refrigerator before using.

Combine all of the ingredients in a blender and blend until smooth. Let the mixture stand for 5 minutes.

For each crêpe, pour about 2 tablespoons batter into a hot, lightly greased crêpe pan or small skillet. Immediately tilt the pan to coat the bottom evenly.

Cook 20-30 seconds, or until the top looks dry. Turn and cook for another 20 seconds.

Stack the crêpes between sheets of waxed paper.

Biscuits *12-15 Biscuits*

3 cups Master Baking Mix, see page 174
⅔ cup milk

Preheat the oven to 425° F.

Lightly mix the ingredients together.

Roll the dough on a floured surface to a ½-inch thickness. Cut into round shapes with a floured biscuit cutter. Place in a greased pan.

Bake for 12-15 minutes.

To reheat biscuits, place them in a well dampened paper bag. Twist the bag closed and place it in a 300° F. oven.

KID BITS

The recipes in Kid Bits have been tested by the young students of Graland Country Day School. As a result, the entrees, breakfasts, snacks and beverages contained in this chapter are sure to please a child's palate. Also, many of these recipes can be prepared by the children themselves.

KID BITS

Apple Annie Pancake
Serves 2-4

1 apple, peeled and finely grated
1 cup pancake mix
1 egg
¾ cup milk
1 tablespoon butter, melted
2 tablespoons vegetable oil

Mix all the ingredients together until well blended.

Cook the pancakes on an oiled skillet until bubbly. Then, turn the pancakes once to cook both sides until golden brown.

Puffy Pancake
Serves 4-6

4 tablespoons butter
½ cup flour, whole wheat or unbleached
pinch of cinnamon
½ cup milk
2 eggs
1 cup fruit, blueberries or chopped apples
3 teaspoons sugar
juice of one lemon

Preheat the oven to 425° F.

In a 10 to 12-inch round baking pan, melt the butter in the oven.

In a bowl, mix the flour, cinnamon, milk and eggs until well blended.

When the butter is melted, pour the mixture into the pan and bake for 15-20 minutes, or until golden brown.

Remove the pan from the oven and sprinkle the pancake with sugar.

Place the pan back in the oven and continue to bake for 5 more minutes.

Remove the pan from the oven and squeeze the lemon juice over the top of the pancake.

Spoon the fruit on top of the pancake. Cut into wedges and serve.

Overnight French Toast
Serves 4-6

1 loaf French bread
4 eggs
1 cup milk
juice of one orange
½ teaspoon vanilla
¼ teaspoon salt
½ teaspoon orange peel, grated
¼ teaspoon nutmeg
butter

Slice the bread in ¾-inch slices.

Beat together the eggs, milk and orange juice. Add the vanilla, salt, orange peel and nutmeg to the mixture.

Dip the bread slices into the mixture and place them in a casserole dish. Pour the remaining mixture over the bread and refrigerate overnight.

Fry the bread in the butter until each side is golden brown.

1 egg
¼ cup milk
¼ teaspoon prepared mustard
pinch of salt
2 slices American cheese
4 slices sandwich bread
2 tablespoons bacon bits
1 tablespoon butter

Breakfast Sandwiches
Serves 2

In a casserole dish, combine the egg, milk, mustard and salt.

Place one slice of the cheese on one slice of the bread. Cover the cheese with one tablespoon of the bacon bits and top with another piece of bread to form a sandwich. Repeat this to form another sandwich.

Carefully dip each sandwich into the egg mixture until the bread is soaked.

Melt the butter in a frying pan and fry each sandwich until golden brown.

Cut the sandwiches into strips and serve.

¾ cup margarine, softened
⅓ cup sugar
1 egg
1 teaspoon vanilla
¾ cup flour
½ teaspoon cinnamon
½ teaspoon baking powder
1½ cups rolled oats
1 cup grated Cheddar cheese
¾ cup chopped raisins
1 cup chopped apple

Breakfast Cookies
24 Cookies

Preheat the oven to 375° F.

Using a large mixing bowl, with the mixer on medium speed, cream the margarine and sugar. Add the egg and the vanilla and mix well.

Add all of the other ingredients. Stir in the apple pieces last.

Drop the dough by tablespoons onto an ungreased cookie sheet.

Bake for 15 minutes.

2 tablespoons butter or margarine
¼ cup brown sugar, firmly packed
⅓ cup chopped nuts
¼ cup coconut, unsweetened
1 large banana
1 8-ounce package refrigerated
 buttermilk biscuits

Graland Country Biscuits
10 Biscuits

Preheat the oven to 450° F.

Place the butter in an 8-inch round cake pan and warm over low heat until the butter melts.

Stir in the brown sugar with a spoon and sprinkle or arrange the nuts in the pan. Sprinkle the raw coconut over the nuts.

Peel the banana and slice it into thin pieces. Place the banana slices over the coconut.

Separate the biscuits into 10 sections. Place the sections over the fruit and nuts and press lightly.

Bake for 10 minutes, or until lightly browned.

Remove the cake pan from the oven and run a knife around the edge of the pan to loosen the biscuits. Immediately turn the pan upside down on a serving plate and let the pan remain over the biscuits for one minute before removing. Serve warm.

KID BITS

Surprise Doughnuts   *Serves 4*

4 cake doughnuts
8 tablespoons honey
8 tablespoons butter
8 tablespoons shredded coconut

Preheat the oven to 350° F.

Split the doughnuts in half.

Whip the honey and the butter together. Spread the mixture on each doughnut half.

Sprinkle each half with one tablespoon of the coconut.

Bake for 5 minutes.

Serve immediately.

Toast Toppers:

Coconut Caramel Toast   *Serves One*

2 tablespoons brown sugar
2 tablespoons flaked coconut
1 tablespoon butter, softened
1 piece toast, unbuttered

Mix the brown sugar, coconut and butter together.

Spread the mixture on the toast and broil until it bubbles.

Serve immediately.

Peanut Butter-Raisin Toast   *Serves One*

¼ cup peanut butter
2 tablespoons chopped raisins
2 tablespoons orange juice
1 piece toast, buttered

Mix the peanut butter, raisins and orange juice together.

Spread the mixture on the buttered toast and broil until it bubbles.

Serve immediately.

Breakfast Treat   *Serves One*

2 teaspoons orange marmalade
1 piece toast, buttered
2 pieces bacon, cooked and crumbled

Spread the marmalade on the toast and top it with the bacon.

Broil until it bubbles.

Serve immediately.

Great Granola
14 Cups

8 cups rolled oats
1 cup brown sugar
1 cup wheat germ
½ cup honey
½ cup sesame seeds
2 cups almonds <u>or</u> cashews
1 teaspoon salt
2 teaspoons vanilla
1½ cups flaked coconut, sweetened <u>or</u> unsweetened

Preheat the oven to 250° F.

Mix all of the ingredients together.

Pour the mixture onto two ungreased cookie sheets.

Bake for about one hour, stirring often, until the mixture is golden brown.

Picture-Frame Egg
Serves One

1 slice bread
1 tablespoon butter
1 egg

Cut a hole out of the center of the bread.

Melt the butter in a frying pan.

Place the bread in the pan and crack the egg into the center of the bread.

Fry over medium heat for one minute. Turn the picture frame and fry for one minute more.

Serve immediately.

Yummy Baked Eggs
Serves One

2 pats butter
1 slice Swiss cheese, grated
1 egg
2 tablespoons grated Parmesan cheese
salt and pepper to taste

Preheat the oven to 350° F.

Coat a ramekin dish with one pat of the butter. Place the second pat in the bottom of the dish.

Add the Swiss cheese.

Beat the egg in another bowl and add the Parmesan cheese. Pour the egg mixture into the ramekin and season with the salt and the pepper.

Bake for 10-12 minutes.

KID BITS

Easy Peanut Butter Cookies *24 Cookies*

1 cup peanut butter,
    smooth <u>or</u> chunky
1 cup sugar
1 egg
1 teaspoon vanilla

Preheat the oven to 300° F.

Mix all of the ingredients together in a medium bowl with your hands or with a spoon.

Form one-inch balls and place them on an ungreased cookie sheet. Using the tines of a fork, press crisscross designs on each cookie.

Bake for 20 minutes, or until set.

Remove the cookies from the oven and cool.

Crunchy Bread *One Loaf*

1⅓ cups milk
⅔ cup Grape-Nuts cereal
1 egg, well beaten
3 tablespoons butter <u>or</u>
    margarine, melted and cooled
1 teaspoon vanilla
2 cups flour
2½ teaspoons baking powder
¼ teaspoon salt
⅔ cup brown sugar, firmly packed

Preheat the oven to 350° F.

Heat the milk and pour it over the Grape-Nuts cereal.

Cool the milk-cereal mixture and add the egg, melted butter and vanilla.

Combine the flour, baking powder, salt and brown sugar.

Add the flour mixture to the milk-cereal mixture, stirring just enough to mix. Do not beat. The mixture should be stiff.

Place the dough in a greased 4"x8"x3" pan.

Bake for 50-60 minutes.

Cool the bread in the pan. Remove when cool. Wrap it in foil and store it in the refrigerator overnight before serving.

Sunflower Seed Bread *One Child-Size Loaf*

1 teaspoon active dry yeast
⅓ cup warm water
2 teaspoons honey
1 teaspoon oil
2 tablespoons non-fat dry milk
½ cup whole-wheat flour
½ cup unbleached white flour
½ teaspoon salt
2 tablespoons sunflower seeds

Preheat the oven to 375° F.

Dissolve the yeast in the warm water. Add the honey, oil and non-fat dry milk.

Blend in the whole wheat flour, white flour, salt and sunflower seeds.

Knead the dough on a floured surface for one minute.

Form the dough into a ball-shaped loaf and let it rise on a cookie sheet for 15-30 minutes.

Bake for 25-30 minutes.

Coconut-Carrot Cupcakes
36 Cupcakes

1 cup honey
1½ cups oil
4 eggs, beaten
1 teaspoon vanilla
2 cups whole-wheat flour
2 teaspoons baking powder
½ teaspoon salt
1 tablespoon cinnamon
1 cup chopped walnuts
1 cup grated fresh coconut
½ cup grated carrot

Preheat the oven to 350° F.

In a large mixing bowl, blend the honey, oil, eggs and vanilla.

In a separate bowl, mix together the flour, baking powder, salt and cinnamon. Add the flour mixture to the liquid and blend well.

Stir in the walnuts, coconut and carrots.

Fill paper-lined cupcake pans half full.

Bake for 30 minutes.

Peanut Butter-Banana Cupcakes
24 Cupcakes

½ cup chunky peanut butter
½ cup margarine, softened
1½ cups sugar
1 cup mashed ripe bananas
2 eggs
2 tablespoons water
2 cups flour
½ teaspoon baking powder
½ teaspoon baking soda
⅛ teaspoon salt

Preheat the oven to 375° F.

Cream the peanut butter, margarine, sugar and bananas until smooth. Add the eggs, one at a time, and then add the water, beating well after each addition.

Sift together the flour, baking powder, baking soda and salt. Add this to the banana mixture.

Spoon into paper-lined or greased muffin pans.

Bake for 20 minutes.

Cool the cupcakes in the pans for 20 minutes before removing.

A coconut shell can be made into a delightful rhythm instrument.

Pierce the eyes of the shell with a sharp pointed instrument and drain the liquid.

Place the drained shell in a vice and saw it in half.

Remove the coconut meat with a knife.

Hold the shell halves by the rounded ends and tap on a hard surface. Horses can be heard riding in the room.

KID BITS

Yummy Banana Muffins
18 Muffins

2 cups flour
1 cup sugar
1 teaspoon baking soda
3 ripe bananas, sliced
½ cup shortening
½ teaspoon salt
1 teaspoon vanilla
1 egg

Preheat the oven to 375° F.

Combine all of the ingredients, except the bananas, and mix with a wooden spoon until well blended.

Add the sliced bananas to the mixture, stirring to mix well. The batter will be exceptionally thick.

Spoon the batter into paper-lined or greased muffin pans.

Bake for 20 minutes, or until done.

A Favorite Snack
Serves One

1 apple
3 tablespoons peanut butter
12 raisins

Wash the apple. Cut it in half and core it.

Mix the peanut butter with the raisins.

Spoon the peanut butter mixture into each hollowed half of the apple.

Banana Split Snack
Serves 2

2 large bananas
1 12-ounce container cottage cheese
1 8¼-ounce can crushed pineapple, undrained
4 maraschino cherries

Peel the bananas and slice them in half lengthwise. Place two halves in each banana split dish or individual salad dish.

Using an ice cream scoop, place one or two scoops of the cottage cheese between the banana halves in each dish.

Spoon the crushed pineapple and the juice over the cottage cheese. Top each scoop of cottage cheese with a cherry.

Cold Weather Fruit Cups
Serves 4

1 banana, peeled and sliced
1 apple, peeled, cored and sliced
½ cup raisins
1 8-ounce can chunk or crushed pineapple
fruit juice
Grape-Nuts cereal
cinnamon

Preheat the oven to 350° F.

Mix the fruit and divide it among four ovenware cups. Put enough fruit in each cup to fill it halfway.

Pour in enough fruit juice to fill ¾ of the cup.

Garnish the cups with the Grape-Nuts and the cinnamon.

Bake uncovered for 20 minutes.

Great Grapes
Serves One

½ cup plain yogurt
1 cup seedless grapes, <u>or</u>
    peaches, <u>or</u> strawberries, sliced
1 tablespoon brown sugar

Mix the yogurt and half of the brown sugar in a small bowl. Add the fruit to the mixture.

Sprinkle the top with the remaining brown sugar and serve.

Identified Fruit Objects
Serves 4

2 oranges
2 cups cubed fresh fruit
wooden skewers <u>or</u> toothpicks

Cut the oranges in half and place the halves cut side down on a plate.

Thread the fruit pieces on the wooden skewers or toothpicks. Insert them into the orange halves.

Cover the fruit and chill until ready to serve.

Peanut Butter and Banana Snack
Serves One

1 banana, peeled
peanut butter
½ cup graham cracker crumbs

This snack can easily be prepared by very young children.

Spread the top half of the banana with the peanut butter.

Dip the banana in the graham cracker crumbs.

Serve immediately.

Rag Doll Salad
Serves One

1 peach half
1 large marshmallow
4 celery sticks
12 raisins
3 maraschino cherries
2 tablespoons grated Cheddar
    cheese
1 lettuce leaf

Fashion the doll by using the peach half as the body; the marshmallow as the head; and the celery sticks as the arms and legs.

Use the raisins and the cherries to create the eyes, mouth and nose.

Use the Cheddar cheese for the hair.

Wrap the lettuce leaf around the lower half of the peach to form a skirt.

KID BITS

Rainbow Jello *48 Rainbows*

Children absolutely love Rainbow Jello. It travels well and stays firmly set for hours without refrigeration. No utensils are required for eating this treat. It is a finger food.

Jello layers:
- 6 3-ounce packages Jello, assorted flavors
- 1¼ cups boiling water for each layer
- 6 small envelopes unflavored gelatin

Milk layers:
- 1 14-ounce can sweetened condensed milk
- 2 packages unflavored gelatin
- 2 cups boiling water

For each layer of the rainbow, mix one box of the Jello, the boiling water and one package of the gelatin together in a bowl.

When the Jello has cooled, but not set, pour it into a 9"x12"x2" pan. Place the pan in the refrigerator and let the Jello set.

Repeat the process with the remaining five packages of the Jello, creating the rainbow by alternating two layers of Jello with one milk layer. Be sure that each layer is firmly set before adding the next layer.

For the milk layer, mix the condensed milk, two packages of the gelatin and the boiling water together in a saucepan. Leave the mixture over low heat on the stove. Use ⅞ cup for each white layer.

When all of the layers have set, cut the Rainbow Jello into 1" x 2" bars.

Zippity Do Dip *1½ Cups*

- 8 ounces cream cheese, softened
- 3 tablespoons mayonnaise
- 3 tablespoons catsup
- 1 teaspoon Worcestershire sauce
- ⅛ teaspoon onion powder
- dash of hot pepper sauce

Combine all of the ingredients in a small bowl. Mix them until they are smooth.

Serve this dip with fresh vegetable sticks, crackers or pretzel sticks.

Frozen Pudding-Wiches
Serves 12

½ cup creamy peanut butter
1½ cups cold milk
1 small package instant pudding
24 graham crackers

Place the peanut butter in a deep, narrow bowl.

Gradually add the milk to the peanut butter and blend until smooth.

Add the pudding mix and beat slowly with a hand beater or at the lowest speed of an electric mixer until well blended, about 2 minutes. Let the mixture stand for 5 minutes.

Spread the filling ½-inch thick on 12 of the crackers. Top with the remaining crackers.

Freeze until firm, about 3 hours.

Fudgsicles
Serves 8

1 package instant chocolate pudding
¼ cup sugar
½ cup heavy cream
1 cup milk
1 cup water

Mix all of the ingredients together thoroughly.

Freeze the mixture in popsicle molds or in paper cups with wooden sticks for handles.

Cheesy Bacon Snack
Serves 8

2 tablespoons mayonnaise
1 teaspoon Worcestershire sauce
¼ teaspoon garlic salt
4 rolls sliced in half
    or 8 crackers
½ pound bacon, cooked and crumbled
2 tomatoes, sliced
½ pound mild Cheddar or Colby cheese, grated

Mix the mayonnaise, Worcestershire sauce and garlic salt in a small bowl.

Spread the mixture on the rolls or the crackers.

Add the bacon and tomatoes to the rolls. Top each roll with the grated cheese.

Place the rolls on an ungreased cookie sheet and broil them until the cheese bubbles.

KID BITS

¼ cup butter
8 slices day-old bread
3 ounces Cheddar cheese, grated

Golden Cheese Crispies *Serves 8*

Preheat the oven to 400° F.

Melt the butter in a small saucepan. Pour half of the butter on a cookie sheet and spread it around evenly.

Remove the bread crusts and place the bread on the cookie sheet.

Pour the remaining butter on each slice of the bread and sprinkle with the cheese.

Bake for 10-15 minutes, or until the bread is crisp and golden.

Remove the crispies from the oven and cut into finger slices. Cookie cutters may also be used to shape the bread into different forms.

Cool the Crispies and serve.

¼ cup butter
¼ cup honey
6 cups freshly popped corn
¾ cup peanuts, shelled

Honey-Nut Popcorn *7 Cups*

Preheat the oven to 350° F.

Melt the butter and the honey in a small saucepan, stirring until well blended.

Mix the popcorn and the peanuts in a bowl. Pour the honey mixture onto the popcorn and the peanuts and stir well.

Spread the popcorn on a baking sheet.

Bake for 10-15 minutes, or until crisp.

Cool the popcorn and serve.

1 cup creamy peanut butter
½ cup honey
1½ cups non-fat dry milk
¼ cup cocoa, optional

Chocolate-Peanut Butter Play Dough *1½ Cups*

Mix the peanut butter, honey, dry milk and cocoa together until the mixture resembles play dough.

Refrigerate the dough for 30 minutes to 1 hour.

Break off pieces of the dough and form them as desired.

Decorate the play dough figures with nuts, raisins, coconut, chocolate chips, sunflower seeds or wheat germ.

Barbecue in a Cup *Serves 10*

1 pound ground beef
½ cup barbecue sauce
¼ cup chopped onion
2 tablespoons brown sugar
1 10-ounce can flaky refrigerated biscuits
½ cup grated Cheddar cheese

Preheat the oven to 400° F.

In a large pan, brown the beef. Drain it well.

Stir in the barbecue sauce, onion and brown sugar. Heat the mixture until bubbly. Remove it from the heat.

Separate the biscuits and place each one into an ungreased muffin cup. Press the dough to cover the bottom and the sides of the cup.

Spoon the hot meat mixture into the cups. Sprinkle the cheese equally over the tops of the cups.

Bake for 10-15 minutes.

Monterey Casserole *Serves 6-8*

1 pound lean ground beef
2 tablespoons chopped onion
¾ teaspoon seasoning salt
16 ounces tomato sauce
4 cups nacho cheese or taco flavor tortilla chips
2 cups grated Cheddar cheese

Preheat the oven to 350° F.

Fry the beef in a skillet for 5 minutes until it is crumbly and light brown in color.

Add the onion, salt and tomato sauce and simmer the mixture for 5 minutes.

Place 3 cups of the tortilla chips in a 2-quart casserole and sprinkle the chips with one cup of the Cheddar cheese.

Pour the meat sauce over the chips and top with the remaining cheese. Then, cover the cheese with the last cup of the chips.

Bake for 15 minutes.

Cheese Dreams *Serves 2*

4 slices bacon
1 English muffin, halved
2 pats butter, softened
½ cup grated Cheddar cheese
2 slices tomato

Cook the bacon slices. Drain them well on a paper towel.

Spread the muffin halves with the butter and broil them until golden brown.

Place the bacon slices on the muffin halves and top with the cheese and the tomato.

Broil until the cheese is melted.

KID BITS

Crescent Sandwiches
Serves 8

1 8-ounce can refrigerated quick crescent rolls
8 slices salami
8 slices Swiss cheese
1 egg white, lightly beaten

Preheat the oven to 375° F.

Separate the dough into triangles and place one slice of the salami on each piece of the dough. Then, place one slice of the cheese on the salami.

Roll up each crescent. Start at the shortest side of the triangle and finish at the opposite point.

Roll each sandwich lightly in the egg white.

Bake for 12-15 minutes on an ungreased cookie sheet.

Hawaiian Sandwich
Serves 2

1 hamburger bun, halved
2 teaspoons butter
1 cup chunk chicken or tuna
2 tablespoons mayonnaise
2 slices pineapple
2 slices Swiss cheese

Spread the bun halves with the butter. Broil them on a cookie sheet until the butter has melted.

Mix the chicken or the tuna with the mayonnaise in a small bowl.

Spread the chicken or tuna mixture on the bun halves. Top with the pineapple and Swiss cheese slices.

Broil until the cheese is melted.

Banana Ginger Ale
Serves 4

2 ripe bananas, peeled
1 cup milk
1 12-ounce bottle ginger ale

Place the bananas in a blender and add the milk. Blend at high speed until smooth.

Add the ginger ale and stir quickly.

Pour the mixture into glasses and serve immediately.

Fresh Fruit Fizz
Serves 4

½ cup fresh fruit, strawberries, peaches or bananas
4 tablespoons honey
½ cup crushed ice
1 8-ounce bottle carbonated water

Combine the fruit, honey and ice in a blender. Purée one minute or until thick.

Gently stir in the carbonated water.

Pour the drink into glasses and serve.

Hot Foamy Lemonade *Serves One*

1 cup lemonade
1 tablespoon raisins
6 mini-marshmallows
1 orange slice

Heat the lemonade.

Place the raisins and the marshmallows in a mug. Add the lemonade.

Squeeze the orange slice into the mug and drop it in.

Stir the drink well.

Serve with a spoon.

Orange Delight *Serves 4*

1 6-ounce can frozen orange juice
2 6-ounce cans water
1 banana
3 ounces plain yogurt

In a blender, combine all of the ingredients. Blend until thick and creamy.

Pour the drink into glasses and serve.

Peachy Cooler *Serves 2-4*

1 cup fresh peaches, strawberries or bananas
2 cups buttermilk
¾ cup raisins

Mix all of the ingredients in a blender on medium speed.

Serve the drink in chilled glasses.

Red Raspberry Rouser *Serves 4*

1 10-ounce package frozen raspberries, thawed
1 8-ounce carton raspberry yogurt
⅓ cup pineapple juice, chilled

Place all of the ingredients in a blender. Blend at medium speed until thick and smooth.

Pour the drink into glasses and serve.

Wow Cow *Serves One*

1 cup milk, cold
¼ cup sliced bananas
2 teaspoons peanut butter
1 tablespoon honey

Mix all of the ingredients in a blender on medium speed.

Pour the drink into a glass and serve immediately.

COOKIE BITS

COOKIE BITS

Almond Cocoa Balls
36 Cookies

½ cup butter, softened
3 tablespoons powdered sugar
⅔ cup plus 2 tablespoons flour
¼ cup unsweetened cocoa
1 cup almonds, finely chopped
powdered sugar

Preheat the oven to 325° F.

Cream the butter and the sugar.

Sift together the flour and the cocoa. Blend them into the butter mixture. Add the almonds and mix well.

Roll the dough into ¾-inch balls. Place the balls on ungreased cookie sheets.

Bake for about 20 minutes, or until firm.

Roll the cookies in the powdered sugar while they are still warm.

Cool the cookies on wire racks.

Best of the Butter Cookies
30 Cookies

½ cup unsalted butter, softened
⅓ cup sugar
2 egg yolks
1 teaspoon vanilla
⅛ teaspoon salt
¼ teaspoon almond extract
⅛ teaspoon nutmeg
1 cup flour, sifted
currant jelly

Icing:
4 ounces semi-sweet baking chocolate
2 tablespoons butter

Cream the butter and the sugar. Beat in the egg yolks, vanilla, salt, almond extract and nutmeg. Add the flour and blend well.

Tightly wrap the dough with plastic wrap. Chill for one hour.

Preheat the oven to 325° F.

Shape the dough into 30 balls. Place the balls on an ungreased cookie sheet about one inch apart. Make an indentation in the center of each cookie with the handle of a wooden spoon. Fill with ¼ teaspoon of the currant jelly.

Bake for approximately 10 minutes, or until the edges are lightly browned.

Cool the cookies on wire racks.

After the cookies have cooled, cover the jelly with the chocolate icing.

To make the icing, blend the chocolate and butter in a double boiler over medium heat.

Almond Cookies

32 Cookies

½ cup unsalted butter, softened
4 tablespoons sugar
1 cup flour, sifted
¼ teaspoon baking powder
2 tablespoons finely chopped almonds
1 teaspoon gin
¼ teaspoon almond extract
sliced almonds

Preheat the oven to 350° F.

Cream the butter and the sugar.

Add the flour and the baking powder and beat until well blended.

Add the chopped almonds, gin and almond extract. Mix the ingredients together thoroughly.

Roll the dough into small balls and place them on a lightly greased cookie sheet. Flatten the balls with a fork and place a sliced almond on top of each.

Bake for approximately 20 minutes, or until lightly browned.

Cool the cookies on wire racks.

Italian Anise Cookies

24 Cookies

⅓ cup butter, softened
½ cup sugar
3 eggs, beaten
1 tablespoon warm water
¼ teaspoon vanilla
1½ tablespoons anise seeds **or**
    1 teaspoon anise extract
2 cups flour
1 teaspoon baking powder

Icing:
1 cup powdered sugar
1 tablespoon boiling water

Preheat the oven to 375° F.

Cream the butter and the sugar. Add the eggs and mix well. Then, add the warm water, vanilla and anise seeds or anise extract. Mix well.

Gradually add the flour, which has been sifted with the baking powder.

Shape the stiff dough into 2-inch balls. To make knots, roll each ball into a rope. Tie each rope into a loose knot. To make crescents, roll each ball into a 3-inch rope and form a crescent. Place them on greased cookie sheets.

Bake for 10-12 minutes, or until lightly browned.

Cool the cookies on wire racks.

Frost the cookies with the powdered sugar icing. To prepare the icing, combine the powdered sugar and the boiling water. If necessary, add more water to achieve the desired spreading consistency.

COOKIE BITS

1 cup butter, softened
½ cup light brown sugar, packed
2 eggs, separated
2 cups flour
1 cup chopped pecans or walnuts

Norwegian Cookies   48 Cookies

Preheat the oven to 300° F.

Cream the butter and the sugar. Add the egg yolks and beat well. Then, blend in the flour.

Roll the dough into one-inch balls. Dip them into the egg whites and then into the chopped nuts. Place the balls on greased cookie sheets.

Bake for 20 minutes.

Cool the cookies on wire racks.

½ cup butter, softened
2 tablespoons sugar
1 teaspoon vanilla
1 cup chopped pecans
1 cup plus 2 tablespoons cake flour
powdered sugar

Pecan Clouds   32 Cookies

Preheat the oven to 300° F.

Cream the butter and the sugar. Add the vanilla.

Mix in the pecans and the flour. Blend well.

Roll the dough into one-inch balls and place them on greased cookie sheets.

Bake for 40 minutes, or until firm.

While the cookies are still warm, roll them in the powdered sugar. For a heavier coating of sugar, roll the cookies in the powdered sugar again, after they have cooled.

1 cup light brown sugar, packed
1 cup butter, softened
1 cup flour
1 teaspoon baking soda
2 cups quick oats
granulated sugar

Punch and Squish Oatmeal Cookies   48 Cookies

Preheat the oven to 350° F.

Combine all of the ingredients in a large bowl. "Punch and squish" the dough until it is soft and well mixed.

Roll the dough into medium balls and place them on ungreased cookie sheets. Flatten the balls with the bottom of a glass dipped in the granulated sugar. If desired, the dough then may be fashioned into interesting shapes.

Bake for 8-10 minutes.

Cool the cookies on wire racks.

The Classic Gingersnap
48 Cookies

¾ cup butter
1 cup sugar
1 egg
¼ cup dark molasses
½ teaspoon lemon flavoring
2 cups flour
2 teaspoons baking soda
½ teaspoon salt
¼ teaspoon ground cloves
½ teaspoon ginger
1 teaspoon cinnamon
granulated sugar

Cream the butter and the sugar. Add the egg, molasses and lemon flavoring. Blend well.

Sift together the dry ingredients. Add them to the mixture, blending well.

Cover the dough tightly with plastic wrap and chill for an hour or more.

Preheat the oven to 350° F.

Form the dough into one-inch balls and place them on greased cookie sheets. Flatten each one with the bottom of a glass dipped in the granulated sugar.

Bake for 8-10 minutes. Watch the cookies carefully to avoid brown edges.

Cool the cookies on the cookie sheets for approximately one minute. Remove them to wire racks.

Walnut Jam Cookies
30 Cookies

½ cup butter, softened
3 ounces cream cheese, softened
1 egg, separated
1 teaspoon vanilla
1 teaspoon grated lemon zest
¼ teaspoon salt
1 cup powdered sugar, sifted
1 cup flour, sifted
1 cup finely chopped walnuts
apricot or raspberry jam

Preheat the oven to 325° F.

Cream the butter, cream cheese, egg yolk, vanilla, lemon zest and salt.

Gradually mix in the powdered sugar and the flour to form a stiff dough. Chill the dough well.

Form the dough into 30 balls. Beat the egg white until foamy. Dip the balls into the egg white and then roll them in the nuts.

Arrange the cookies on ungreased cookie sheets. Make an indentation in the center of each cookie with the handle of a wooden spoon. Fill each indentation with ¼ teaspoon of the jam.

Bake for 15 minutes, or until the cookies begin to brown on the bottom.

Remove the cookies to wire racks and cool them thoroughly.

Lemon or orange zest is the thin outer skin of the lemon or orange. The zest can be removed with a vegetable peeler or a fine grater.

COOKIE BITS

Almond Meringue Bars *30 Bars*

Crust:
1 cup butter, softened
½ cup almond paste
½ cup light brown sugar, packed
1 egg
2 cups flour

Filling:
1 cup raspberry jam
lemon juice, optional

Topping:
3 egg whites
¾ cup sugar
½ cup slivered almonds

Preheat the oven to 325° F.

To prepare the crust, cream the butter and the almond paste. Gradually beat in the brown sugar and the egg.

Blend in the flour.

Firmly press the dough into a lightly greased 9"x13"x2" pan.

Bake for 20 minutes.

Spread the crust with the raspberry jam. If the jam is too sweet, add lemon juice to taste.

To prepare the topping, beat the egg whites until they are frothy. Gradually beat in the sugar until a stiff meringue is formed. Do not overbeat.

Fold in the slivered almonds. Spread the meringue over the jam.

Return the pan to the oven and bake for 20 minutes, or until the peaks are a pale brown.

Cut into 2-inch squares when completely cooled. Store the bars in an airtight container with wax paper between the layers.

Backpacker's Delight *30 Bars*

Crust:
1 cup butter, softened
1 cup sugar
2 cups whole wheat flour

Filling:
2 eggs
1 teaspoon baking powder
2 tablespoons whole-wheat flour
1 teaspoon vanilla
½ teaspoon salt
1 cup sugar
1 cup chopped walnuts
1 cup unsweetened coconut
6 ounces semi-sweet chocolate chips, optional

Preheat the oven to 350° F.

To prepare the crust, cream the butter and the sugar.

Blend in the flour.

Firmly press the dough into an ungreased 9"x13"x2" pan.

Bake for 25 minutes.

To prepare the filling, mix all of the remaining ingredients together and spread over the crust.

Bake for another 20-25 minutes, or until the filling is set.

Cut into bars while still warm. When completely cooled, remove the bars from the pan.

Extraordinary Chocolate Bars *24 Bars*

Crust:
½ cup butter, softened
¼ cup sugar
1 egg
1½ cups flour

Filling:
12 ounces semi-sweet chocolate chips **or** apricot preserves

Topping:
2 eggs
¾ cup sugar
6 tablespoons butter, melted
2 teaspoons vanilla
2 cups finely chopped walnuts

Preheat the oven to 350° F.

To prepare the crust, cream the butter and the sugar. Add the egg and mix well.

Add the flour gradually to form a soft dough.

Firmly press the crust into a greased 9"x13"x2" pan.

Bake the crust for 10 minutes. Remove from the oven.

Sprinkle the crust with the chocolate chips. Return the pan to the oven for one minute to melt the chips. Remove the pan from the oven and spread the melted chocolate chips over the crust.

To prepare the topping, beat the eggs until thick. Add the sugar, butter, vanilla and walnuts. Beat well.

Spread the topping over the chocolate layer.

Bake for 30-35 minutes.

Cut into bars while still warm. When completely cooled, remove the bars from the pan.

Oatmeal-Raspberry Bars *20 Bars*

1½ cups flour
1 teaspoon baking powder
¼ teaspoon salt
¾ cup light brown sugar, packed
1½ cups old fashioned rolled oats
¾ cup unsalted butter
1 cup raspberry jam
lemon juice, optional

Preheat the oven to 350° F.

Sift together the flour, baking powder and salt. Add the brown sugar and the rolled oats.

Cut in the butter. Then, mix the dough with your hands. Reserve one cup of the oat mixture for the topping.

Firmly press the remaining oat mixture into a 7"x11"x1½" pan. Spread with the raspberry jam. If the jam is too sweet, add lemon juice to taste. Top with the crumb mixture.

Bake for 25 minutes.

Cut into 2-inch bars when completely cooled.

COOKIE BITS

Outrageous Brownies *30 Bars*

1 cup butter
4 ounces unsweetened baking chocolate
1¾ cups sugar
3 eggs
1 teaspoon vanilla
1 cup flour
1½ cups chopped blanched almonds
6 ounces semi-sweet chocolate chips

Preheat the oven to 350° F.

Melt the butter and the chocolate in a double boiler over medium heat.

Beat in the sugar with a wooden spoon. Add the eggs, one at a time, beating well after each addition.

Stir in the vanilla, and then the flour. Blend well. Add one cup of the nuts to the batter.

Pour the batter into a greased 9"x13"x2" pan. Combine the chocolate chips and the remaining nuts. Sprinkle them over the top of the batter.

Bake for 35 minutes. Do not overbake.

Cut into 2-inch bars when completely cooled.

Plantation Brownies *20 Bars*

½ cup unsalted butter, softened
1¼ cups dark brown sugar, packed
2 eggs
1 tablespoon light molasses
1 teaspoon vanilla
1 cup flour
½ cup chopped walnuts

Icing:
2 tablespoons powdered sugar
¼ teaspoon instant coffee powder
½ teaspoon or more warm water

Preheat the oven to 350° F.

Cream the butter and the sugar. Add the eggs, molasses and vanilla. Beat the mixture well.

Fold in the flour and the walnuts.

Pour the batter into a greased 9"x9"x2" pan.

Bake for approximately 30-35 minutes. Do not overbake.

While the brownies are cooling, prepare the icing by combining the powdered sugar, coffee and water.

Add more water, if needed, to obtain the correct drizzling consistency of the icing.

Drizzle the icing back and forth in a fine, zigzag line on the cooled brownies.

Cut the brownies into squares.

Shortbread Plus
20 Bars

Crust:
1¼ cups flour
½ cup sugar
½ cup butter

Filling:
apricot or raspberry jam,
    approximately ⅔ cup

Topping:
2 eggs
½ cup light brown sugar, packed
1 teaspoon vanilla
2 tablespoons flour
⅛ teaspoon baking soda
1 cup chopped walnuts

Preheat the oven to 350° F.

To prepare the crust, combine the flour and the sugar. Cut in the butter with a pastry blender until the mixture resembles fine meal. Firmly press the mixture into a greased 9"x9"x2" pan.

Bake for 20 minutes, or until the edges are lightly browned.

Spread the crust with apricot or raspberry jam.

To prepare the topping, beat the eggs with the brown sugar and the vanilla until well blended. Stir in the flour, salt and baking soda. Fold in the walnuts.

Spoon the topping over the jam and return the pan to the oven.

Bake for 20-25 minutes, or until the topping is set.

Cut the bars while still warm. When completely cooled, remove the bars from the pan.

Simply Shortbread
30 Bars

1 cup unsalted butter, softened
⅔ cup superfine sugar
3 cups flour

Preheat the oven to 325° F.

Beat the butter until creamy. Gradually add the sugar and beat until fluffy.

Blend in the flour with a wooden spoon until a dough is formed. Use as little flour as possible to make the dough. The amount of flour may vary, depending on the moisture content of the butter and the flour.

Firmly press the dough to an even thickness in an ungreased 9"x13"x2" pan. Before baking, use a serrated knife to cut the dough into 2-inch bars.

Bake for 30 minutes or until the edges begin to brown slightly.

Cut the bars apart when almost cooled.

Blend granulated sugar in a blender jar for a short time to get fine-grained sugar. If blended for a longer time, it will approximate powdered sugar.

COOKIE BITS

Turtle Temptations
30 Bars

Crust:
½ cup butter, softened
1 cup dark brown sugar, packed
2 cups flour
1 cup walnuts <u>or</u> pecan halves

Caramel layer:
⅔ cup butter
½ cup dark brown sugar, packed
½ teaspoon vanilla

Chocolate topping:
6 ounces semi-sweet chocolate chips

Preheat the oven to 350° F.

To prepare the crust, cream the butter and the sugar. Blend in the flour.

Firmly press the dough into an ungreased 9"x13"x2" pan. Sprinkle the nuts over the unbaked crust.

To prepare the caramel layer, melt the butter and the sugar in a heavy pan over medium heat. Stir constantly until the mixture boils. Continue to boil and stir for ½ to 1 minute.

Remove the pan from the heat and stir in the vanilla. Pour the mixture over the nuts.

Bake for 18-22 minutes, or until the crust is light brown and the caramel is bubbling.

Remove the pan from the oven and sprinkle with the chocolate chips. Let the chips melt for 3 minutes. Then, slightly swirl the chips to give a marbled effect.

Cut into bars while warm. When completely cooled, remove the bars from the pan.

Chocolate Chip Meringues
24 Cookies

2 egg whites, at room temperature
¾ cup sugar
½ teaspoon vanilla <u>or</u>
    ½ teaspoon peppermint extract
6 ounces semi-sweet chocolate chips
1 cup chopped pecans <u>or</u> walnuts

Preheat the oven to 350° F.

Beat the egg whites until they are stiff. Gradually add the sugar and beat for about 10 minutes, or until stiff peaks form.

Fold in the flavoring. Gently add the chocolate chips and the nuts.

Drop the batter by teaspoonfuls on foil-lined cookie sheets.

Place in the oven and then TURN OFF THE OVEN. Leave the cookies in the oven overnight, or for at least 4 hours.

These delicate cookies should be stored in airtight containers with wax paper between the layers.

Chocolate Crowns

42 Cookies

½ cup butter
2 ounces semi-sweet baking chocolate
1 cup sugar
2 eggs
2 teaspoons vanilla
1 cup plus 2 tablespoons flour
½ teaspoon baking soda
¼ teaspoon salt
¼ teaspoon almond extract
2½ cups coarsely chopped walnuts

Icing:
4 ounces semi-sweet baking chocolate
2 tablespoons butter
walnut halves

Preheat the oven to 350° F.

Melt the butter and the chocolate in a double boiler over medium heat.

Remove the mixture from the heat and blend in the sugar. Beat in the eggs and the vanilla until the mixture is smooth.

Stir in the flour, baking soda, salt and almond extract. Fold in the nuts.

Drop by rounded teaspoonfuls on greased cookie sheets.

Bake for 10-12 minutes, or until firm. For best results, bake one sheet at a time in the center of the oven.

Cool the cookies on wire racks.

To prepare the icing, melt the chocolate and the butter in a double boiler over low heat. Blend well. For easy spreading, keep the icing over the hot water.

Frost the center of each cookie and place a walnut half on top.

Chocolate Indulgence Cookies

54 Cookies

6 tablespoons butter
8 ounces semi-sweet baking chocolate
3 ounces unsweetened baking chocolate
3 eggs
1 cup sugar
2 teaspoons vanilla
⅓ cup flour
¼ teaspoon salt
12 ounces semi-sweet chocolate chips
1½ cups chopped pecans
1½ cups chopped walnuts

Preheat the oven to 350° F.

Melt the butter and both the semi-sweet and unsweetened chocolates in a double boiler over medium heat. Blend well and cool.

Beat the eggs, sugar and vanilla. Add the melted chocolates and blend. Then add the flour and the salt. Blend well. Stir in the chocolate chips and the nuts.

Drop by tablespoonfuls on greased cookie sheets.

Bake for 8-10 minutes. The centers should be fudge-like.

Cool the cookies slightly on the cookie sheets. Then, transfer them to wire racks.

COOKIE BITS

Currant Cookies *48 Cookies*

½ cup dried currants
2 tablespoons rum
½ cup butter, softened
¼ teaspoon salt
¾ cup sugar
2 eggs
1½ cups flour

Soak the currants in the rum for at least 30 minutes.

Preheat the oven to 350° F.

Cream the butter and the salt. Gradually blend in the sugar. Beat in the eggs. Add the currants and the rum, mixing well. Gradually stir in the flour.

Drop by teaspoonfuls on greased cookie sheets.

Bake for 8-10 minutes, or until the edges are lightly browned.

Cool the cookies on wire racks.

Granny's Ribbon Cane Syrup Cookies *60 Cookies*

The flavor and the texture of these old-fashioned cookies are improved if they are allowed to mellow in a covered jar for a few days.

1 cup sugar
1 cup margarine
2 eggs, beaten
1 cup ribbon cane syrup
4 cups flour
⅛ teaspoon baking powder
1 teaspoon baking soda
½ teaspoon ginger
1 teaspoon allspice
1¼ teaspoons cinnamon
½ teaspoon salt
1 cup chopped walnuts or pecans

Preheat the oven to 350° F.

Cream the sugar and the margarine.

Add the eggs and the syrup and continue to beat until well blended.

Combine the flour, baking powder, baking soda, ginger, allspice, cinnamon and salt. Blend the dry mixture into the wet mixture one cup at a time.

Add the nuts and stir into the batter.

Drop by rounded teaspoonfuls onto a greased or teflon-coated cookie sheet.

Bake 12-13 minutes, or until golden brown.

Marie Antoinette's Lace Cookies
20 Cookies

½ cup butter
½ cup sugar
1 tablespoon flour
¾ cup blanched almonds, finely ground
2 tablespoons milk
¼ teaspoon almond extract
4 ounces semi-sweet baking chocolate

Preheat the oven to 350° F.

In a skillet, melt the butter over medium heat. Add the sugar and the flour stirring until the sugar dissolves.

Mix in the almonds and the milk. Stir until the mixture thickens slightly.

Remove the skillet from the heat and blend in the almond extract. Cool the batter slightly.

Drop the batter by half-teaspoonfuls on greased teflon cookie sheets. Space the cookies 3-4 inches apart.

Bake for 5-7 minutes, or until the edges are golden. Watch the cookies carefully.

Cool the cookies on the cookie sheets for 1-2 minutes. Remove them to wire racks. If the cookies stick to the cookie sheets or break, you have waited too long to remove them. Briefly return them to the oven to soften.

Melt the chocolate in a double boiler over medium heat. With the chocolate over warm water, spread a layer of it on the bottom side of one cookie. Cover with the bottom side of another cookie to form a sandwich.

Cool the cookies on the wire racks until the chocolate has set.

Store the cookies in airtight containers and serve within a few hours of baking time or freeze them until ready for use.

Soft Sugar Cookies
64 Cookies

⅔ cup butter, softened
1½ cups sugar
2 eggs
1 cup sour cream **or** buttermilk
1 teaspoon vanilla
2¾ cups flour
1 teaspoon baking soda
1 teaspoon baking powder
¼ teaspoon salt
raisins
granulated sugar

Preheat the oven to 375° F.

Cream the butter and the sugar. Add the eggs, one at a time, and beat well after each addition. Blend in the sour cream, *or* the buttermilk, and the vanilla.

Sift together the dry ingredients and add them to the mixture. Blend well.

Drop the batter by teaspoonfuls on lightly greased cookie sheets, leaving about 2½ inches between the cookies. Put one raisin in the center of each cookie and sprinkle with the granulated sugar.

Bake for 8-10 minutes or until the edges are lightly browned.

Cool the cookies on wire racks.

COOKIE BITS

½ cup butter
1 cup sugar
1 egg
1 tablespoon grated lemon zest
1 tablespoon or more lemon juice
2 cups flour, sifted
1 teaspoon baking powder
1 cup chopped pecans

Lemon Icebox Cookies *72 Cookies*

Cream the butter and the sugar. Add the egg, lemon zest and lemon juice. Beat well.

Sift together the dry ingredients and add them to the creamed mixture. Blend well. Stir in the chopped pecans.

Shape the dough into rolls 1½ inches in diameter and cover tightly with plastic wrap. Chill thoroughly.

Preheat the oven to 350° F.

Slice the rolls thinly and place the slices on a greased cookie sheet.

Bake for 10 minutes.

Cool the cookies on wire racks.

1 cup unsalted butter, softened
1 cup sugar
1 egg yolk
zest of one orange, coarsely grated
¼ teaspoon salt
½ teaspoon nutmeg
2 cups flour
¼ cup poppy seeds

Orange-Poppy Seed Cookies *60 Cookies*

Cream the butter and the sugar. Blend in the egg yolk.

Add the orange zest, salt, nutmeg and flour. Blend the ingredients well. Add the poppy seeds and blend again.

Divide the dough into four equal portions. Using sheets of plastic wrap, shape the dough into 2"x4" rolls. Wrap tightly. Refrigerate the rolls until firm, approximately one hour.

Preheat the oven to 350° F.

Cut the dough into ¼-inch slices and place them on ungreased cookie sheets.

Bake for approximately 8 minutes, or until the edges are lightly browned.

Cool the cookies on wire racks.

English Tea Biscuits
78 Biscuits

1¼ cups flour
¾ cup old fashioned rolled oats
½ cup superfine sugar
¾ cup butter
1-2 tablespoons milk

Preheat the oven to 350° F.

Mix the flour, oats, sugar and butter with fingertips until the mixture becomes crumbly. Add the milk gradually, working the mixture into a cohesive dough. Add the least amount of milk possible.

Knead the dough briefly and place it on a lightly floured surface. Roll it out to a ⅛-inch to ¼-inch thickness.

Cut the dough into 2-inch rounds. Place the biscuits on greased cookie sheets and prick the centers with a fork.

Bake for approximately 20 minutes, or until the biscuits are firm and pale in color.

Cool the biscuits on wire racks.

Gingerbread Children and Their Friends
42 Cookies

½ cup unsalted butter, softened
½ cup shortening
2 cups sugar
2 eggs
½ cup dark molasses
4 cups flour
2 teaspoons cinnamon
1 teaspoon ginger
1 teaspoon nutmeg
1 teaspoon baking soda
⅛ teaspoon salt

Cream the butter, shortening and sugar. Blend in the eggs, one at a time, beating after each addition. Mix in the molasses.

Sift together the dry ingredients, evenly distributing the spices throughout the flour. Gradually add the dry ingredients to the liquid mixture, blending well.

Divide the dough into 3 or 4 large balls. Cover the balls tightly with plastic wrap and chill thoroughly.

Preheat the oven to 325° F.

On a lightly floured surface, roll the dough to a ¼-inch thickness. Use a variety of cookie cutters to form the gingerbread children and their friends. Place the cookies on greased cookie sheets.

For ornaments, use a plastic straw to make holes at the top of each cookie before baking.

Bake for 10-12 minutes.

Cool the cookies on wire racks. The cookies may be decorated in any way desired.

COOKIE BITS

Ischl Cookies
30 Cookies

2 cups flour
⅔ cup sugar
½ teaspoon cinnamon
¼ teaspoon ground cloves
4 ounces unblanched almonds or hazelnuts, ground
1¼ cups butter, chilled and cut into pieces
currant or raspberry jelly
powdered sugar

Preheat the oven to 325° F.

Sift together the flour, sugar, cinnamon and cloves. Mix in the nuts.

Cut in the butter. Then knead the dough lightly until the mixture holds together. Shape it into 2 balls.

For the cookie bottoms, roll half of the dough to a ⅛-inch thickness on a lightly floured surface. Cut out the bottoms with a 2-inch round cookie cutter. Place them on ungreased cookie sheets.

For the cookie tops, roll the other half of the dough to a ⅛-inch thickness. Cut out the tops with the 2-inch round cutter. Then, with a ½-inch cookie cutter, cut out the centers of the tops. Place the rounds on ungreased cookie sheets.

Bake both bottoms and tops for 10-12 minutes. Do not let them brown.

Cool the cookies on wire racks.

Spread the cookie bottoms with the jelly. Cover the bottoms with the cookie tops.

Sprinkle the cookies with a light dusting of powdered sugar.

Regal Tea Cookies
60 Cookies

2 cups butter, softened
1 cup sugar
2 eggs
4½ cups flour
⅛ teaspoon salt

Icing:
1 cup powdered sugar
1 tablespoon boiling water, or more, to achieve spreading consistency
raspberry jam
candied cherries, halved

Preheat the oven to 325° F.

Cream the butter and the sugar.

Beat in the eggs. Then, add the flour and the salt.

On a lightly floured surface, roll out the dough to a ¼-inch thickness. Cut the dough into 2-inch rounds.

Bake for 15-20 minutes, or until the bottoms are golden brown.

Cool the cookies on wire racks.

To prepare the icing, combine the powdered sugar and the water. Keep the icing over hot water in a double boiler for 10-15 minutes to remove its raw taste.

Form a sandwich cookie by spreading the raspberry jam between the bottoms of two cookies. Cover the jam with the bottomsides of the remaining cookies.

Frost the cookies with the icing and place a halved cherry in the center of each cookie.

Almond Shells

50 Tarts

1 cup butter
1 cup plus 2 tablespoons sugar
1 egg
4 ounces almonds, finely ground
½ teaspoon almond extract
3 cups cake flour, sifted

Preheat the oven to 350° F.

Cream the butter and sugar. Add the egg, ground almonds and almond extract and beat well.

Add the flour, a little at a time, mixing until well blended.

Firmly press small amounts of the dough into fluted muffin tins or miniature tart pans, forming crusts as thin as possible. Prick the sides and the bottom of each shell with a fork.

Bake for 5 minutes.

Remove the shells from the oven and prick the bottoms again. Return the shells to the oven and bake until pale brown, about 3 minutes.

Cool the shells before removing them from the pans.

Fill the cooled shells with lemon curd or chocolate mousse.

Lemon Curd

6 eggs, well beaten
2 cups sugar
½ cup fresh lemon juice
¼ cup butter

Combine all of the ingredients in the top of a double boiler and cook over medium heat until the mixture thickens.

Chocolate Mousse

12 ounces semi-sweet chocolate chips
4 tablespoons sugar
6 tablespoons milk
2 teaspoons vanilla
6 egg yolks
8 egg whites

Melt the chocolate chips, sugar and milk in the top of a double boiler over hot water.

Cool the mixture slightly and beat in the vanilla and the egg yolks one at a time.

Beat the egg whites until stiff.

Fold in the chocolate mixture.

Almond shells filled with Chocolate Mousse freeze well.

COOKIE BITS

Crust:
½ cup butter, softened
3 ounces cream cheese, softened
⅓ cup sugar
¾ cup flour
¼ cup unsweetened cocoa

Filling:
2 ounces unsweetened baking chocolate
2 tablespoons butter
½ cup sugar
1 egg
1 teaspoon vanilla
1 tablespoon Kahlua <u>or</u> any other liqueur

Chocolate Kahlua Tarts *24 Tarts*

To prepare the crust, cream the butter and the cream cheese. Add the sugar and beat until fluffy.

Sift together the flour and the cocoa. Add this to the creamed mixture and blend well.

Cover the dough tightly with plastic wrap and chill for approximately one hour.

Preheat the oven to 325° F.

Divide the dough into 24 balls. Press each ball into the bottom and the sides of greased miniature muffin tins or miniature tart pans. For easiest removal, use teflon pans.

To prepare the filling, melt the chocolate and the butter over low heat. Remove the pan from the heat and stir in the sugar, egg, vanilla and liqueur.

Divide the filling evenly among the tart shells.

Bake for 25-30 minutes, or until the filling has set.

Cool the tarts in the pans briefly before removing them to wire racks.

MERRY BITS

Transforming that ordinary party for a child or young teen into a memorable "happening" will be easier with the assistance of this chapter. Whether the occasion involves a birthday celebration or merely a gathering of friends, Merry Bits will suggest themes, invitations, decorations, activities and food selections.

MERRY BITS

Teddy Bears' Party

Age
3-7 years

Invitations
Make an invitation in the shape of a teddy bear, providing all of the party information. Encourage the guests to bring their teddy bears or any other favorite stuffed animals to the party.

Favors
Stickers, stationery or pencils with bear designs

Copies of *Winnie-the-Pooh* or *Paddington Bear*

Decorations
In the party room, arrange teddy bears and other stuffed animals.

Activities
Let the children decorate previously prepared bear-shaped cookies.

Let the children make teddy bears out of Chocolate Peanut Butter Play Dough. See page 188 for the recipe. They can eat them at the party or take them home.

Arrange to have an adult appear dressed as a bear to tell stories.

Party Foods
Frozen Pudding-Wiches, see page 187

Banana Ginger Ale, see page 190

Beach Party

Age	5-8 years
Invitations	Attach a written note to a fly swatter or small shovel, or place an invitation in a sand pail and deliver it.
Favors	Shovels and pails Beach balls Sand-painting kits Sea shell figurines Child's snorkel masks
Activities	On tagboard, have the children write their names or make a picture with glue and sand. Colored sand can be purchased in hobby shops. Have the children guess the number of sea shells in a large container. Allow the children to run through sprinklers or swim, if a pool is available.
Party Foods	Hot dogs or hamburgers on the grill Corn on the cob Watermelon Ice cream and cookies Toasted marshmallows

MERRY BITS

Clown Party

Age
5-8 years

Invitations
With paper, fashion a clown hat, a big shoe or a balloon and provide the party information on it. Ask the guests to wear circus costumes.

Favors
Bag of peanuts
Box of popcorn
Clown hats
Balloons

Decorations
Drape crepe paper streamers from the center to the outside edges of the ceiling in the party room to give a circus tent effect. Place balloons and circus posters around the room. Use picnic benches for seating.

Activities
Ask the guests to do face painting on each other.

Teach the children how to juggle three objects, such as balls or plastic bowling pins.

Ask each guest to perform a circus act based on his or her costume.

Party Foods
Balloon Cake: On a sheet cake covered with white frosting, outline balloons with thin strings of licorice and fill them in with brightly colored frosting.

Ice cream clown heads: Use a scoop of ice cream for the clown's face, an upside down sugar cone for his hat, jelly beans for his eyes and nose and red string licorice for his mouth.

Honey-Nut Popcorn, see page 188

High Energy Punch, see page 134

Little Girls' Dress-Up Party

Little girls love to dress up. At this party, the mother should be dressed up, too.

Age

5-8 years

Invitations

Place a picture of a fashionably dressed young girl on pink construction paper. Provide the pertinent party information and ask that the guests dress up for the party.

Favors

Inexpensive jewelry from a dime store or thrift shop

Beads and elastic thread for make-your-own necklaces and bracelets

Child's cologne or make-up

Fancy soap

Activities

Provide materials for jewelry making.

Provide materials for making tissue paper and pipe cleaner flowers.

Take Polaroid pictures of each child upon arrival. Send the picture home with the child.

Party Foods

Fancy finger sandwiches

Fancy cookies and petits fours

Punch or soft drinks

Chocolates

For younger children, design the party games to make every child a winner.

MERRY BITS

Pirate Party

Ages — 5-9 years

Invitations — Using black ink, draw treasure maps to the party address, marking the spot with an "X". Tear or burn the edges of the paper.

Favors

- Bandanas
- Eye patches
- Earrings
- Shovels
- Pails
- Small telescopes
- Gold-covered chocolate coins
- Pirate flags
- Rubber knives
- The book *Treasure Island*

Decorations — Draw a skull and crossbones for the front door or place black flags with skull and crossbones along the approach to the house.

Activities — Prepare bags or pails with bandanas, eye patches or the materials for making earrings. The children can begin to make their earrings upon arrival. Use cardboard circles and cover them with aluminum foil. Hang the earrings by strings looped over the ears.

Begin a treasure hunt with individual burnt-edged maps or make treasure maps in puzzle pieces which each child can assemble. There should be a separate treasure buried for each child. Alternatively, one large treasure with enough booty for all of the children can be hidden. An adult can lead the treasure hunt by reading from a letter or a scroll. Have the first clue read to the children just as they finish their food. Then, give a different clue for each child. Bury the treasure in advance and supply shovels for digging.

On the driveway, draw a narrow rectangular plank with chalk. Draw a small island about 8 to 10 feet from the end of the plank. Blindfold a child, turn him or her around several times and position him or her at the start of the plank. Allow one minute for each child to walk the plank and try to make his or her way to the island. When a child's time is up, remove the blindfold and let him or her stay in place as an obstacle for the remaining children.

Party Foods

Shipwreck sandwiches	Submarine sandwiches
Chicken bones	Chicken legs
Seaweed	Green beans
Fish	Fish crackers
Booty	Banana and pineapple kabobs
Islands	Ice cream surrounded by chocolate syrup
Ale	Frosty mugs of ginger ale or root beer

MERRY BITS

Break the Bank Party

Age

5-10 years

Invitations

On play money, paste the birthday child's picture over the President's picture. Write the party information on a blank piece of paper and glue it to the back of the play money.

Favors

Gold-covered chocolate money

Play money

Piggy banks

Personalized fabric wallets or change purses

A few small denomination foreign coins

Decorations

Design money trees. Use branches trimmed from trees or make fake ones out of cardboard. Tape play dollar bills on the branches. Decorate the walls with the money branches or set them in flower pots in the party room.

Decorate the party room to resemble the inside of a bank. Fashion the teller's cage out of a large cardboard box.

Decorate the party room with green balloons.

Hang-up a piñata shaped like a piggy bank. Fill the piñata with chocolate coins, gold nuggets and bubble gum.

Activities

Break the piñata.

Give each child a specific amount of paper money. Provide party favors that the children can purchase at the teller's cage. Also, award paper money to the winners of games at the party. Then, the children can also spend it at the teller's cage.

Use play money to bid on surprise packages.

Have a hunt for small-denomination coins.

Party Foods

Barbecue in a Cup, see page 189

Cold Weather Fruit Cups, see page 184

Hot Foamy Lemonade, see page 191

Man's Best Friend Party

This party can be adapted to any family pet. It is a good spur-of-the-moment party for a rainy day when the neighborhood children need an activity.

Age

6-8 years

Invitations

Make a paper invitation in the shape of a dog. Provide all of the party information and suggest that each guest bring a rubber toy, an old tennis ball or a sock as a gift.

Favors

Bone-shaped cookies which are made at the party

Varnished dog milk bones with holes poked in one end and a ribbon inserted

Books with a dog as the central character

Activities

Have the guests prepare and decorate cookies cut out with a bone-shaped cookie cutter. Give them a doggie bag in which to take their bones home.

Have each guest tell his or her favorite funny dog or animal story.

Show an interesting film about a domestic animal.

Have the guest of honor display any tricks or obedient dog routines which he or she can do.

Party Foods

Cookies or brownies

Lemonade

MERRY BITS

Back to School Party

Age
6-10 years

Invitations
Cut a large apple out of red or green paper or make a paper report card. Provide the necessary party information.

Favors
Ball point pens
Crayons
Pencils inscribed with each guest's name
Pencil cases
Fancy erasers
Spiral notebooks
Small appointment calendars

Activities
Place "spider webs" all around the house. Wind strings around the house or backyard, over and under chairs and tables, and up and down staircases. Each guest can follow a separate string and, at the end of the string, he or she finds a favor.

Have a shoe scramble. Place the guests' shoes and additional shoes in a pile. Ask each child to find his or her shoes. The first child to find his or her own shoes is the winner.

Have a spelling bee using silly words.

Party Foods
Pack a school lunch in a brown paper bag for each guest:
Sandwiches
Fresh vegetables and dips
Rainbow Jello, see page 186
Apples
Individual packs of potato chips
Cookies
Individual cans of fruit juice

Field Day Party at the Park

Age	6-10 years
Invitations	Make an invitation in the shape of a medal with gold metallic paper. Supply the party information on the back.
Favors	Frisbees Paint-your-own tee shirts with athletic motifs Posters with athletes' pictures
Activities	Backwards race — Relay race Three-legged race — Obstacle course race Distance race — Soccer ball kick Sack race — Baseball throw
Party Foods	Tortilla sandwiches, see pages 136 to 137 Fresh vegetables and dips Fresh fruit kabobs Punch and Squish Oatmeal Cookies, see page 196 Fruit juices and soda pop

Airplane Party

Age	6-11 years
Invitations	Make a paper airplane and give all of the party information on it.
Favors	Construction kits for making simple airplanes.
Activities	Provide instructions for building several types of paper airplanes. The library, local bookstore or hobby shop is a good source of this information. Have plenty of paper and scissors on hand. Encourage the guests to pick and choose the type or types of planes they would like to create. Have various contests after the construction is finished. Determine which plane can fly the farthest, the highest or perform small stunts. A large inside or outside area is needed for this activity. Arrange a trip to the local airport for a guided tour by a major airline.
Party Foods	Prepare a meal or snack to be served on a tray in airline fashion.

MERRY BITS

Gingerbread House Party

This is a nice way to begin the winter holiday season.

Age
6-10 years

Invitations
Make an invitation in the shape of a gingerbread house with brown paper. Decorate the house with Christmas stickers and provide all of the party information.

Favors
Gingerbread houses made by the guests at the party

Decorations
Traditional Christmas decorations may be used.

Activities
The main activity at this party is the making of a gingerbread house by each guest.

Build the house on a rectangular cardboard base which has been covered with festive wrapping paper or aluminum foil.

To prepare the icing glue which is used to assemble and decorate the house, beat 3 egg whites until stiff. Gradually add one pound of powdered sugar, beating continually. Remove any icing spills immediately.

For each house, 6½ double-square graham crackers will be needed. Glue one double-square graham cracker to the covered base to make the floor. Glue one double-square graham cracker to each side and one single-square graham cracker to each end to form the walls. Cut 2 triangles from one single-square graham cracker to form the gables which are then glued on the front and back of the house at the roof line. Use 2 double-square graham crackers glued at a slant to form the roof.

Allow the houses to dry. Then, using more of the icing glue, decorate them with a variety of candies, gum, miniature marshmallows, nuts, sugar cubes, pretzels or other edible items.

For very young guests, consider making the houses in advance of the party. Then, have the guests decorate them.

Party Foods
Assorted Christmas cookies

Hot cider with cinnamon-stick stirrers

Prehistoric Party

Age
6-10 years

Invitations
Make a dinosaur on construction paper and supply all of the party information on it.

Favors
Small books on dinosaurs

Plastic dinosaurs

Activities
Have guests try to outline the real size of a dinosaur using a string.

Pin the tail on the dinosaur.

Have each child make a fossil footprint. Obtain a package of materials and instructions at a toy or craft store.

Party Foods
Dinosaur-shaped sandwiches made with cookie cutters.

Juice or punch

Ice-Age Cake: Place ice cream between 2 cake layers. Frost the cake with softened ice cream and place plastic dinosaurs all over the cake. Keep the cake frozen until ready to use.

Good sources of interesting party favors are novelty companies, craft stores, thrift shops, army surplus stores, religious stores, nurseries, discount stores and the gift shops at art museums, natural history museums, botanic gardens, historical societies and zoos.

MERRY BITS

Space Party

Age
6-10 years

Invitations
Make a paper invitation in the shape of a space ship or a celestial body. In giving the party information, use space language. The time of the party is the blast-off time. The place of the party is the launching pad. The hosts and hostesses of the party are the crew.

Favors
Make space helmets using five gallon ice cream containers for each guest. Cut out a face piece and cover it with cellophane. Write each child's name on the front of the helmet.

Activities
Let each guest decorate his helmet with pipe cleaners, styrofoam balls, stickers, glitter glue and markers.

Have a space hunt. Divide the group in half and provide a number of clues. Spray-painted gold rocks, space theme candy or small plastic robots make good treasures.

Have the guests build asteroids. Provide them with gumdrops, toothpicks and a piece of cardboard to serve as the base for their construction.

Party Foods
Moonscape Cake: Decorate a sheetcake with fluffy, white frosting to suggest a moonscape. Place plastic space figures on the cake.

Identified Fruit Objects, see page 185

Punch served in a bowl with dry ice

Backyard Campout

Age

6-12 years

Invitations

Make a tent with heavy brown paper. Decorate it and supply the party information. Make sure the information mentions the need for a sleeping bag, pillow, pajamas and grubby camping clothes.

Favors

Tee shirts

Tin cups or Sierra cups

Flashlights

Canteens

Equipment

Barbecue grill

Small or large tents which can be rented from sporting goods stores

Insect repellent

Skewers or green sticks for roasting marshmallows or hot dogs

Activities

Have the guests cook their own food on the grill.

Tell ghost stories in the dark.

Have the guests look at the stars and try to locate the Big Dipper, the Little Dipper, the North Star and other constellations.

Have a flashlight hike around the block with Mom and Dad.

Party Foods

Dinner:

Hot dogs or hamburgers

Corn or baked beans

Unbaked dinner rolls placed on a stick and cooked over the fire

Backpacker's Delight, see page 198

Watermelon

Toasted marshmallows

Breakfast:

Orange juice

Eggs or pancakes

Bacon or sausage

Peanut Butter-Banana Cupcakes, see page 183

Hot chocolate

MERRY BITS

Silly Supper

Silly Supper revolves around the selection and eating of a meal. It can be adapted to breakfast, lunch or dinner. It can be easily combined with other activities such as skating, movies, plays or slumber parties. Be sure to have plenty of help available when it is time to serve the meal.

Age

7-12 years

Invitations

Make an invitation that looks like a menu or write the party information on a paper napkin or paper bib.

Favors

Scratch-and-sniff stickers

Silly stickers

Bandana napkins

Play dishes

Real dishes

Activities and Party Foods

This silly supper is the main activity! Before the party, the menu must be selected and then a silly name devised for each food item and eating utensil. Every child receives a menu with his or her name on it. The menu contains only the silly names of the foods and utensils to be served. These names appear on the menu in random order and do not reveal the real identity of the item. The child must then choose any six items by marking his or her menu. There will be three courses with six menu items per course. The child should indicate with a 1-6 designation the order in which each item should be brought to the table. The children will be very surprised if they receive a plate of food and they have nothing with which to eat it. Remove everything after each course. After all of the children have been served from the silly menu, give them the opportunity to fill their plates in traditional style if they wish.

Menu examples are:

George Washington Carver	knife
Warty Wonders	pickles
Colonel Gold	corn
Hollywood Specialty	cocktail hot dogs
Satan's Tool	fork
Silver Pool	spoon
Woodpeckers	toothpicks
Survival of Ocean Waves	water
Gurgly Broth	Kool Aid
Greasy Wheat	bread and butter
Salty Log	pretzel sticks
Sweet Little Helper	mints
Over the Rainbow	rainbow sherbet
Golden Sliver	carrot sticks
Green Jungle	salad
Stained Glass	jello
Lucy, Linas, Charley Brown	peanuts
Strings and Things	spaghetti and sauce

Breakfast Come-As-You-Are Party

Invite the class to breakfast the morning after a big school event or on a day when there is no school. A video tape of the school event provides amusing entertainment for the party guests.

Age

9-14 years

Invitations

Make an invitation in the shape of a cereal box, cup or doughnut. Provide all of the party information and ask the guests to dress for breakfast.

Activities

Replay the video tape of the night-before school activity.

Play a game of charades.

Set up 4 or 5 board games for use as desired by the guests.

Party Foods

Fruits and juices

Yogurt sprinkled with granola

Puffy Pancakes, see page 178

Make-your-own omelets

Bacon and sausage

Graland Country Biscuits, see page 179

Hot chocolate or milk

MERRY BITS

Literary Party

Age
10-13 years

Invitations
Write the invitation on a paper bookmark. Tell the guests to come dressed as their favorite character from a book or a play. Also, tell them to be prepared to give a 2-3 minute presentation depicting their chosen character. Ask the guests to keep their choice of character confidential so that the other party guests will be surprised.

Favors
Books
Bookplates
Book jackets
Bound blank books

Decorations
Arrange a stage for the character presentations. This can be done outdoors by using badminton stakes decorated with balloons and crepe paper or indoors by running crepe paper streamers from ceiling to floor to outline a stage.

Activities
Allow each guest to present his or her character on the stage which has been designed for that use. The remaining guests watch the presentation and try to guess the identity of the character.

Party Foods
Prepare box lunches or suppers which can be eaten after the characters make their presentations. Place a bookplate with a guest's name on each box.

PARITY BITS

All of the recipes in this book have been tested in Denver—the "Mile-High City"—which is 5,280 feet above sea level. In Parity Bits, there are hints for converting other recipes for use at varying altitudes. For busy cooks who must frequently revise recipes to fit available ingredients, this chapter also includes measure equivalents, ingredient equivalents and ingredient substitutions.

PARITY BITS

Ingredient Substitutions

broth
1 cup broth = 1 cup water + 1 teaspoon granular stock base or 1 bouillon cube

chocolate
1 ounce unsweetened chocclate = 3 tablespoons cocoa + 1 tablespoon butter or margarine

1 ounce semi-sweet chocolate = 1 ounce unsweetened chocolate + 4 teaspoons sugar

dried foods, herbs and spices
1 part dry = 3 parts fresh

eggs
1 whole egg for custards and sauces = 2 egg yolks

1 whole egg for thickening = 1 tablespoon cornstarch or 2 tablespoons flour

flours
1 cup cake flour = 1 cup minus 2 tablespoons all-purpose flour

1 cup all-purpose flour = 1 cup cornmeal

1 cup all-purpose flour = 1½ cups rye flour

1 cup all-purpose flour = ¾ cup + 2 tablespoons whole-wheat flour or graham flour

garlic
1 clove fresh garlic = ⅛ teaspoon garlic powder

ginger
1 tablespoon candied ginger = 1 slice fresh ginger root or ¼ teaspoon powdered ginger

leavening agents
1 teaspoon baking powder = ¼ teaspoon baking soda + ½ cup sour milk, yogurt, or buttermilk. Reduce liquid in recipe by ½ cup.

1 teaspoon baking powder = ⅓ teaspoon baking soda + ½ teaspoon cream of tartar

milk products
1 cup whole milk = ½ cup evaporated milk + ½ cup water

1 cup whole milk = 1 cup reconstituted non-fat dry milk + 2 tablespoons butter or margarine

1 cup buttermilk = 1 cup yogurt or 1 cup sour milk

1 cup sour milk or buttermilk = 1 tablespoon lemon juice or vinegar + warm milk to make 1 cup. Let stand 5 minutes.

1 cup light cream or half and half = 1 cup evaporated milk

1 cup heavy cream, not for whipping = ¾ cup milk + ⅓ cup butter or margarine

1 cup sour cream for dips = 1 cup creamed cottage cheese puréed in blender with 1 tablespoon lemon juice

1 cup sour cream for dips = 1 cup yogurt + 2 tablespoons mayonnaise

1 cup sour cream for cooking = ¾ cup sour milk or buttermilk + ⅓ cup butter or margarine

1 cup sour cream for cooking = ½ cup evaporated milk + 1 tablespoon mild vinegar. Let stand 5 minutes.

1 cup yogurt = 1 cup buttermilk, or 1 cup sour milk or 1 cup sour cream

onions 1 medium onion = 1 tablespoon chopped dehydrated onion

shortening and fats 1 cup butter or margarine = 1 cup hydrogenated shortening + ½ teaspoon salt

1 cup butter or margarine = ⅞ cup cooking oil

sweeteners 1 cup honey = 1¼ cups granulated sugar + ¼ cup liquid

1 cup granulated sugar for cakes and cookies = ⅞ cup honey. Reduce oven temperature 25° F.

1 cup granulated sugar for bread and rolls = 1 cup honey. Reduce oven temperature 25° F.

1 cup granulated sugar = ½ cup maple syrup + ¼ cup corn syrup. Reduce liquid in recipe by 2 tablespoons and reduce oven temperature 25° F.

1 cup granulated sugar = 1 cup corn syrup. Reduce liquid in recipe by ¼ cup.

1 cup granulated sugar = 1 cup packed brown sugar

1 cup granulated sugar, not for baking = 1¾ cups powdered sugar.

thickening agents To thicken 1 cup liquid to a medium consistency use:
    2 tablespoons all purpose flour or
    1 tablespoon cornstarch or
    3 egg yolks or
    2 teaspoons arrowroot starch or
    4 teaspoons quick tapioca or
    4 teaspoons cream of wheat or rice

tomatoes 1 cup tomato juice = ½ cup tomato sauce + ½ cup water

1 cup catsup or chili sauce = 1 cup tomato sauce + ½ cup sugar + 2 tablespoons vinegar

yeast 1 packet dry active yeast = 1 pack quick rise yeast. Reduce rising time by 50%.

PARITY BITS

Ingredient Equivalents

almonds, shelled	4 ounces = 1 cup
almonds, unshelled	1 pound = 1¼ cups
apples, fresh	1 pound = 3 cups sliced
apples, dried	1 pound = 5 cups cooked
apricots, dried	1 pound = 3 cups cooked
bananas	1 pound or 3 medium = 1 cup mashed or 2½ cups sliced
beans, dried	1 pound = 6 cups cooked
beans, fresh green	1 pound = 3½ cups cooked
blueberries, fresh	1 pound = 4 cups
broccoli, fresh	1 pound = 5 cups cooked
butter or margarine	1 pound = 2 cups 1 stick = ½ cup
cabbage	1 pound or 1 small head = 5 cups shredded
carrots	1 pound or 6-8 medium = 3 cups shredded or 2½ cups chopped
cauliflower	1 pound = 5 cups cooked
celery	1 pound = 4½ cups chopped
cherries, dark sweet	1 pound = 2 cups, pitted
cheese, Cheddar or Swiss	1 pound = 4 cups grated
cheese, cottage	1 pound = 2 cups
chocolate	1 square = 1 ounce
coconut, shredded	1 pound = 4-5 cups
cornmeal	1 pound = 3 cups
cranberries	1 pound = 3 cups cooked
cream, whipping	1 cup = 2 cups whipped
crumbs, bread	1 slice = ¾ cup soft or ¼ cup dry
crumbs, Saltines	28 crackers = 1 cup finely crushed
crumbs, rich round	24 crackers = 1 cup finely crushed
crumbs, graham	14 squares = 1 cup finely crushed
dates	1 pound = 2 cups chopped, pitted
eggs	2 large = 3 small
flour, all-purpose	1 pound = 4 cups, sifted
flour, cake	1 pound = 4¾ - 5 cups, sifted

flour, whole-wheat	1 pound = 3½ cups, unsifted
garlic	1 clove = ¼ teaspoon, minced
grapes	1 pound = 2¾ cups
green pepper	1 medium = 1 cup chopped
lemons	1 medium = 3 tablespoons juice 1 medium = 2 teaspoons grated peel
lettuce	1 medium head = 5 cups torn leaves
limes	1 medium = 2 tablespoons juice 1 medium = 1½ teaspoons grated peel
macaroni	1 cup = 2½ cups cooked
meat, raw boneless	1 pound = 2 cups cooked, chopped
meat, cooked	1 pound = 3 cups chopped
meat, bone-in	1 pound = ¼-½ cup cooked, chopped
mushrooms	1 pound = 5-6 cups sliced 1 pound = 2 cups cooked
onions	1 medium = ½ cup chopped
oranges	1 medium or 6 ounces = ¼-⅓ cup juice 1 medium = 4 teaspoons grated peel
peaches, pears	1 medium or 4 ounces = ½ cup sliced
popcorn	¼ cup = 5 cups popped
potatoes	1 pound or 3-4 medium = 3 cups chopped = 2 cups mashed
raisins	1 pound = 3 cups
rhubarb	1 pound = 4 cups chopped
rice, regular long grain	1 cup = 3 cups cooked
rice, quick	1 cup = 2 cups cooked
spinach, fresh	1 pound or 12 cups = 1½ cups cooked
strawberries	1 pint basket = 3 cups whole = 2 cups sliced = 1½ cups pureed
sugar, brown	1 pound = 2¼ cups packed
sugar, granulated	1 pound = 2 cups
sugar, powdered	1 pound = 3½ cups, sifted
tomatoes	1 pound or 4 medium = 2 cups chopped
walnuts	1 pound in shell = 1½ cups shelled

PARITY BITS

Equivalent Measures

Dash	⅛ teaspoon
1 teaspoon	⅓ tablespoon
1 tablespoon	3 teaspoons
1 ounce, liquid	2 tablespoons
¼ cup	4 tablespoons or 2 ounces
⅓ cup	5 tablespoons + 1 teaspoon or 2¾ ounces
1 cup	16 tablespoons or 8 ounces
1 pint	2 cups or 16 ounces
1 quart	4 cups or 2 pints or 32 ounces
1 gallon	4 quarts or 16 cups or 128 ounces
¼ pound	4 ounces
½ pound	8 ounces
1 pound	16 ounces

High Altitude Cooking and Baking Tips

general comments

Do not assume that a sea level recipe will fail when prepared at higher altitudes. In general, the more complicated the recipe, the greater are the chances of failure. Cake recipes, for example, are much more difficult to adapt than recipes for muffins, biscuits or quick breads.

It is best to try a favorite sea level recipe without alteration before experimenting with possible adaptation methods.

cooking

At higher altitudes, where atmospheric pressure is lower, water boils at lower temperatures. The boiling point of water is approximately 1° F. lower for each increase of 550 feet in altitude.

Foods cooked over or in boiling water will take longer to cook at high altitudes than at sea level. For example, a 3-minute egg at sea level will take 4 minutes to cook at 5,000 feet.

If a particular food requires a prolonged cooking period, additional water may be needed.

Cooking time may have to be increased by 15% to 25%.

Sugar mixtures such as syrups, candies and jellies concentrate more rapidly at high altitudes. Therefore, they require less cooking time. Reduce cooking temperature by about 2° F. for each 1,000 feet of increased altitude.

baking

Cornstarch or flour-based cream fillings, sauces and puddings should be prepared over low but direct heat rather than in a double boiler. Because of the lower boiling point of water, the temperature in a double boiler may not be hot enough to cook the mixture properly, and it may not thicken.

When slow cookers are used, increase the recipe temperature by 15° to 25° F. and avoid removing the cover of the cooker. Thaw all foods completely before starting to cook.

Deep-fat frying temperatures should be decreased by about 3° F. for each 1,000 feet to prevent food from overcooking on the outside while undercooking on the inside.

The reduced air pressure at high altitudes causes leavened batters and doughs to rise faster than they do at sea level.

For baked goods, begin recipe adjustment by first reducing the leavening agent, such as baking powder, baking soda or cream of tartar. Liquid, flour or sugar adjustment may not be necessary after the leavening has been changed. This can be determined only by trial and error.

Avoid overbeating whole eggs, yolks or whites when eggs are used as a leavening agent in a recipe.

Because yeast dough rises faster at high altitudes, the flavor and gluten do not always develop properly. Punch down yeast doughs twice rather than once to improve the texture and the flavor.

Oven temperature will need to be increased when baking at high altitudes.

High Altitude Adjustments for Sea Level Recipes

	At 3,000 feet	At 5,000 feet	At 7,000 feet
For each teaspoon of baking powder, baking soda or cream of tartar in the recipe, decrease same by:	⅛ teaspoon	⅛-¼ teaspoon	¼-½ teaspoon
For each cup of liquid in the recipe, increase same by:	1-2 tablespoons	2-4 tablespoons	3-4 tablespoons
For each cup of flour in the recipe, increase same by:	no increase	1 tablespoon	2 tablespoons
For each cup of sugar in the recipe, decrease same by:	0-1 tablespoon	0-2 tablespoons	1-3 tablespoons
Increase the recipe baking temperature by:	15° F.	15°-25° F.	25° F.
Approximate temperature at which water boils:	206.5° F.	202.6° F.	199.2° F.

Contributors:

Dorcas Albaugh
Linda Alcott
Claudia Alexander
Craig Allen
Karen Allen
Sally Allen
Lieba Alpert
Carol Altman
Connie Ankelein
Christian Anschutz
Libby Anschutz
Nancy Anschutz
Sarah Anschutz
Mrs. Steven B. Armstrong
Marilyn Atler
Deanna Austin
Gaetano Austin
Adam Averbach
Linda Averbach
Rosie Backes
Florence Baker
Marlin Barad
Jessica Bard
Elaine Barkin
Suky Barkin
Joan Baronberg
Joan Barton
Jan Baucum
Eric Baumheier
David Beasley
Leslie Beasley
Susan Beasley
Betsy Beatty
Faye Bender
Marge Bender
Lucy Benedict
Patsy Benedict
Denise Bennett
Laura Benson
Joan Betz
Marjorie Beusse
Denese Bjornson
Kim Bleakley
Nicole Bleakley
Phyllis Bollman
Kathy Borgen
Carolyn Borus
Jean Bright
Jody Broughton
Linda Broughton
Lindsay Broughton
Chris Brown
Knobby Brown
Margaret Brown
Wava Brown
Betty Brownson
Edie Buchanan
Sarah Buchanan
Aaron Burgamy
Dana Busch
Joan Byrne
Sue Byrne
Constance Cain
Joann Cannon
Charla Cannon
Jan Cantrill

Hilary Carlson
Kathy Carty-Mullen
David Caulkins
Ellie Caulkins
Mary Caulkins
Max Caulkins
Bev Chew
Erika Chiles
Wendy Christensen
Snooky Claussen
Dorothy S. Coakley
Elizabeth Cohen
Leslie Cohen
Mareen Comi
Shannon Connery
Sharon Cook
Zabelle Cook
Mary Corson
Grandma Covey
T. Cox
Natalie Cross
Jill Crow
Mrs. Michael Cudahy, Jr.
Clara Cytron
Jane Dahlstrom-Quinn
Vivian David
Brett DeBoer
Kathryn Dines
Jane Dodd
Katharine Dodge
Mary Dominick
Meg Dorn
Maureen Douglass
Sara Drucker
Lara Duboff
Dre Dufford-Anjo
Marlene Edgerly
Hilda Eichenberger
Nan Eklund
Charlie Eldridge
Sharon Elfenbein
Timothy Elfenbein
Carol Elliott
Donald Elliott
Mary Eiseman
Ginny Ennis
Alandra Epperson
Gordon R. Epperson
Laura Epperson
Pat Epperson
Susan Epstein
Rosemary Esty
Regina Falbo
Cathy Falk
Chris Fascilla
Cindy Ferguson
Sharon Ferlic
Suzanne Ferlic
Violet Fisher
Joan Flautt
Carolyn Fodrea
Greg Fodrea
Marilyn Marranzino Foster
Karen Frankel
Nancy Franks
Barbara Freeman

Andy Friedman
Susan Friedman
Patricia Gabow
Deborah Gaensbauer
Jamie Gaensbauer
Judith Gallegos
Faye Gardenswartz
Peltner Garnet
Charles Gates
Mrs. Charles Gates
Susie Ganzenmuller
Andrew Givens
Gary Givens
Judy Givens
Katherine Givens
Susan Givens
Fred Glick
Dianna Goldberg
Linda Goldstein
Karen Goodman
Michelle Goodman
Pat Goodman
Ruth Gorham
Karen Gralow
Zell Greene
Holly Grogan
Colette Guiberteau
Linda Gutin
Pat Hall
Anne Halverson
Barbara Hamilton
Barbara Hamman
Richard Hamman
Kay Hanson
Melissa Hart
Jennifer Hatcner
Norma Heinschel
Sara Heitler
Susan Heitler
Carol Heller
David Heller
Betty Hemmel
Kitty Henry
Jeannie Herrick-Stare
Judy Hertz
Marc Hertz
A. Barry Hirschfeld, Sr.
Arlene Hirschfeld
Barry Hirschfeld
Dorothy Hirschfeld
Hayden Hirschfeld
Mary Jo Hitchens
Sarah Hite
Diane Hoagland
Kimberly Hodge
Eula Hoff
Elizabeth Holman
Libba Holman
Rebecca Holman
Robert Holman
Missy Hoster
Cheryle Houlihan
Beth Hower
Karen Howsam
Harriet Hull
Donna Hultin

Julie Hunter
Carl Hutchins
Diane Huttner
Julie Huttner
Michael Huttner
Stephanie Huttner
Cheryl Issel
Betty Jeffries
Marty Jensen
Cindy Jessop
Gretchen Johnson
Jennifer Johnson
Julie Johnson
Kate Johnson
Kathy Johnson
Nancy Johnson
Kathryn Johnston
Martina Jones
Mary Jones
Peter Jones
Ainsley Kasten
Lauren Kasten
Mallary Kasten
Elise Katch
Charlotte Katz
Fred Katz
Gail Katz
Eileen Kay
Brad Keller
Debbie Keller
Jonathan Keller
Lilo Kinaman
Urling Kingery
Wally Kennaugh
Priscilla Kirshbaum
Ginny Kitch
Joe Kitch
Marilyn Kitch
Jeannie Kithil
Lisa Klapper
Betty Klemmer
Phyllis Knight
Chase Knott
Julie Konrad
Cathy Kosal
Evelyn Kroymann
Alice Laber
Evelyne Lafond
Doris Lane
Ed Lane
Margi Lane
Gay Lasher
Eleanor Lauer
Bev Levine
Bonnie Levitan
Valerie Lewis
Karen Lichtenstein
Ulla Lidman
Gutin Lindu
Amy Lipschuetz
Sallie Lipschuetz
Paulette Louie
Nancy Lubchenco
Janice Lane Lucas
Thomas Lucas
Alex MacPhee

Lois MacPhee
Jan Mallory
Laraine Mandel
Brian Mankwitz
Brooke Mankwitz
Joni Mankwitz
Pam Marcum
Dianne Mariash
Pasquale Marranzino
Chartan Martin
Joyce Martin
Rich Martin
Sister Julie Mary
Barbara Polnick Maryatt
Jenny Matthews
Linda Matthews
Linda McCabe
Carol McCain
Jan McCulloch
Mary McGuire
Peg McKechnie
Peter McLaughlin
Lynne McMurtry
Marilyn McWilliams
Wilma Megill
Carolyn Miller
Frederick Miller
Ida Miller
Joanna Miller
Nancy Miller
Rachel Miller
Mrs. Thomas Mills, Jr.
Genca Mischke
Jan Mitchell
Michelle Mixson
Cheston Mizel
Courtney Mizel
Hadley Moore
Gegertha Mozia
Nancy Mullen
Rosemarie Murane
Janie Narcisi
Barbara Neider
Laurie Nelson
Nancy Neusteter
Claudia Newcomb
Lavern Newton
Edmond Noel
Johanna Noel
Linda Ferguson Norton
Barbara O'Shaughnessy
Wendy Oaks
Karen Oldham
Nancy Orcutt
Jan Orsini
The Overy Family
Elizabeth Owen
Pauline Owen
Mrs. Pauline Owens
Langdon Page
Mrs. Horace Palmerone
Judy Pappas
Judy Parcel
Lucile Parker
Nancy Parker
Elizabeth Peck

Grace Peck
Mary Peck
Vonnee Pell
Mary Perry
Ann Petkun
Harry Pforzheimer
Pam Powell
Judy Prakken
Judy Prasad
Mike Prasad
Susie Precourt
Marilyn Press
Betsy Price
Nancy Priest
Erin Pritchard
Judy Proctor
Mary Pugh
E.J. Pulis
Karen Quandt
Donald Quinn
Gayle Quinn
Barbara Radosevich
Mrs. Donald Raudenbush
Gayle Renick
Jill Renick
Michele Right
Ron Ritchhart
Elizabeth Robbins
Mary Robbins
Chris Roberts
Nichole Roberts
Peggy Robertson
Jill Robinson
Candi Rogers
Mrs. Walter Rosenberry
Sharon Sadlak
Ann Salyards
Jane Sanders
Jennifer Sansing
Kendall Sansing
Dorothy Schilling
Marie Schilling
Carol Schmidt
Dee Schranz
Tanna Schwarz
Thelma Schwarz
Cindy Scott
Nancy Scott
Nicole Seeds
Gretchen Shaffer
Diane Shafroth
Kathleen Sheldon
Mrs. Harris Sherman
Valerie Francis Simons
Nathalie Simsak
Jane Sindon
Richard Sindon
David Singer
Sylvia Singer
Laura Snapp
Judith Snyder
Mary Ellen Snyder
Margaret Spencer
Gene Spiritus
Tom Stahl
Kit Stanford

Barbara Stanton
Louise Stanton
Steven Stearns
Brian Stein
Karen Stein
Anna Steinbrecher
Ruth Stielstra
Carole Stolper
Elaine Stolper
Lisa Stolper
Jean Sullivan
Judith Sullivan
Ladawn Sullivan
Ellen Susman
Margaret Tennille
Jane Thalman
Don Thomas
Kate Toll
Barbara Reed Tolve
Kristin Tracy
Mary Trescott
Betty Tuchman
Ilga Tyler
Kresta Tyler
Addie Valentine
Kimberly Valentine
Muffy Valentine
Dorothy Van Vleet
Beth Van De Water
Karen Van De Water
Beth Vinton
Cynthia Vivian
Alexander Volpe
Barbara Volpe
Lane Volpe
Les Volpe
Diane Vosilus
Robert Vosilus
Barb Wagner
Greg Waldbaum
Roberta Waldbaum
Gert Waldman
Pamela Warner
Janet Warren
Eugenie Waters
Molly Waters
Andrea Watson
Connie Watts
Polly Weil
Gail Weingast
Diane Duke Whitfield
Joy Wilhelm
Susan Willson
Lisa Woodman
Jackie Wylde
Jan York
Christine Yoshinaga
Karen Zimmerman
Sara Zimmerman
Ali Zinn
Gus Zinn

INDEX

A Cake for All Seasons, 41
Acknowledgements, 5
A Different Rice, 167
A Favorite Snack, 184
Almond(s)
    Almond Cocoa Balls, 194
    Almond Cookies, 195
    Almond Meringue Bars, 198
    Almond Shells, 209
    Walnut and Almond Torte, 110
Any Season Chicken Salad, 139
Appetizers, See Hors d'Oeuvres and Appetizers
Apple(s)
    A Favorite Snack, 184
    Apple Annie Pancakes, 178
    Apple Cake, 171
    Apple Tart, 96
    Apple-Filled Squash, 169
    Breakfast Cookies, 179
    Hot Apple Wine, 118
    Pork Chops and Apples, 162
    Waldorf Chicken Salad, 141
Apricot(s)
    Apricot Rice, 40
    Lamb With Apricots, 97
Artichoke(s)
    Artichoke and Oyster Soup, 66
    Cañon Salad, 124
    Chicken and Artichoke Casserole, 157
    Flagstaff Casserole, 18
Asparagus With Olive Oil, Steamed, 31
Avocado
    Avocado and Papaya Salad, 112
    Avocado Dressing, 124
    Caviar Supreme, 14
    Guacamole-Tortilla Sandwiches, 136
    Palm Hearts, Avocado and Lettuce Salad, 44
    Pueblo Cream, 29
    Red Cabbage Salad, 149
Backpacker's Delight, 198
Bacon
    BLT Pitas, 135
    Breakfast Sandwich, 179
    Breakfast Treat, 180
    Cheese Dreams, 189
    Cheese Tart, 164
    Cheesy Bacon Snack, 187
    Green Onion Cakes, 89
    Stuffed Figs, 13
Baked Cheese and Ham Sandwiches, 118
Baked Honey Chicken, 157
Baked Pineapple with Sauce Natillas, 116
Baked Rice, 28
Baked Snapper on Lettuce, 31
Baked Stuffed Fish, 150
Banana(s)
    Banana Ginger Ale, 190
    Banana Split Snack, 184
    Cold Weather Fruit Cups, 184
    Fresh Banana Chutney, 99
    Graland Country Biscuits, 179
    Orange Delight, 191
    Peanut Butter and Banana Snack, 185
    Peanut Butter Banana Cupcakes, 183
    Wow Cow, 191
    Yummy Banana Muffins, 184
Barbecue
    Barbecue in a Cup, 189
    Barbecue Sauce, 109
    Barbecued Leg of Lamb, 49
    Brisket of Beef with Barbecue Sauce, 109
Barley and Mushrooms, 49
Basic Italian Sauce, 153
Basiled Vegetables, 68
Basque Cassoulet, 160
Bean Sprout and Carrot Salad, 105
Bean Sprout Salad, 90
Beans
    Basque Cassoulet, 160
    Sausage and Bean Chowder, 147
    Western Baked Beans, 121
Bearnaise Cream Sauce, 68
Beef
    Beef Rolls, 12
    Beefy Sandwiches, 138
    Braised Tongue, 71
    Brisket of Beef with Barbecue Sauce, 109
    Cabernet Pot Roast, 154
    Carpaccio, 36
    Cowgirl Casserole, 155
    Denver Beef, 74
    Eldorado Beef Casserole, 156
    Flank Steak in Mushroom Sauce, 156
    Green Chile Stew, 112
    Here's The Beef Sandwiches, 119
    Lasagne Pie, 163
    Lemon Sirloin Steak, 123
    Make-Ahead Beef Wellingtons, 67
    Mexican Beef Soup, 146
    Pepper Beef with Sweet and Sour Sauce, 91
    Steak Magnifique, 154
    Stir-Fry Beef and Vegetables, 154
    Stuffed Grape Leaves, 84
    Szechwan Beef, 92
    Taco Pie, 155
    Tortilla-Wrapped Flank Steak, 137
    Tournedos of Beef with Roquefort Sauce, 95
Beer Batter Fried Fish, 150
Beet and Watercress Salad, 62
Beet Soup, Cold, 131
Belgian Endive and Hot Walnut Salad, 68
Best of the Butter Cookies, 194
Beverages
    Banana Ginger Ale, 190
    Country Lane Hot Chocolate, 120
    Fresh Fruit Fizz, 190
    High Energy Punch, 134
    Hot Apple Wine, 118
    Hot Foamy Lemonade, 191
    Kir Double Royale, 20
    Milk-With-A-Punch, 18
    Orange Delight, 191
    Peachy Cooler, 191
    Red Raspberry Rouser, 191
    Wow Cow, 191
Bibb Lettuce Salad with Roquefort Cheese Dressing, 75
Biscuits, 176
Biscuits, Graland Country, 179
Black Bottom Pie, 61
Blender Potato Bake, 166
BLT Pitas, 135
Blue River Liver, 161
Blueberries
    Blueberry Cake, 122
    Blueberry Chicken, 43
    Reversible Cobbler, 173
    Summer Berries, 47
Braised Quail, 63
Braised Scallions, 38
Braised Tongue, 71
Brandied Hearts of Palm, 80
Breads
    Biscuits, 176
    Cinnamon Pitas, 21
    Corn Pone Piggies, 175
    Crunchy Bread, 182
    Filled Corn Muffins, 124
    Graland Country Biscuits, 179
    Herbed Pita Toast, 26
    Muffins, 175
    Overnight French Toast, 178
    Pumpkin Bread, 176
    Strawberry Bread, 19
    Sunflower Seed Bread, 182
    Yummy Banana Muffins, 184
Breakfast
    Apple Annie Pancakes, 178
    Biscuits, 176
    Breakfast Cookies, 179
    Breakfast Sandwiches, 179
    Breakfast Treat, 180
    Coconut Caramel Toast, 180
    Corn Pone Piggies, 175
    Crunchy Bread, 182
    Easy Crepes, 176
    Graland Country Biscuits, 179
    Great Granola, 181
    Muffins, 175
    Overnight French Toast, 178
    Pancakes or Waffles, 173
    Peanut Butter Raisin Toast, 180
    Picture-Frame Egg, 181
    Puffy Pancakes, 178
    Pumpkin Pancakes with Sautéed Apples, 174
    Sunflower Seed Bread, 182
    Surprise Doughnuts, 180
    Toast Toppers, 180
    Yummy Baked Eggs, 181

Yummy Banana Muffins, 184
Breckenridge Pineapple
    Pudding, 166
Brisket of Beef with Barbecue
    Sauce, 109
Broccoli Salad, Marinated, 144
Brochettes of Shrimp and
    Zucchini, 40
Broiled Fish with Dill, 149
Broiled Sherried Tomatoes, 170
Brownie Torte, 125
Brownies, German Chocolate, 130

Brunch
    Baked Pineapple with Sauce
        Natillas, 116
    Breckenridge Pineapple
        Pudding, 166
    Brunch Pie, 164
    Cheese Tart, 164
    Chocolate Tea Cake, 19
    Cinnamon Pitas, 21
    Coffee Cake, 175
    Easy Crepes, 176
    Easy Sopaipillas, 116
    Egg Curry, 20
    Filled Corn Muffins, 124
    Flagstaff Casserole, 18
    Lasagne Pie, 163
    Milk-With-A-Punch, 18
    Poppy Seed Cake, 21
    Potato Crust Quiche, 165
    Pumpkin Bread, 176
    Spinach and Sausage
        Frittata, 165
    Strawberry Bread, 19
    Tofu Enchiladas, 164
Brussels Sprouts with Chestnuts, 95
Brussels Sprouts with Herb Butter, 72
Bulgur Pilaf, 86
Buttered Egg Noodles, 46

Cabbage
    Norwegian Slaw, 119
    Pineapple and Cabbage
        Salad, 148
    Red Cabbage Salad, 149
Cabernet Pot Roast, 154

Cakes and Tortes
    A Cake For All Seasons, 41
    Apple Cake, 171
    Blueberry Cake, 122
    Brownie Torte, 125
    Chocolate Pudding Cake, 171
    Chocolate Tea Cake, 19
    Coconut-Carrot Cupcakes, 183
    Coffee Cake, 175
    Peanut Butter Banana
        Cupcakes, 183
    Poppy Seed Cake, 21
    Pound Cake, 41
    Saronno Torte, 24
    Sesame Pound Cake, 107
    Spice Cake, 100
    Walnut and Almond Torte, 110
Canon Salad, 124
Capillini with Caviar, 79

Carpaccio, 36

Carrot(s)
    Bean Sprout and Carrot
        Salad, 105
    Carrot and Celery Curls, 134
    Carrot and Lemon Salad, 21
    Carrot Pudding, 60
    Coconut-Carrot Cupcakes, 183
    Crudites, 94
    Honey-Glazed Carrots, 168
    Italian Marinated Carrots, 148
    Julienne of Carrots and Celery, 75
    Sweet and Sour Carrots, 55

Casseroles
    Basque Cassoulet, 160
    Chicken and Artichoke
        Casserole, 157
    Chicken Enchiladas, 115
    Chicken Parmigiana, 160
    Chile Relleno Casserole, 115
    Cowgirl Casserole, 155
    Eldorado Beef Casserole, 156
    Flagstaff Casserole, 18
    Lasagne Pie, 163
    Lemon Chicken and
        Potatoes, 156
    Mexican Chicken, 111
    Monterey Casserole, 189
    Pork Chops and Apples, 162
    Seafood Lasagne, 54
    Taco Pie, 155
Cauliflower Soup, 30

Caviar
    Capillini with Caviar, 79
    Caviar in Kumquat Shells, 13
    Caviar Supreme, 14
    Eggs-ecutive, The, 131

Cereal
    Great Granola, 181

Cheese
    Baked Cheese and Ham
        Sandwiches, 118
    Breakfast Cookies, 179
    Breakfast Sandwich, 179
    Cheese and Herb Soup, 146
    Cheese Dreams, 189
    Cheese Tart, 164
    Cheesy Bacon Snack, 187
    Crescent Sandwiches, 190
    Golden Cheese Crispies, 188
    Lasagne Pie, 163
    Monterey Casserole, 189
    Papaya Baked with Cheese, 25
    Ricotta Cheese Filling, 41
    Salad Gruyere, 45
    Tofu Enchiladas, 164
    Yummy Baked Eggs, 181
Cheesecake, 104
Cheesy Bacon Snack, 187

Chicken
    Any Season Chicken Salad, 139
    Baked Honey Chicken, 157
    Basque Cassoulet, 160
    Blueberry Chicken, 43

    Chicken and Artichoke
        Casserole, 157
    Chicken Curry, 98
    Chicken Enchiladas, 115
    Chicken in a Basket, 126
    Chicken Marsala, 158
    Chicken Parmigiana, 160
    Chicken Soup with Matzoh
        Balls, 108
    Chicken with Spinach and
        Linguine, 158
    Hawaiian Sandwich, 190
    Hearty Chicken Soup, 147
    Lemon Chicken and
        Potatoes, 156
    Lobster and Chicken
        Marengo, 37
    Mexican Chicken, 111
    Moroccan Bastillo, 16
    Oven-Fried Chicken, 159
    Peachy Chicken Salad, 129
    Picnic Chicken Salad, 140
    Rocky Ford Chicken Salad, 140
    Spiced Chicken Wings, 88
    Spicy Orange Chicken, 90
    Stir-Fry Cashew Chicken, 159
    Swiss Chicken, 159
    Waldorf Chicken Salad, 141
    Yakitori, 105
Chile Relleno Casserole, 115
Chinese Chews, 92
Chinese Fried Cookies, 92

Chocolate
    Almond Cocoa Balls, 194
    Backpacker's Delight, 198
    Black Bottom Pie, 61
    Brownie Torte, 125
    Chocolate Chip Meringues, 202
    Chocolate Cream Torte, 53
    Chocolate Crowns, 203
    Chocolate Filling, 57
    Chocolate Frosting, 41
    Chocolate Indulgence
        Cookies, 203
    Chocolate Kahlua Tarts, 210
    Chocolate Mousse, 209
    Chocolate Peanut Butter Play
        Dough, 188
    Chocolate Pots de Creme, 128
    Chocolate Pudding Cake, 171
    Chocolate Tea Cake, 19
    Country Lane Hot Chocolate, 120
    Extraordinary Chocolate
        Bars, 199
    Frozen Chocolate Mousse
        Torte, 76
    Fudgsicles, 187
    German Chocolate Brownies, 130
    Marie Antoinette's Lace
        Cookies, 205
    Opera House Pie, 38
    Outrageous Brownies, 200
    Toffee Bars, 119
    Turtle Temptations, 202
Chutney, Fresh Banana, 99

Chutney, Fresh mint, 99
Cinnamon Pitas, 21
Citrus Filling, 56
Coconut
    Backpacker's Delight, 198
    Chinese Fried Cookies, 92
    Coconut Caramel Toast, 180
    Coconut-Carrot Cupcakes, 183
    Spice Cake, 100
    Surprise Doughnuts, 180
Coconut-Carrot Cupcakes, 183
Coffee Cake, 175
Cold Weather Fruit Cups, 184
Colorado Corn Soup, 129
Columbine Consomme, 79
Confetti Pasta Salad, 143
Contributors, List of, 236
Cookie Bits, 193-210
Cookies and Bars
    Almond Cocoa Balls, 194
    Almond Cookies, 195
    Almond Meringue Bars, 198
    Almond Shells, 209
    Backpacker's Delight, 198
    Best of the Butter Cookies, 194
    Breakfast Cookies, 179
    Chinese Chews, 92
    Chinese Fried Cookies, 92
    Chocolate Chip Meringues, 202
    Chocolate Crowns, 203
    Chocolate Indulgence Cookies, 203
    Chocolate Kahlua Tarts, 210
    Currant Cookies, 204
    Easy Peanut Butter Cookies, 182
    English Tea Biscuits, 207
    Extraordinary Chocolate Bars, 199
    German Chocolate Brownies, 130
    Gingerbread Children and Their Friends, 207
    Granny's Ribbon Cane Syrup Cookies, 204
    Ischl Cookies, 208
    Italian Anise Cookies, 195
    Khourabia, 87
    Lemon Icebox Cookies, 206
    Marie Antoinette's Lace Cookies, 205
    Norwegian Cookies, 196
    Oatmeal-Raspberry Bars, 199
    Orange-Poppy Seed Cookies, 206
    Outrageous Brownies, 200
    Pecan Clouds, 196
    Plantation Brownies, 200
    Punch and Squish Oatmeal Cookies, 196
    Regal Tea Cookies, 208
    Shortbread Plus, 201
    Simply Shortbread, 201
    Soft Sugar Cookies, 205
    The Classic Gingersnap, 197
    Toffee Bars, 119
    Turtle Temptations, 202
    Walnut Jam Cookies, 197

Corn Custard, 43
Corn Muffins, Filled, 124
Corn Pone Piggies, 175
Corn Soup, Colorado, 129
Country Lane Hot Chocolate, 120
Cowgirl Casserole, 155
Crab
    Crab Gumbo, 146
    Marinated Crab Claws, 17
    Southwestern Sole with Crab Sauce, 23
Cream Cheese
    Cheesecake, 104
    Kennedy Crackers, 15
    Noodle Kugel, 109
    Stuffed Figs, 13
    Sweet Cheese Fondue, 65
    Zippity Do Dip, 186
Cream Fondue, 15
Cream of Salsa Soup, 111
Cream of Sorrel Soup, 93
Creamy Cucumber and Dill Filling, 127
Crepes, Easy, 176
Crescent Sandwiches, 190
Crudites, 94
Crunchy Bread, 182
Crustless Pumpkin Pie, 172
Cucumbers
    Creamy Cucumber and Dill Filling, 127
    Crudites, 95
    Cucumber Salad, 99
    Cucumber-Watercress Soup, 33
    Cucumbers in Cream, 95
    Sauteed English Cucumbers, 60
    Tabouleh Salad, 86
    Yogurt Soup, 87
Currant Cookies, 204
Curried Egg Salad Sandwiches, 138
Curry
    Chicken Curry, 98
    Curried Egg Salad Sandwiches, 138
    Egg Curry, 20
Denver Beef, 74
Desserts
    Baked Pineapple with Sauce Natillas, 116
    Cakes, See Cakes and Tortes
    Cheesecake, 104
    Chocolate Frosting, 41
    Chocolate Mousse, 209
    Chocolate Pots de Creme, 128
    Cookies, See Cookies and Bars
    Flan, 113
    Frozen Chocolate Mousse Torte, 76
    Frozen Pudding-wiches, 187
    Frozen Yogurt, 134
    Fruit, See Fruit, Mixed
    Fudgsicles, 187
    Great Grapes, 185
    Lemon Curd, 209

    Persimmon Pudding with Hard Sauce, 81
    Pies, See Pies and Tarts
    Pistachio-Almond Sundaes, 78
    Poached Pears with Raspberry Sauce, 69
    Pueblo Cream, 29
    Raspberries Sabayon, 50
    Reversible Cobbler, 173
    Sherry-Macaroon Freeze, 72
    Sopaipillas, Easy, 116
    Spiced Pecans, 132
    Strawberry-Orange Sorbet, 32
    Summer Berries, 47
    Sweet Cheese Fondue, 65
    Sweet Vermicelli Cake, 104
    Tarts, See Pies and Tarts
    White Chocolate Strawberries, 35
Dips, See Hors d'Oeuvres
Duck, Plum Good, 52
Durango Salad, 144
Easy Crepes, 176
Easy Peanut Butter Cookies, 182
Easy Sopaipillas, 116
Egg Curry, 20
Egg, Picture-Frame, 181
Eggplant
    Eggplant Caponata, 101
    Eggplant Relish, 15
    Eggplant with Sun-Dried Tomatoes, 47
    Lamb and Eggplant, 85
Eggs
    Curried Egg Salad Sandwiches, 138
    Egg Curry, 20
    Eggs-ecutive, The, 131
    Picture-Frame Egg, 181
    Scotch Eggs, 120
    Yummy Baked Eggs, 181
Eldorado Beef Casserole, 156
Elegant Bits, 11-81
Endive
    Belgian Endive and Hot Walnut Salad, 68
    Endive and Pomegranate Salad, 55
    Ham and Belgian Endive Roulade, 51
    Mushroom and Endive Cheese Bites, 13
English Tea Biscuits, 207
Equivalent Measures, 234
Equivalents, Ingredient, 231-233
Extraordinary Chocolate Bars, 199
Family Bits, 145-176
Fast Rhubarb Pie, 172
Fennel Salad on Tomato Slices, 26
Filled Corn Muffins, 124
Fillings
    Chocolate Filling, 57
    Citrus Filling, 56
    Ricotta Cheese Filling, 41
    Vanilla Filling, 57

Fish
    Baked Snapper on Lettuce, 31
    Baked Stuffed Fish, 150
    Beer Batter Fried Fish, 150
    Broiled Fish with Dill, 149
    Grilled Swordfish, 152
    Hot Tub Trout, 153
    Marinated Herring, 58
    Marinated Salmon Steaks, 152
    Salmon Florentine, 151
    Saute of Sole with Lemon, 152
    Southwestern Sole with Crab Sauce, 23
    Steamed Red Snapper, 150
    Swordfish Soup, 64
Flagstaff Casserole, 18
Flan, 113
Flank Steak in Mushroom Sauce, 156
Florentine Soup, 102
Fondue, Cream, 15
Fondue, Sweet Cheese, 65
French Peas, 80
French Toast, Overnight, 178
Fresh Fruit Fizz, 190
Fried Tomatoes with Parmesan Cheese, 170
Frosting, Chocolate, 41
Frozen Chocolate Mousse Torte, 76
Frozen Pudding-wiches, 187
Frozen Yogurt, 134
Fruit, See Specific Fruits
Fruits, Mixed
    Cold Water Fruit Cups, 184
    Fresh Fruit Fizz, 190
    Fruit Salad with Pecan Dressing, 122
    Honeyed Fruit Marnier, 132
    Identified Fruit Objects, 185
    Marmalade Melange, 128
Fudgsicles, 187
Garam Masala, 98
Garlic Mayonnaise, 142
German Chocolate Brownies, 130
Gingerbread Children and Their Friends, 207
Gingered Pork and Cauliflower, 91
Gingersnap, The Classic, 197
Global Bits, 83-116
Golden Cheese Crispies, 188
Graland Country Biscuits, 179
Granny's Ribbon Cane Syrup Cookies, 204
Granola, Great, 181
Grape Leaves, Stuffed, 84
Grapes, Great, 185
Grated Zucchini, 29
Green Beans
    Canon Salad, 124
    Green Beans with Hazelnuts, 168
    Green Beans with Walnuts and Feta, 130
    Italian Green Bean Filling, 127
    Steamed Green Beans and Turnips, 63

Green Chile
    Chicken Enchiladas, 115
    Chile Relleno Casserole, 115
    Eldorado Beef Casserole, 156
    Green Chile Stew, 112
    Mexican Chicken, 111
    Taco Pie, 155
Green Onion Cakes, 89
Green Pepper-Mushroom Medley, 168
Grilled Swordfish, 152
Ground Beef
    Barbecue in a Cup, 189
    Beefy Sandwiches, 138
    Cowgirl Casserole, 155
    Eldorado Beef Casserole, 156
    Lasagne Pie, 163
    Mexican Beef Soup, 146
    Monterey Casserole, 189
    Stuffed Grape Leaves, 84
    Taco Pie, 155
Guacamole Tortilla Sandwiches, 136
Ham
    Baked Cheese and Ham Sandwiches, 118
    Flagstaff Casserole, 18
    Ham and Belgian Endive Roulade, 51
    Ham Pin Wheel Sandwiches, 138
    Ham and Orange Salad, 141
Hard Sauce, 81
Hawaiian Sandwich, 190
Hazelnuts
    Green Beans with Hazelnuts, 168
    Ischl Cookies, 208
    Pork Tenderloin with Hazelnuts, 80
Hearts of Palm, Avocado and Lettuce Salad, 44
Hearts of Palm, Brandied, 80
Hearty Chicken Soup, 147
Herb Butter, 72
Herbed Pita Toast, 26
Here's The Beef Sandwiches, 119
Herring, Marinated, 58
High Altitude Adjustments for Sea Level Recipes, 235
High Altitude Cooking and Baking Tips, 234
High Energy Punch, 134
High Strawberry Pie, 172
Honey Nut Popcorn, 188
Honey-Glazed Carrots, 168
Honeyed Fruit Marnier, 132
Hors d'Oeuvres and Appetizers
    Beef Rolls, 12
    Carpaccio, 36
    Caviar in Kumquat Shells, 13
    Caviar Supreme, 14
    Cream Fondue, 15
    Eggplant Caponata, 101
    Eggplant Relish, 15
    Green Onion Cakes, 89
    Hummus with Pita Bread, 85
    Kennedy Crackers, 15

    Marinated Crab Claws, 17
    Marinated Herring, 58
    Melon and Prosciutto, 77
    Mexican Pinwheels, 114
    Moroccan Bastillo, 16-17
    Mushroom and Endive Cheese Bites, 13
    Snail and Walnut Stuffed Mushrooms, 13
    Spiced Chicken Wings, 88
    Stuffed Figs, 13
    Tomato-Shrimp Mold, 12
    Zippity Do Dip, 186
Hot and Sour Soup, 89
Hot Apple Wine, 118
Hot Foamy Lemonade, 191
Hot Tub Trout, 153
Hummus with Pita Bread, 85
Ice Cream
    Pistachio-Almond Sundaes, 78
    Sherry Macaroon Freeze, 72
Identified Fruit Objects, 185
Ingredient Equivalents, 231-233
Ingredient Substitutions, 230
Inventive Tarts, 56
Ischl Cookies, 208
Israeli Salad, 110
Italian Anise Cookies, 195
Italian Green Bean Filling, 127
Italian Marinated Carrots, 148
Italian Steamed Rice, 37
Jello, Rainbow, 186
Julienne of Carrots and Celery, 75
Kennedy Crackers, 15
Khourabia, 87
Kid Bits, 177-191
Kir Double Royale, 20
Lamb
    Barbecued Leg of Lamb, 49
    Lamb and Eggplant, 85
    Lamb Chops in Paper, 59
    Lamb Patties with Dill Sauce, 162
    Lamb with Apricots, 97
    Lemon Lamb Chops with Rice, 161
Lasagne Chips, 133
Lasagne Pie, 163
Lasagne, Seafood, 54
Leek Salad, 27
Leeks, Marinated, 48
Lemon
    Carrot and Lemon Salad, 21
    Hot Foamy Lemonade, 191
    Lemon Chicken and Potatoes, 156
    Lemon Consomme, 25
    Lemon Curd, 209
    Lemon Herbed New Potatoes, 166
    Lemon Icebox Cookies, 206
    Lemon Lamb Chops with Rice, 161
    Lemon Rice, 167
    Lemon Sirloin Steak, 123
Lemonade, Hot Foamy, 191

Lettuce and Orange Salad, 38
Lime Dressing, 140
Liver, Blue River, 161
Lobster and Chicken Marengo, 37
Make-Ahead Beef Wellingtons, 67
Mango-Tuna Spread, 139
Mangoes with Lime, 19
Marie Antoinette's Lace
    Cookies, 205

Marinades
    Grilled Swordfish, 152
    Lemon Sirloin Steak, 123
    Marinated Salmon Steaks, 152
    Steak Magnifique, 154
Marinated Broccoli Salad, 144
Marinated Crab Claws, 17
Marinated Herring, 58
Marinated Leeks, 48
Marinated Salmon Steaks, 152
Marmalade Melange, 128
Master Baking Mix, 174
Matzoh Balls, 108
Meats, See Specific Meats
Mediterranean Salad Pitas, 135
Melon and Prosciutto, 77
Melon Balls Melba, 123

Menus
    Armenian Buffet, 84
    Aspen Alfresco, 33
    Aspen-Turning Supper, 51
    Autumn Buffet, 54
    Blake Street Brunch, 20
    Bolder Boulder Breakfast, 18
    Boulder Tailgate Picnic, 118
    Bronco Tailgate Picnic, 120
    Celebration Dinner, 66
    Central City Supper, 36
    Cherry Creek Luncheon, 22
    Chinese Banquet, 88
    Concert in the Park Picnic, 129
    Fireside Dinner, 70
    French Dinner, 93
    Grand Lake Regatta Supper, 39
    Indian Dinner, 97
    Italian Dinner, 101
    Japanese Dinner, 105
    Jewish Family Dinner, 108
    Loveland Luncheon, 25
    Mexican Brunch, 114
    Mexican Dinner, 111
    Mountain Weekend Dinner, 27
    Picnic at the Zoo, 133
    Ranch Barbecue, 123
    Red Rocks Concert Picnic, 126
    Seventeenth Street Brown
        Bag, 131
    Springtime Supper, 30
    Stock Show Dinner, 73
    Summer Reunion Dinner, 42
    Symphony Supper, 45
    Tech Center Company Dinner, 58
    Telluride Barbecue, 48
    Upland Hunter's Dinner, 62
    Vail Apres Ski Dinner, 64

    Winter Carnival Dinner, 77
    Winter Holiday Dinner, 79
Merry Bits, 211-228
Mexican Beef Soup, 146
Mexican Chicken, 111
Mexican Pinwheels, 114
Milk-With-A-Punch, 18

Mint
    Fresh Mint Chutney, 99
    Lamb and Eggplant, 85
    Tabouleh Salad, 86

Mixes
    Basic Italian Sauce, 153
    Master Baking Mix, 174
    Stir-Fry Sauce Mix, 151
Monterey Casserole, 189
Moroccan Bastillo, 16
Muffins, 175
Muffins, Filled Corn, 124

Mushrooms
    Barley and Mushrooms, 49
    Flank Steak in Mushroom
        Sauce, 156
    Green Pepper-Mushroom
        Medley, 168
    Mushroom and Endive Cheese
        Bites, 13
    Snail and Walnut Stuffed
        Mushrooms, 13
Noodle Kugel, 109
Noodles, See Pasta
Norwegian Cookies, 196
Norwegian Slaw, 119
Oatmeal Cookies, Punch and
    Squish, 196
Oatmeal-Raspberry Bars, 199
Onion Cakes, Green, 89
Opera House Pie, 38

Orange(s)
    Ham and Orange Salad, 141
    Lettuce and Orange Salad, 38
    Orange Delight, 191
    Orange Salad Dressing, 38
    Orange-Glazed Pork Chops, 162
    Orange-Peanut Butter
        Sandwiches, 133
    Orange-Poppy Seed
        Cookies, 206
    Spicy Orange Chicken, 90
Oriental Shrimp Salad, 142
Oriental Tuna Spread, 139
Outrageous Brownies, 200
Oven-Fried Chicken, 159
Oven-Fried Potatoes, 167
Overnight French Toast, 178

Pancakes
    Apple Annie Pancakes, 178
    Pancakes or Waffles, 173
    Puffy Pancakes, 178
    Pumpkin Pancakes with Sauteed
        Apples, 174

Papaya
    Avocado and Papaya Salad, 112
    Papaya Baked with Cheese, 25

    Sauteed Papaya with Lime
        Juice, 168
Parity Bits, 229-235

Parsnips
    Parsnip Slaw, 149
    Parsnip Soup, 70
    Pureed Parsnips and Potatoes, 52

Parties, 211-228
    Airplane Party, 221
    Back To School Party, 220
    Backyard Campout, 225
    Beach Party, 213
    Break The Bank Party, 218
    Breakfast Come-As-You-Are
        Party, 227
    Clown Party, 214
    Field Day Party at the Park, 221
    Gingerbread House Party, 222
    Literary Party, 228
    Little Girls' Dress-Up Party, 215
    Man's Best Friend Party, 219
    Pirate Party, 216-217
    Prehistoric Party, 223
    Silly Supper, 226-227
    Space Party, 224
    Teddy Bears' Party, 212

Pasta
    Buttered Egg Noodles, 46
    Capillini with Caviar, 79
    Chicken with Spinach and
        Linguine, 158
    Lasagne Chips, 133
    Noodle Kugel, 109
    Pasta Primavera Salad, 143
    Pasta Salad, Confetti, 143
    Pasta with Pesto Sauce, 102
    Rice with Vermicelli, 71
    Seafood Lasagne, 54
    Shrimp and Pasta Salad, 144
    Sweet Vermicelli Cake, 104

Peach(es)
    Peachy Chicken Salad, 129
    Peachy Cooler, 191
    Rag Doll Salad, 185
    Sunny Side Up Peach Pie, 173

Peanut Butter
    A Favorite Snack, 184
    Chocolate Peanut Butter Play
        Dough, 188
    Easy Peanut Butter Cookies, 182
    Frozen Pudding-Wiches, 187
    Orange-Peanut Butter
        Sandwiches, 133
    Peanut Butter and Banana
        Snack, 185
    Peanut Butter Banana
        Cupcakes, 183
    Peanut Butter Raisin Toast, 180

Peanut(s)
    Chinese Fried Cookies, 92
    Durango Salad, 144
    Honey Nut Popcorn, 188
Pears with Raspberry Sauce,
    Poached, 69

Pea(s)
    Canon Salad, 124
    Durango Salad, 144
    French Peas, 80
Pecan(s)
    Pecan Clouds, 196
    Pecan Dressing, 122
    Spiced Pecans, 132
Pepper Beef with Sweet and Sour Sauce, 91
Persimmon Pudding with Hard Sauce, 81
Picnic Chicken Salad, 140
Picnics, See Portable Bits
Picture-Frame Egg, 181
Pie Crust, 100-Watt, 172
Pies and Tarts
    Almond Shells, 209
    Apple Tart, 96
    Black Bottom Pie, 61
    Chocolate Kahlua Tarts, 210
    Crustless Pumpkin Pie, 172
    Fast Rhubarb Pie, 172
    High Strawberry Pie, 172
    Inventive Tarts, 56
    Opera House Pie, 38
    Strawberry Tart, 44
    Sunny Side Up Peach Pie, 173
Pineapple
    Baked Pineapple with Sauce Natillas, 116
    Breckenridge Pineapple Pudding, 166
    Hawaiian Sandwich, 190
    High Energy Punch, 134
    Marmalade Melange, 128
    Oriental Tuna Spread, 139
    Pineapple and Cabbage Salad, 148
    Stir-Fry Shrimp and Pineapple, 151
Pistachio Soup, 39
Pistachio-Almond Sundaes, 78
Pita Bread
    BLT Pitas, 135
    Cinnamon Pitas, 21
    Herbed Pita Toast, 26
    Mediterranean Salad Pitas, 135
    Shrimp Pitas, 135
    Turkey Pitas, 136
Plantation Brownies, 200
Plum Good Duck, 52
Plum Soup, Chilled, 22
Poached Pears with Raspberry Sauce, 69
Poppy Seed(s)
    Orange-Poppy Seed Cookies, 206
    Poppy Seed Cake, 21
    Poppy Seed Dressing, 149
Pork
    Gingered Pork and Cauliflower, 91
    Hot and Sour Soup, 89
    Orange-Glazed Pork Chops, 162

    Pork Chops and Apples, 162
    Pork Tenderloin with Hazelnuts, 80
    Stir-Fry Pork, 163
Portable Bits, 117-144
Potato(es)
    Lemon Chicken and Potatoes, 156
    Lemon Herbed New Potatoes, 166
    Oven-Fried Potatoes, 167
    Potato Casserole, 167
    Potato Crust Quiche, 165
    Potato Latkes, 110
    Pureed Parsnips and Potatoes, 52
    Tarragon Sauteed New Potatoes, 31
Pound Cake, 41
Pueblo Cream, 29
Puffy Pancakes, 178
Pumpkin
    Crustless Pumpkin Pie, 172
    Pumpkin Bread, 176
    Pumpkin Pancakes with Sauteed Apples, 174
Punch and Squish Oatmeal Cookies, 196
Pureed Parsnips and Potatoes, 52
Quail, Braised, 63
Quiche
    Brunch Pie, 164
    Potato Crust Quiche, 165
Rag Doll Salad, 185
Rainbow Jello, 186
Raspberry(ies)
    Melon Balls Melba, 123
    Oatmeal-Raspberry Bars, 199
    Poached Pears with Raspberry Sauce, 69
    Raspberries Sabayon, 50
    Red Raspberry Rouser, 191
    Reversible Cobbler, 173
Red Cabbage Salad, 149
Regal Tea Cookies, 208
Reversible Cobbler, 173
Rice
    A Different Rice, 167
    Apricot Rice, 40
    Baked Rice, 28
    Italian Steamed Rice, 37
    Lemon Rice, 167
    Rice with Vermicelli, 71
    Shrimp and Rice Salad, 142
    Steamed Rice, 74
    Stuffed Grape Leaves, 84
    Wild Rice, 63
Ricotta Cheese Filling, 41
Rocky Ford Chicken Salad, 140
Rodeo Soup, 73
Roquefort Cheese Dressing, 75
Salad Dressings
    Avocado Dressing, 124
    Garlic Mayonnaise, 142
    Lime Dressing, 140
    Mint Dressing, 130

    Orange Salad Dressing, 38
    Pecan Dressing, 122
    Poppy Seed Dressing, 149
    Roquefort Cheese Dressing, 75
    Sherried Dressing, 65
Salad(s), Fruit
    Avocado and Papaya Salad, 112
    Fruit Salad with Pecan Dressing, 122
    Honeyed Fruit Marnier, 132
    Marmalade Melange, 128
    Melon Balls Melba, 123
    Pineapple and Cabbage Salad, 148
    Rag Doll Salad, 185
Salad(s), Main Course
    Any Season Chicken Salad, 139
    Ham and Orange Salad, 141
    Oriental Shrimp Salad, 142
    Pasta Salad, Confetti, 143
    Peachy Chicken Salad, 129
    Picnic Chicken Salad, 140
    Rocky Ford Chicken Salad, 140
    Shrimp and Pasta Salad, 144
    Shrimp and Rice Salad, 142
    Waldorf Chicken Salad, 141
Salad(s), Tossed
    Bibb Lettuce Salad with Roquefort Cheese Dressing, 75
    Canon Salad, 124
    Endive and Pomegranate Salad, 55
    Lettuce and Orange Salad, 38
    Palm Hearts, Avocado and Lettuce Salad, 44
    Spicy Spinach Salad, 148
    Strawberry and Spinach Salad, 24
Salad(s), Vegetable
    Bean Sprout and Carrot Salad, 105
    Bean Sprout Salad, 90
    Beet and Watercress Salad, 62
    Belgian Endive and Hot Walnut Salad, 68
    Carrot and Celery Curls, 134
    Carrot and Lemon Salad, 21
    Crudites, 94
    Cucumber Salad, 99
    Durango Salad, 144
    Fennel Salad on Tomato Slices, 26
    Green Beans with Walnuts and Feta, 130
    Israeli Salad, 110
    Italian Marinated Carrots, 148
    Leek Salad, 27
    Marinated Broccoli Salad, 144
    Norwegian Slaw, 119
    Parsnip Slaw, 149
    Pasta Primavera Salad, 143
    Red Cabbage Salad, 149
    Salad Gruyere, 45
    Sissar Salad, 86
    Stuffed Tomato Salad, 126
    Tabouleh Salad, 86

Vegetable Salad with Sherried Dressing, 65
Salami-Tortilla Roll-Ups, 136
Salmon Florentine, 151
Salmon, Marinated, 152
Sandwiches
  Baked Cheese and Ham Sandwiches, 118
  Beefy Sandwiches, 138
  BLT Pitas, 135
  Breakfast Sandwich, 179
  Cheese Dreams, 189
  Crescent Sandwiches, 190
  Curried Egg Salad Sandwiches, 138
  Guacamole-Tortilla Sandwiches, 136
  Ham Pin Wheel Sandwiches, 138
  Hawaiian Sandwich, 190
  Here's The Beef Sandwiches, 119
  Mango-Tuna Spread, 139
  Mediterranean Salad Pitas, 135
  Orange-Peanut Butter Sandwiches, 133
  Oriental Tuna Spread, 139
  Salami-Tortilla Roll-Ups, 136
  Shrimp Pitas, 135
  Soda Bread Sandwiches, 121
  The Eggs-ecutive, 131
  Tortilla-Wrapped Flank Steak, 137
  Tuna Tortillas, 137
  Turkey Pitas, 136
Saronno Torte, 24
Sauces
  Barbecue Sauce, 109
  Basic Italian Sauce, 153
  Bearnaise Cream Sauce, 68
  Hard Sauce, 81
  Herb Butter, 72
  Sauce Natillas, 116
  Stir-Fry Sauce Mix, 151
  Sweet and Sour Sauce, 91
Sausage
  Basque Cassoulet, 160
  Corn Pone Piggies, 175
  Hearty Chicken Soup, 147
  Sausage and Bean Chowder, 147
  Scotch Eggs, 120
  Shrimp and Sausage Arezzo, 78
  Spinach and Sausage Frittata, 165
Saute of Sole with Lemon, 152
Sauteed Cherry Tomatoes, 40
Sauteed English Cucumbers, 60
Sauteed Escarole and Red Peppers, 53
Sauteed Papaya with Lime Juice, 168
Scallions, Braised, 38
Scallops
  Scallops in Mushroom-Tomato Cream, 28
  Sea Scallops with Sake Sauce, 106
  Seafood Lasagne, 54

Scotch Eggs, 120
Sea Scallops with Sake Sauce, 106
Seafood Lasagne, 54
Sesame Pound Cake, 107
Sherried Dressing, 65
Sherry Macaroon Freeze, 72
Shortbread Plus, 201
Shortbread, Simply, 201
Shrimp
  Brochettes of Shrimp and Zucchini, 40
  Oriental Shrimp Salad, 142
  Seafood Lasagne, 54
  Shrimp and Pasta Salad, 144
  Shrimp and Rice Salad, 142
  Shrimp and Sausage Arezzo, 78
  Shrimp Pitas, 135
  Stir-Fry Shrimp and Pineapple, 151
  Tomato-Shrimp Mold, 12
Simply Shortbread, 201
Sissar Salad, 86
Snacks
  A Favorite Snack, 184
  Banana Split Snack, 184
  Carrot and Celery Curls, 134
  Cheesy Bacon Snack, 187
  Chocolate Peanut Butter Play Dough, 188
  Coconut-Carrot Cupcakes, 183
  Cold Weather Fruit Cups, 184
  Crunchy Bread, 182
  Easy Peanut Butter Cookies, 182
  Frozen Pudding-wiches, 187
  Frozen Yogurt, 134
  Fudgsicles, 187
  Golden Cheese Crispies, 188
  Great Granola, 181
  Great Grapes, 185
  Honey Nut Popcorn, 188
  Identified Fruit Objects, 185
  Lasagne Chips, 133
  Peanut Butter and Banana Snack, 185
  Peanut Butter Banana Cupcakes, 183
  Rag Doll Salad, 185
  Rainbow Jello, 186
  Spiced Pecans, 132
  Sunflower Seed Bread, 182
  Yummy Banana Muffins, 184
  Zippity Do Dip, 186
Snail and Walnut Stuffed Mushrooms, 13
Soda Bread Sandwiches, 121
Soft Sugar Cookies, 205
Sopaipillas, Easy, 116
Soups, Cold
  Chilled Plum Soup, 22
  Chilled Tomato-Dill Soup, 42
  Cold Beet Soup, 131
  Colorado Corn Soup, 129
  Cucumber-Watercress Soup, 33
  Lemon Consomme, 25

Pistachio Soup, 39
Yogurt Soup, 87
Soups, Hot
  Artichoke and Oyster Soup, 66
  Cauliflower Soup, 30
  Cheese and Herb Soup, 146
  Chicken Soup with Matzoh Balls, 108
  Columbine Consomme, 79
  Crab Gumbo, 146
  Cream of Salsa Soup, 111
  Cream of Sorrel Soup, 93
  Florentine Soup, 102
  Green Chile Stew, 112
  Hearty Chicken Soup, 147
  Hot and Sour Soup, 89
  Lemon Consomme, 25
  Mexican Beef Soup, 146
  Parsnip Soup, 70
  Rodeo Soup, 73
  Sausage and Bean Chowder, 147
  Swordfish Soup, 64
Southwestern Sole with Crab Sauce, 23
Spice Cake, 100
Spiced Chicken Wings, 88
Spiced Pecans, 132
Spicy Orange Chicken, 90
Spicy Spinach Salad, 148
Spinach
  Brunch Pie, 164
  Chicken with Spinach and Linguine, 158
  Florentine Soup, 102
  Salmon Florentine, 151
  Spicy Spinach Salad, 148
  Spinach and Sausage Frittata, 165
  Spinach Souffle, 169
  Spinach with Red Onions, 50
  Stir-Fried Spinach, 106
  Strawberry and Spinach Salad, 24
Squash
  Apple-Filled Squash, 169
  Squash Patties, 169
  Stuffed Spaghetti Squash, 170
Steak Magnifique, 154
Steak, See Beef
Steamed Asparagus with Olive Oil, 31
Steamed Green Beans and Turnips, 63
Steamed Red Snapper, 150
Steamed Rice, 74
Stir-Fried Spinach, 106
Stir-Fry
  Gingered Pork and Cauliflower, 91
  Pepper Beef with Sweet and Sour Sauce, 91
  Spicy Orange Chicken, 90
  Stir-Fried Spinach, 106
  Stir-Fry Beef and Vegetables, 154
  Stir-Fry Cashew Chicken, 159
  Stir-Fry Pork, 163

Stir-Fry Sauce Mix, 151
Stir-Fry Shrimp and Pineapple, 151
Szechwan Beef, 92
Strawberry(ies)
    High Strawberry Pie, 172
    Marmalade Melange, 128
    Strawberry and Spinach Salad, 24
    Strawberry Bread, 19
    Strawberry Tart, 44
    Strawberry-Orange Sorbet, 32
    Summer Berries, 47
    White Chocolate Strawberries, 35
Stuffed Figs, 13
Stuffed Grape Leaves, 84
Stuffed Spaghetti Squash, 170
Stuffed Tomato Salad, 126
Substitutions, Ingredient, 230
Summer Berries, 47
Sunflower Seed Bread, 182
Sunny Side Up Peach Pie, 173
Surprise Doughnuts, 180
Sweet and Sour Carrots, 55
Sweet and Sour Sauce, 91
Sweet Cheese Fondue, 65
Sweet Vermicelli Cake, 104
Swiss Chicken, 159
Swordfish, Grilled, 152
Swordfish Soup, 64
Szechwan Beef, 92
Tabouleh Salad, 86
Taco Pie, 155
Tarragon Sauteed New Potatoes, 31
Tarts, See Pies and Tarts
Testers, List of, 8
The Classic Gingersnap, 197
The Eggs-ecutive, 131
Toast Toppers, 180
Toast, Coconut Caramel, 180
Toast, Overnight French, 178
Toast, Peanut Butter Raisin, 180
Toffee Bars, 119
Tofu Enchiladas, 164
Tomato-Shrimp Mold, 12
Tomatoes
    Basic Italian Sauce, 153
    Broiled Sherried Tomatoes, 170
    Chilled Tomato-Dill Soup, 42
    Crudites, 94
    Eggplant with Sun-Dried Tomatoes, 47
    Fennel Salad on Tomato Slices, 26
    Fried Tomatoes with Parmesan Cheese, 170
    Sauteed Cherry Tomatoes, 40
    Stuffed Tomato Salad, 126
    Tabouleh Salad, 86
    Tomatoes Provencal, 34
Tongue, Braised, 71
Tortes, See Cakes
Tortilla(s)
    Chicken Enchiladas, 115
    Green Onion Cakes, 89
    Guacamole Tortilla Sandwiches, 136
    Mexican Pinwheels, 114
    Salami-Tortilla Roll-Ups, 136
    Tofu Enchiladas, 164
    Tortilla-Wrapped Flank Steak, 137
    Tuna Tortillas, 137
    Zucchini Tostadas, 114
Tournedos of Beef with Roquefort Sauce, 95
Trout, Hot Tub, 153
Tuna Spread, Oriental, 139
Tuna Tortillas, 137
Turkey Pitas, 136
Turtle Temptations, 202
Vanilla Filling, 57
Veal
    Braised Tongue, 71
    Veal with Prosciutto, 46
    Veal with Red Pepper Sauce, 103
    Vitello Tonnato, 34
Vegetable Salad with Sherried Dressing, 65
Vegetables, Basiled, 68
Vitello Tonnato, 34
Waldorf Chicken Salad, 141
Walnut(s)
    Belgian Endive and Hot Walnut Salad, 68
    Snail and Walnut Stuffed Mushrooms, 13
    Walnut and Almond Torte, 110
    Walnut Jam Cookies, 197
Watercress
    Beet and Watercress Salad, 62
    Cucumber-Watercress Soup, 33
    Endive and Pomegranate Salad, 55
Western Baked Beans, 121
White Chocolate Strawberries, 35
Why Bytes?, 9
Wild Rice, 63
Wow Cow, 191
Yakitori, 105
Yogurt Soup, 87
Yogurt, Frozen, 134
Yummy Baked Eggs, 181
Yummy Banana Muffins, 184
Zippity Do Dip, 186
Zucchini
    Brochettes of Shrimp and Zucchini, 40
    Grated Zucchini, 29
    Squash Patties, 169
    Zucchini Strips with Parmesan, 78
    Zucchini Tostadas, 114

BYTES
COLORADO'S FAMILY-FRIENDLY COOKBOOK

To order additional copies of BYTES, complete one of the forms below and send it to: BYTES, 30 Birch Street, Denver, Colorado 80220

Name of Purchaser _____ Phone _____

Address _____

City/State/Zip _____

MAIL TO: (if different than above) _____

Address _____

City/State/Zip _____

☐ Check enclosed (payable to Graland Country Day School)
☐ Charge to   ☐ MasterCard   ☐ VISA

Card Number _____ Expiration Date _____

Signature _____

Item	Quantity	Unit Price	Total Price
BYTES		$11.95	
Gift Wrap		$ .75	
Postage/Handling		$ 1.50	
Sales Tax (CO residents only)		.44	
Amount Due			

Name of Purchaser _____ Phone _____

Address _____

City/State/Zip _____

MAIL TO: (if different than above) _____

Address _____

City/State/Zip _____

☐ Check enclosed (payable to Graland Country Day School)
☐ Charge to   ☐ MasterCard   ☐ VISA

Card Number _____ Expiration Date _____

Signature _____

Item	Quantity	Unit Price	Total Price
BYTES		$11.95	
Gift Wrap		$ .75	
Postage/Handling		$ 1.50	
Sales Tax (CO residents only)		.44	
Amount Due			

Send to: BYTES, 30 Birch Street
            Denver, Colorado 80220